The Pacific Gardener

by A.R.Willis

B. COM.

GRAY'S PUBLISHING LTD.

Sidney, British Columbia, Canada

Foreword

One problem that faces every would-be gardener in our part of the country is where to find a garden book which will give authoritative guidance under the climatic conditions of the Pacific Northwest. There are garden books aplenty, but most of them published in North America are written with the Atlantic seaboard states in mind, and their instructions are not always applicable here.

Our growing season is as long as that of Virginia or the Carolinas, and much longer than in any of the midwest states or the prairie provinces, but our nights are cool while theirs are stifling; heat-loving plants which thrive under Eastern conditions will often fail to mature here, while our favorite plant varieties shrivel and die in the intense sunshine and baking heat of an Eastern summer.

English garden books come closer to our needs, but there is one vital difference in the climates—the distribution of the annual rainfall. Wet summers are fairly common in England, whereas we can usually count on a prolonged period of midsummer drought. British garden books are not very helpful with drought-combatting techniques. English books on fruit-growing make mention of fruit varieties which are almost unknown here.

We have long needed a book written specifically for the Pacific Northwest gardener—written with *our* climate and *our* kinds of soil in mind and about *our* kinds of plants and shrubs and trees. Almost any kind of a book slanted in our general direction would have been welcome; one as comprehensive and authoritative as "The Pacific Gardener" is almost more than we deserve.

M. V. CHESNUT, F.R.H.S.

ACKNOWLEDGMENT

Among my many gardener friends, professional and amateur, who have encouraged me during the production of this book, I am particularly grateful to Prof. Mark Bell of the University of Victoria for his constructive criticism and useful suggestions, to A. E. Richman, R.H.S., Saanich Parks Superintendent, and Geo. A. Wiggan, secretary of the Victoria Horticultural Society, for photographs and other assistance.

I extend my special thanks to M.V. Chesnut, F.R.H.S., well-known gardening authority, for reviewing my manuscript in embryo, and for his kind remarks in the Foreword.

A.R.W.

S.B.N.0-88826-047-4

1st Edition 1964
2nd Edition 1966
3rd Edition 1968
4th Edition 1970
5th Edition 1972
6th Edition 1973
7th Edition 1975
8th Edition 1978
9th Impression 1980

Table of Contents

TABLE OF CONTENTS—(Cont'd)

Preface

During my past twenty years as a gardener and nurseryman on Vancouver Island, I have been bombarded with thousands of questions related to the growing of plants.

"How far apart should I plant peas?"

"When is the best time to set out fruit trees?"

"Something's chewing the leaves off my roses. What should I do?"

"The leaves of my rhododendron are yellowing and it won't bloom. Why?"

How? When? What? Why?

Scores of books have been written on gardening by more qualified authorities than myself, dealing with every aspect of horticulture, and I don't presume to challenge them. But I do feel there is need for a simplified, yet comprehensive, guide to which the home gardener can refer without floundering through a score of detailed volumes to find answers to a few simple questions.

So I have tried to write a sort of primer-encyclopedia, outlining the main facts concerning garden plants and gardening activities in the Pacific northwest area, to help Joe and Mary Doakes make gardening less frustrating and more fun.

ARTHUR R. WILLIS, B.COM.

Illustrations

Plus 14 photographs.

Introduction . . .

Some Definitions

Horticultural terminology is often confusing, but a knowledge of basic terms is necessary, even to interpret a seed catalogue, so let's begin with a brief outline of the A. B. C's.

The field of horticulture may be conveniently divided into three parts:

"POMOLOGY", the study of the various phases of fruit-growing, including small fruits, and nuts.

"OLERICULTURE", the growing and harvesting of vegetables.

"ORNAMENTAL HORTICULTURE", the art and science of propagating, growing, cultivating and displaying ornamental plants of all sorts, from bulbs to trees.

All plants in the above three groups are either annuals, biennials, or perennials.

"ANNUALS" are plants that mature seed in one season and die after flowering. Most vegetables like peas, beans and corn, and many flowers such as petunias, nasturtiums and zinnias come under this category.

"BIENNIALS" are plants that make one season's growth, survive the winter in a dormant state, produce seed the following year, then die. Mustard, cabbage, hollyhocks and wallflowers fall into this group.

"PERENNIALS" are plants that persist from year to year, some not producing seeds for a long time after planting, like fir trees, others producing seeds year after year, like delphiniums or roses,

Perennials embrace such a wide range of plant material that it helps to classify them.

1. HERBACIOUS PERENNIALS, like asparagus and peonies, have tops that die down every season, while the roots persist. Bulbs and grasses fit into this group.

2. WOODY PERENNIALS, like blackberries or raspberries, have tops that last two seasons, with year old canes that fruit the second season and then die.

3. TREES AND SHRUBS are completely woody plants that persist from year to year, adding growth to the plant body previously produced. If they shed their leaves and are completely bare during one season of each yearly cycle, they are termed "deciduous". If they shed leaves or needles so gradually that they have leaves on them at every season of the year, they are known as "evergreen" plants, and may either be "broad-leaved evergreens" like laurel, rhododendrons, or holly, or "coniferous evergreens" like the pines, firs and junipers.

So much, then, for definitions. There are many more, but those just mentioned crop up fairly frequently in any discussion of gardening, and you would be wise to fix them firmly in your mind.

The Components of Gardening

Gardening, as a subject, might be likened to a large pie, divided into eight slices: tools and equipment, soils and fertilizers, planning and planting, propagation, watering and cultivation, pruning, spraying, harvesting and storage. Let us munch each slice slowly, with relish, and avoid indigestion.

(a) Tools and Equipment

To the beginner this can be a fascinating, and if he's not careful, an expensive subject. Garden centres these days are filled with a bewildering array of glittering garden gadgets and power equipment, designed to produce a carrot or a cabbage from seed to harvest, almost untouched by human hand, like a loaf of bread. Some of them are interesting, even useful. Many are unnecessary. Much of the value of gardening should come from the physical exercise it provides, particularly to the sedentary worker, but if he persists in loading himself with a lot of expensive power equipment he no longer becomes an amateur gardener, but an amateur mechanic. However, there are a number of essential items, and we will deal with them.

One important item neglected by most beginning gardeners, and many with experience, is the soil testing kit. As we will see later, the condition of the soil is the cornerstone upon which we build our gardening hopes, and our knowledge of its acidity and fertility often spells the difference between success and failure. It's possible and desirable to send soil samples to our provincial or state agricultural agencies, where free analyses are made, but to possess a soil testing kit of one's own is advantageous for several reasons. Even in a small area soils often vary, and a number of samples should be tested to provide a complete picture. Soils change, too, from year to year, even from month to month, as we add lime, peat moss or fertilizers to make desirable corrections. It is not convenient to keep sending samples in any quantity to a government agency, not to mention the usual delay involved. A few dollars invested in a simple testing kit will avoid this, and provide a fascinating do-it-yourself project for rainy evenings.

For preparing the soil by hand only three tools are needed, a digging fork, a spade, and a rake. Needless to say they should be of good quality, short or long handled to suit your height, and kept free of rust with an occasional coating of light grease.

If you find it desirable to purchase a power tiller, by all means obtain one with sufficient horse power to do the job. There is nothing more frustrating or exhausting than to find yourself fighting a machine that simply was not constructed to do what you think it should, or what you want. In soils of average texture three horsepower is the minimum needed to do the work without stress, and in heavier soils four or even five horsepower are necessary. Many machines on the market today are nothing but surface scratchers. Don't be hasty in making a purchase, and

1

don't let price be the main deciding factor. Try out various machines on your own property until you find the one that really digs in and does the job without you having to wrestle it back and forth across the yard. It should penetrate at least eight inches, which is only the depth of a digging fork, and should break up the soil without pulverizing it too fine. One fault with rototilling practice in general is that it tends to fluff up the soil, like meringue on a pie, filling it with air. Of course air is essential in soils, but too much dries soil out too quickly, preventing bacterial action and decay of humus. A happy balance of air and moisture is essential for perfect soil texture and for this it is hard to improve on careful hand digging.

(b) Transplanting and Planting

Once the soil has been conditioned, by hand or machine, the fun of transplanting begins, for which only a few inexpensive tools are required. A spade, of course, is a must for digging holes for trees and shrubs, a trowel for setting out items like tomatoes or zinnias, a dibber for planting bulbs, and a ridger of some sort for row planting. Drills may be made in the time honored way with the back of a rake or the edge of a hoe, but a ridger, which is a miniature plowshare on a handle, makes the job easier and it's a tool that can be used later for hilling beans or potatoes.

(c) Cultivating and Weeding

For cultivating or weeding, all you need is a three or five-pronged cultivator, a Dutch hoe, or if you prefer, the swan neck hoe like gran'pa used to use, only with a lighter, more modern blade. Here again, if you are power-minded, you can indulge in a rotary power hoe or cultivator which can be either a separate machine or an attachment to your tiller. But if you intend using a power tool for cultivation, you must remember to plant the rows far enough apart to go through them easily, and leave room at each end to turn around. Such spacing means more reduction of your planting area and it's questionable in the average backyard garden whether or not a power cultivator is an asset. Even after machine cultivation you have to work between the plants with a hand tool,

and often you can do the whole area by hand as quickly and as easily as you can manoeuvre a machine through it, not to mention the saving in gas and oil.

(d) Spraying and Pruning

Once the crop is up and growing, we come inevitably to the necessity of spraying and, in the case of large subjects, pruning as well.

Spray equipment can be cheap and simple or expensive and elaborate, depending upon your requirements and the size of your purse. For the average home operation the power sprayer is a luxury, and we will not discuss it here. If you have one as an attachable unit to other equipment, more power to you, but we will not be too envious. Ordinary hand operated equipment will serve us well.

This may be of three types, the pressure tank sprayer, the hand operated sliding pump, or the nozzle attachment sprayer for the hose. Each have their advantages and disadvantages. The pressure tank, with a capacity of from two to ten or more gallons, constructed of galvanized metal or brass, has the pump on the top or side as an integral part of the tank itself and may be equipped with one shoulder sling, shoulder straps like a knapsack, or in the larger sizes set upon a two-wheeled push cart. It is compact, mobile, and once pumped up sprays for several minutes without recharging. If you purchase this type it will certainly pay in the long run to get one with a brass tank. The galvanized tanks rarely last more than two or three years, even if conscientiously cleaned after use. Some spare parts are available for most models but if the pump cylinder should leak, as happens occasionally, it is difficult to repair, and you may be faced with the full loss of your investment, even though the tank is still intact.

This doesn't hold true for the sliding pump type, where your pump is separate from the container. These pumps are constructed of brass and will function for years with a bit of grease and a few spare washers. Though they spray well enough, the hand pumping action must be continuous and becomes tiresome when prolonged. Also there is the nuisance of moving the container (usually a galvanized pail from two to five gallons capacity) from place to place.

The most recent development in garden spraying is the nozzle attachment to the garden hose, with a small jar containing the concentrated spray solution which dilutes under water pressure through the nozzle. This is simply an adaptation of the paint sprayer, and it does a good job wherever you can reach with the hose. It is a bit tiring holding up the container but certainly easier than using the sliding pump, though somewhat more expensive. This is because you tend to use more solution than with the other two methods, though this may not be the extravagance it seems. Often the tendency is to underspray. Too much is better than too little.

No matter what kind of sprayer you decide on, there is one cardinal rule to remember when using it: keep both container and liquid free of grit and scale. Nothing can be more aggravating than having to stop in the middle of spraying operations to clear a clogged nozzle, screen or valve. A thorough cleansing of equipment after each period of use will save time and temper.

When we come to pruning, tool requirements are simple and not too expensive. The most indispensable item is the hand pruner, or secateur, which may be the anvil type or the scissors type. The former has one sharp blade which presses down on a soft brass or aluminum "anvil" to make the cut. It has a tendency to squeeze the bark or stem on the anvil side, but if the blade is kept sharp and if the tool is not used on heavy branches (over ⅜") it will do a good job and last for a long time.

The scissors type of secateur, as it suggests, has two sharpened blades that cut into the branch from both sides, and if working perfectly this tool makes a cleaner cut than the other. If, however, there is the slightest opening between the blades when they meet, it will tend to fold or tear the subject. So if you're buying this type be sure to get one with an adjustable nut on the blade screw. The slight extra cost will be well justified.

If your property has fruit or ornamental trees and shrubs of any size, you will need a pair of long handled lopping pruners. Pruners with hardwood or tubular steel handles twenty-four inches long will **sever**
branches an inch in diameter without difficulty, and last many years. Anything over an inch should be sawn, and a small pruning saw will be worth every cent you paid for it. Make sure you keep it sharp, and that goes without saying for the pruners.

A hedge brings special pruning problems. A pair of sharp grass clippers might suffice for boxwood or barberry, but when we get into laurels, cedars and cypress, a pair of strong hedge shears is a must, and you need a pair of strong hands to use them. If you get discouraged with the chore of hedge trimming and feel affluent enough to buy power hedge clippers, please remember that most of them are designed for the soft growth hedges like lonicera, yew and boxwood. Don't try cutting heavy laurel or cedar branches with them or you'll burn up your motor and your money.

(e) Watering

On the face of it you wouldn't think that watering would present any complicated tool and equipment problem, and it doesn't. Yet manufacturers have had a field day in this particular branch of gardening, with hoses and sprinklers *ad infinitum*. Not too long ago an adjustable hose nozzle, a perforated disc and a whirlygig, plus the good old watering can, were about the limit of choice in water dispensers. And you can still get by nicely with them. But let's examine a few of the newer items.

One with considerable merit for lawn or border watering is the underground plastic pipe sprinkling system, with adjustable sprinkler heads spaced to take care of a given area. Plastic pipe will not rust, rot, corrode or split from frost, and can be installed with a pocket knife, screwdriver and a spade. The cost is not a great deal more than that of hose and sprinkler needs for the same area, and it's a permanent, trouble free system, provided you have ample water pressure and carefully install it according to manufacturers directions.

A substitute for this, with equivalent results, is watering through perforated plastic hose, either single or double-barrelled. Unfortunately plastic hose isn't as foolproof as plastic pipe. Too much pressure inevitably widens holes, making spraying uneven, or blows out a connection and you are obliged to discard it. Of course regular plastic hose is more durable, with manufacturer's guarantees of five to ten years. It is still easier to repair a break or a tap connection on rubber hose, but for ease of handling and durability the plastic has it beaten and no doubt will soon replace it altogether.

Sprinklers are a matter of personal choice, for there are many adequate ones. However, one good adjustable whirlygig type and one half-moon or round pin cushion type, plus a good hose nozzle, will serve the average garden. There is no need to go overboard for walkie-wigglers or jet propulsion unless you feel a bounden duty to stimulate the general economy.

(f) Lawn Care

When we think of lawns we think of mowers, and here again confusion fogs the tyro. With your decision made for a hand operated mower the problem is fairly simple, and selection a matter of price versus efficiency. If there is an argument with yourself between a hand mower or a power machine, look at it sensibly. When your lawn is, figuratively speaking, postage stamp size, you don't need a power mower, even if Jim Smith next door has one. On the other hand, if your lawn looks to you like the first fairway at The Country Club, there is some justification for your desire for power. Of all jobs least likely to be enjoyed by gardeners, amateur or professional, mowing the lawn wins in a breeze. Perhaps it is the deadly endless monotony, besides the hard work. Other plants grow and bloom, or become edible, but grass just grows. And it must be cut, often.

Whether you purchase a rotary type mower or the reel type is not too important provided, in either case, you get one of quality. Yet there are a few things you should remember. If your lawn isn't perfectly level and is plagued with humps and hollows, even small ones, the rotary mower tends to scalp the high spots more than the reel type. And in the cheaper rotary machines the blade doesn't always revolve at high enough speed to cut clean, and leaves a chewed effect, especially if it isn't sharp. However a good high speed rotary mower does a good job.

It can get right to the edge of the grass and chops up the cuttings very fine and spreads them almost unnoticed across the lawn. It is easier to service and sharpen than the reel type, but it has been the cause of a few fatal accidents from throwing up bits of metal.

Besides a mower, hand or power operated, there are a couple of other items you should have for lawn maintenance, an edger and an aerator. You can keep lawn borders fairly neat by clipping with shears, but an edger does a better job. The simplest and cheapest is simply a sharp half moon blade on a handle. There is another type with a cutting wheel on the side, which revolves and cuts as you push. Both, of course, must be kept sharp at all times.

If your lawn tends to compact, and many lawns do, you will find an aerator of great value. Lack of air at the roots not only kills grass but encourages moss, fungi and general soil sourness. An aerator is simply a small spiked spindle that punctures the soil to a depth of two or three inches as it's pushed along. If this is done twice a year on a lawn, preferably just before fertilization, the results will amaze you. You can, of course, punch holes in a lawn with a digging fork, but it's a bit of a chore on a large area.

For cleaning up around the garden, moving soil, fertilizer, or what-have-you, it is difficult to get along without a wheelbarrow. Here again let your need and your purse be your guides. It is always well to remember that garden equipment is not purchased for style, but utility. Quality tools, properly cared for, will last years, even a lifetime. Cheap tools are not cheap in the long run.

SUMMARY
HAND TOOLS

A. FOR PREPARING THE SOIL
1. Soil test kit.
2. Digging fork.
3. Spade.
4. Rake.

B. FOR TRANSPLANTING AND PLANTING
1. Spade.
2. Trowel.
3. Dibber (closed trowel).
4. Ridger.

4

C. For Cultivating and Weeding
  1. Three or five-pronged cultivator.
  2. Dutch hoe, or swan-neck hoe.

D. For Spraying and Pruning
  1. Tank, pump, or hose sprayer.
  2. Hand secateurs (anvil or scissors type).
  3. Long-handled pruners.
  4. Pruning saw.
  5. Hedge clippers.

E. For Watering
  1. Plastic pipe sprinkling system.
  2. Perforated plastic hose.
  3. Plastic or rubber garden hose.
  4. Nozzles and sprinklers.
  5. Watering can.

F. For Lawn Care
  1. Reel-type mower.
  2. Edger.
  3. Aerator.

G. Miscellaneous
  1. Wheelbarrow.
  2. Files, whetstone, oil can, etc.

POWER TOOLS

Rotary tiller.
Rotary hoe or cultivator attachment.
Power sprayer.
Electric hedge clippers.
Rotary or reel type mower.

NOTE: The recent invention of rotary trimmers using nylon fishing line has saved gardeners a lot of stooping and tedious hand trimming. They come in either electrically operated or gas powered units and are very effective. However the nylon spools have to be replaced frequently if they are given much use.

A BRIEF WORD ON ORGANICS

With the upsurge of ecological and environmental concerns during the past few years, there has followed a parallel interest in organically grown foods and organic gardening. Health food stores are springing up like organically grown mushrooms and are being patronized by increasing numbers of people who don't mind paying 25% more for fruits or vegetables presumably grown with manure, et al, unsprayed, as opposed to those grown with chemical fertilizers and sprayed with insecticides or fungicides more or less toxic.

Which is fine if we don't lose perspective and refuse to face the facts. First of all, organic farming is not new. Two thousand years ago the Aztecs of Mexico found that, by burying a fish under a hill of maize, they could increase their yield appreciably. And the Chinese, even before that, added "night soil" to their impoverished land to keep up its fertility, and still do.

The value of manure as a fertilizer and soil conditioner is without question, the only problem being, for the home gardener, or anyone, for that matter, where to obtain it in sufficient quantity. The best most of us can do is to provide a bit of processed sewage, seaweed derivative, or compost from kitchen and garden waste—never nearly enough to supply sufficient fertility to keep the soil in top productivity. We are simply forced to add some chemical fertilizer as a supplement, unless we are prepared to pay an unjustifiable amount of money.

But don't be too alarmed. There is no scientific proof that a tomato grown with chemical fertilizer, hydroponically (without soil), is any less nutritious than one grown with cow manure in your back yard. Yours may taste better, or you may think it does, but the main value of your tomato against a 'store' bought one is the pride of home production and the exercise it provided while producing it.

Use organics if and when you can, but don't make a fetish out of it.

Soils and Fertilizers

These are the raw materials of gardening and without a basic knowledge of them, gardening success becomes merely a matter of chance.

(1) Soil Structure and Drainage

If it's possible to define soil briefly, we might say that it is "vitalized earth". As we know from our school days, soil may be composed of fine mineral particles (clay) or coarse mineral particles (sand), in various proportions. But it is dead or inert unless it contains organisms, decaying vegetable matter (humus), plus air and water. An ideal soil contains, by volume, 25% water, 25% air, 45% mineral matter and 5% organic material. Soil with this critical 5% of organic matter holds large quantities of moisture and provides a happy home for fungi, bacteria and earthworms. These attack the organic material and produce carbon dioxide in solution. This in turn dissolves minerals required for plant nutrition. Ammonifying bacteria convert organic protein from humus to ammonia. Nitrifying bacteria convert ammonia to nitrite, and nitrite to nitrate, which is the main form of nitrogen uptake by plants. Earthworms aerate the soil, sweeten it with calcium, and their castings add valuable fertilizers. Thus, as long as humus is present, soil becomes a continuous chemical factory, producing plant food. The maintenance of organic matter is therefore of prime importance.

Almost equally important to soil vitality is drainage. Movement of water is the result of a number of factors, the texture of the soil, presence of worm holes and decayed root channels, height of water table, and the slope of ground. While some plants are more tolerant of "wet feet" than others, all suffer if the soil is in a saturated or waterlogged condition for long. The roots actually suffocate from lack of oxygen, and rot.

If the structure of the soil is at fault (i.e., too much clay is present) some correction can be made by the addition of sand, sawdust, peat moss, or coarse manure. Sawdust is the cheapest material in the Pacific Northwest area, and a couple of inches thoroughly incorporated every three or four years will definitely improve the friability of a heavy soil.

If soil saturation is a question of slope or high water table, the area should be drained. (See Fig. 1.) Examine your property twenty-four hours after a heavy rain and mark the obviously wet or spongy areas. Or dig down and take soil samples. If it's impossible to lower your winter water table below eighteen inches, you should restrict your plantings to annuals, perennials and shrubs. Most deeply-rooted trees will not be happy there.

(2) Acidity and the pH Scale

The problem of soil acidity is directly associated with drainage. In the humid climate of the Pacific Northwest more water moves down through the soil than up to the surface, especially during the winter. Thus

SOIL DRAINAGE, USING TILE

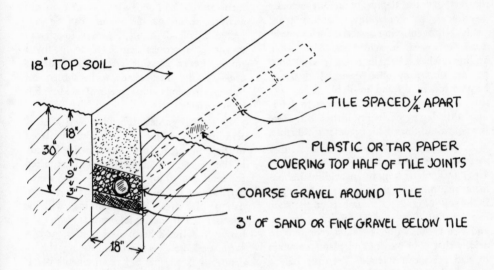

18" TOP SOIL

TILE SPACED $\frac{1}{4}$" APART

PLASTIC OR TAR PAPER
COVERING TOP HALF OF TILE JOINTS

COARSE GRAVEL AROUND TILE

3" OF SAND OR FINE GRAVEL BELOW TILE

18"
30"
9"
3"

18"

SOIL DRAINAGE, USING RUBBLE

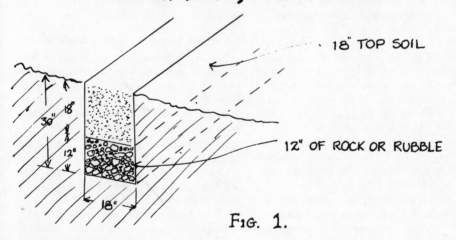

18" TOP SOIL

12" OF ROCK OR RUBBLE

18"
30"
12"

18"

FIG. 1.

soluble salts not removed by crops tend to be leached away. One of the most soluble of these is calcium, or lime. Up to 300 lbs. of lime per acre annually is lost in this way. As the calcium content of the soil diminishes, the acidity rises, and the degree of acidity directly affects the growth of various plants. Such growth is affected not only by the lack of lime, which is itself a plant food, but by the fact that the degree of acidity actually determines the availability of other plant foods. Nitrogen-fixing bacteria, for example, don't work well in acid soils. Also, when acidity reaches a certain point, phosphorus, potash, and many other essential elements, become locked up and insoluble. Therefore it is very important to the gardener to determine this degree of acidity in his soil. Here is where a soil-testing kit becomes invaluable.

As such a kit will show you, an acidity measuring device has been developed, called a pH scale. It is simply an acidity thermometer that measures the quantity of hydrogen in the soil. (Fig. 2.) As numbers on the scale rise, acidity decreases, alkalinity increases, and vice versa. Values below 4 represent an acidity that only mosses and plants common to acid peats can tolerate. Yet only half a point higher, at 4.5, blueberries, azaleas, and rhododendrons find their optimum acidity. Another half a point higher we can grow potatoes, strawberries and raspberries. In soils of moderate acidity, between 5.0 and 6.0 on the scale, a host of plants thrive, including grain crops, garden vegetables like tomatoes and squash, fruit and ornamental trees, and deciduous shrubs. In the so-called "neutral" zone, between 6.0 and 7.0 the brassicas (cabbage, cauliflower, sprouts) and leafy vegetables like lettuce and spinach, are happiest, together with peas, beets and the clovers. After we pass 7.0 on the pH scale, soil becomes alkaline, and for the majority of plant subjects, needs acidifying.

To correct either alkalinity or acidity is not difficult. A quick way to reduce alkalinity is to apply either ammonium sulphate or sulphur. Six pounds of ammonium sulphate to 100 square feet on heavier soils, and three pounds on sandy soils, will cut the pH one full point. Two pounds of sulphur will usually do the same. A slower but a better way

is by the addition of oak leaf mold or peat moss.

All that is necessary to correct acidity is to add a liming material that will form calcium bicarbonate in the soil solution. Pure ground limestone will do this, but it takes time. A quicker acting material is hydrated lime, or "agricultural lime", sold by garden centres and feed stores everywhere. The lime requirement of your soil depends on your own soil analysis, so no specific amount can be suggested. It is inadviseable, however, to attempt to correct a serious degree of acidity by a single, heavy dressing. Apply a moderate dressing the first year, with subsequent lighter dressings until the soil acidity has been corrected.

In a small garden difficulties will arise if acid-loving and lime-loving plants are placed in the same area. This can be avoided easily in the vegetable plot where lime is required for most everything but potatoes and strawberries. But in the flower borders and foundation plantings, some planning will be necessary. For example, azaleas won't be happy in a limed herbacious border, or carnations planted between acid-loving rhododendrons. Study the pH requirements of all plants before setting them out, and keep them together as far as possible in areas of pH compatability. You will avoid no end of disappointments if you follow this general rule.

(3) Plant Structure and Requirements

Before we proceed to a discussion of fertilizers, it might be wise to determine just what a plant is, and how it functions. We all know that, structurally, a plant consists of roots, stems, leaves, flowers and fruit, but what about its chemical composition?

Its skeleton, or framework, consists of an insoluble carbohydrate, cellulose. In woody plants, and even in grasses and legumes, this cellulose is strengthened by another compound called lignin. The cells of the plant hold other important carbon compounds, solid or in solution, such as fats, starches, sugars and vitamins. All these carbon compounds are built by the plant from carbon, hydrogen and oxygen. Another one, protein, contains nitrogen, sulphur, and sometimes phosphorus. All are manufactured by the

THE pH SCALE

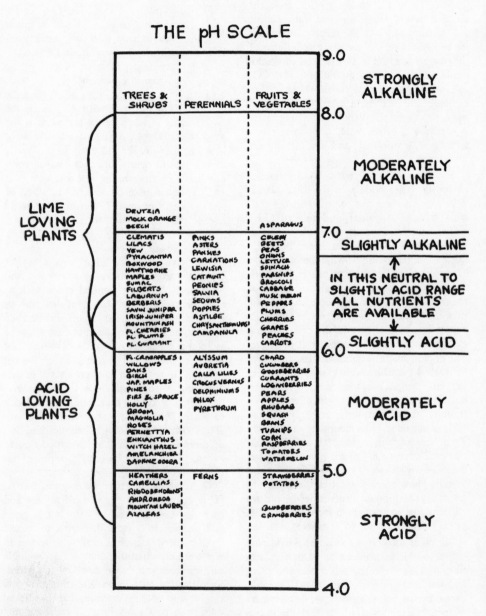

Fig. 2.

plant by absorption through the leaves or roots.

Leaves might be likened to solar batteries. The green leaf pigment, chlorophyll, is energized by the sun to change to CO_2 from the air and water from the soil into simple sugars, from which all the carbon compounds we've mentioned are manufactured. Some of the oxygen released in this process of photosynthesis is used in respiration. The CO_2 released by respiration, with water, forms carbonic acid which, in turn, dissolves soil minerals to feed the plant roots. This process is continuous, often rapid, as long as moisture, light, temperature and soil fertility are in balance.

The proportion of water to dry matter obviously varies widely in different plants. A lush green plant like celery or lettuce contains at least 90% water, and only 10% dry matter, whereas a woody plant like a fir tree might contain only 20% water and 80% dry matter. But regardless of what the percentage of water might be, the dry matter is constituted much the same. It contains a balance of roughly nine parts of organic matter to one part inorganic. In fact, the only inorganic matter in plants is that in the cell solution, and is not part of the actual cell structure. The organic matter (carbohydrates, fats, proteins, etc.) contain mainly carbon, hydrogen, oxygen, nitrogen, and calcium, with lesser, but important, amounts of magnesium, potassium, phosphorus, sulphur, copper, iron, zinc, manganese, molybdenum and boron. These elements, then, in total, are the main chemical constituents of all plants. Requirements of each element vary in different plant species, since every plant has the ability to select the nutrition elements it needs, and we will examine some of these variations shortly, as we come to a study of fertilizers.

No other subject in horticulture has come under so much discussion as plant fertilization, because the relationship between plant and soil is so complex. Plant growth is influenced by so many climatic and biological factors, besides soil fertility, that the causes for success or failure are often difficult to determine. However, both plant and soil analyses provide a good guide to nutrition requirements, and once we have a reasonably accurate picture of our soil's fertility, or lack of it, we can plan our fertilization program to fit the need.

(4) Organic Fertilizers

Fertilizers may be divided into two classes, organic materials, such as animal or plant residues, or inorganic materials, i.e. chemicals. Two schools of thought, almost irreconcileable, have arisen in favor of one or the other, and there are convincing arguments on both sides. Actually, no matter what the original form of the fertilizer applied, the end product as taken up by the plant is the same. For example, if you were to use dried blood or manure, the plant would eventually absorb the nitrogen from these in the form of nitrates or ammonium, just the same as if you applied nitrate of soda or sulphate of ammonia as chemicals. Therefore they should not be considered competitive, but complementary, and the advantages of each combined to benefit the whole.

We have mentioned the importance of organic matter (humus) in keeping a soil "vitalized". Under perennial crops such as trees or grass, nature takes care of this by constantly adding dead leaves or decayed roots to the soil, but where crops are removed as food a deficiency obviously develops. The best known, and still in first place on the list of valuable organic fertilizers, is stable manure, but unfortunately for the home gardener it is becoming more and more difficult to obtain. And often, even when it is available, much of the good has been leached out, or there is too much litter in proportion to excreta. This brings its cost, in terms of results, quite high.

On the Pacific coast poultry manure is fairly easy to get, but if allowed to heat and then dry out, the loss of nitrogen is rapid and serious. It is best, therefore, to spread fresh poultry manure directly on the soil in wet weather, when the ammonia and soluble nitrogen compounds are absorbed and speedily converted to nitrates. Of course, if you can obtain poultry manure that has dried quickly in peat moss litter, it can be stored indefinitely without much nitrogen loss.

Compost is another valuable organic fertilizer, if properly prepared, and every gardener should have a compost bin. A bin eight

10

feet square, made of two by six cedar planks, divided in half by a removable partition, will provide a lot of compost as time goes by. Use one half for "green" material, leaves, grass clippings, vegetable waste, etc. and the other half for storing the "ripe" compost for use. There are many methods of making it, but the simplest is to start with about six inches of compacted green matter, add a couple of inches of soil, a light sprinkling of a complete chemical fertilizer, another layer of green matter and soil, a sprinkling of lime or wood ashes, and repeat. If you are in a hurry you can speed up the rate of decomposition by using a compost activator, of which there are many on the market. The material should be kept moist at all times and turned over occasionally as decay sets in. A burlap sack spread on top will help keep it from drying out, and at the same time allow air and water to pass through.

Those living adjacent to the ocean should not overlook seaweed as a valuable organic fertilizer. Pound for pound, it actually contains more nitrogen and potassium than manure, though less phosphorus, and in addition a valuable content of "trace" elements, which we will see in a moment are vital for plant health. Seaweed is also free from disease organisms and weed seeds. Since it is 70-80% water, it has little fibre, and decomposes rapidly into gases and soluble compounds, so should not be exposed to prolonged weathering. Apply it to the land, and dig it in, immediately after gathering, or better still, use it for composting material. Those unable to obtain the seaweed itself can now buy a liquid concentrate which has been proven of great value as an organic foliar feed and root fertilizer.

The organic fertilizers we have mentioned so far: manures, compost, and seaweed, may be considered more or less as "complete" fertilizers, inasmuch as they all contain three of the chief elements for plant growth—nitrogen, phosphorus and potassium. But there are several other organic materials that contain only one or two of these elements in any amount. Dried blood and processed sewage provide chiefly nitrogen; bone meal mostly phosphorus. Peat moss contains no fertilizer at all but is a valuable soil condi-

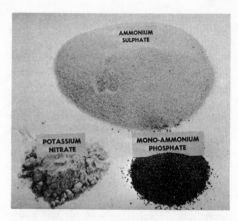

tioner and, like seaweed, is free from weed seeds and disease organisms. We mustn't forget that it is very acid, and unless we are using it specifically to acidify the soil, some liming material must be added as a corrective. There are a number of peat moss products on the market, containing fish or whale solubles, thus increasing their value as important organic materials.

So much, then, for the most important organic fertilizers. Their main advantage, in addition to providing plant nutrients, is their ability to supply the soil with humus. Their main disadvantages are the slow, uncertain rate at which they supply their nutrients, and their high cost compared to chemicals.

(5) Chemical Fertilizers

Nitrogen, phosphorus and potassium are the main elements commonly applied to soils in the form of chemical fertilizers. When we hear or read of an 8-10-5 fertilizer, for example, it simply means that in every hundred pounds of mix there is 8%, by weight, of some form of chemical nitrogen (N), 10% of chemical phosphorus in the form of phosphate (P_2O_5), and 5% of chemical potassium in the form of potash (K_2O). Different amounts of each of these can be combined for the varied requirements of different soils and plants, and for various degrees of solubility or acidity.

Nitrogen encourages leafy growth, which is of prime importance. The amount of nitrogen contained in crops may vary from 50 to 200 pounds per acre, but all of it comes from the soil unless the plants have been fed with

11

nitrogenous foliar sprays. A lack of it becomes evident from the pale color of plant leaves, and stunted growth. (See Fig. 3.) But too much of it results in overdevelopment of foliage at the expense of root, fruit, or seed.

Some of the most important nitrogenous compounds used as fertilizers are nitrate of soda (16% N), sulphate of ammonia (20% N), ammonium nitrate (35% N), and urea (46% N). The first has an alkaline reaction, the second acid, and the last two are neutral or only slightly acid. All are quickly soluble in water, which is desireable when quick results are wanted, but a disadvantage when we would like nitrogen liberated slowly and steadily over a longer period. For example, an application of nitrate of soda will turn a fading lawn green almost overnight, but after a few rains or waterings the effect disappears. Recent experiments and research, however, have developed urea compounds that release nitrogen at a steady rate for months, and have proven ideal for plants like grasses with a long growing season. The decision as to the best nitrogen fertilizer to use, depends upon the soil and the crop in question. For instance, lettuce, a lime-loving plant, would prefer nitrate of soda to sulphate of ammonia, but acid-loving blueberries would prefer the latter.

Phosphorus deficiency is not easy to detect, but weak growth and dull purple-tinted leaves are indications. The most obvious results from adding phosphorus to a soil are an acceleration of root development, especially in seedlings, and the promotion of fruit and seed production. Some crops like turnips, corn and tomatoes respond more definitely than others to liberal applications of phosphate, but all plants require a generous supply and that is why, in most combinations of "complete" chemical fertilizers, the percentage of phosphate is the greatest.

Bone meal is an excellent source of organic phosphorus, but is slow acting and becoming increasingly expensive. The most common source of chemical phosphorus is rock phosphate, which may contain as high as 50%. When treated with sulphuric acid it yields superphosphate (20% P_2O_5) and by other chemical processes produces ammonium phosphate, with as high as 60% phosphorus content and a fair amount of nitrogen as well. Unlike the highly soluble nitrogen chemicals, the phosphates are not easily soluble in water. Different types of soils react defferently, but all will remove a soluble phosphate from solution, and in the case of acid soils, "lock" it up until the acidity is rectified. This is called "phosphate fixation". Even under the most favorable soil conditions it has been proven that the recovery of added phosphorus is less than 10%. Since freshly applied phosphate is likely to remain relatively soluble for a few weeks, it is better to apply little and often than to give a massive dressing at one time.

The third most important chemical element required for plant growth is potassium. Nitrogen, we have said, promotes leaf development, and phosphorus promotes seed and fruit. Potassium is important in the formation of carbohydrates within the plant structure. Root crops such as turnips, beets and poatoes, high in starch or sugar content, benefit particularly from potash fertilizers.

Potassium deficiency is most common in sandy soils, and the chief evidence of its lack is marginal leaf scorch. Potassium fertilizers are sold on the basis of their content of potassium oxide (K_2O), commonly called potash. The two most commonly used are muriate of potash (50% K_2O), and sulphate of potash (48% K_2O). Both are soluble in water but often tend, like the phosphates, to change to forms unavailable to plants. Consequently, the total potassium in a soil isn't a reliable measure of what may be utilized by the plant. Crop recovery of potassium added to the soil is only about 50%. Clay soils, notably high in potassium, may not yield it to the plants unless lime, nitrates and phosphates are present in proper balance.

Before leaving the discussion of chemical fertilizers, we should make some mention of a group of minor elements essential to plant health. Iron, magnesium, and sulphur should not, perhaps, be referred to as "minor" elements in the sense that they are unimportant, but rather because they present a minor problem to the gardener, inasmuch as they are

HOW SOIL NUTRIENTS AFFECT PLANT GROWTH

COMPLETE

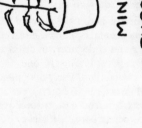

MINUS POTASSIUM

MINUS PHOSPHORUS

MINUS NITROGEN

Fig. 3.

present in most soils in sufficient quantity and availability.

Symptoms of iron deficiency (bleached leaves, green veins) usually occur in soils containing an excess of lime, a condition not often found in the Pacific Northwest. Since soil conditions are at fault, little is to be gained by adding soluble iron salts to the soil. Spraying affected plants with a solution of ferrous sulphate, 1 lb. to 40 gal., will usually help.

Magnesium deficiency (mottled, yellowish leaves) is most likely to occur on light soils in areas of heavy rainfall, because it is easily leached out. The best permanent cure is to reduce acidity in the soil gradually with ground limestone. To save a growing crop suffering from magnesium deficiency, spray with a 25% solution of Epsom salts.

Sulphur deficiency, fortunately, is rare. Although the element is a major nutrient, there is usually a good deal of sulphate in the soil solutions, and sulphates are present in the most commonly used fertilizers.

Besides iron, magnesium and sulphur, and The Big Three (nitrogen, phosphorus and potassium), there is another small group of essential elements, commonly called "trace" elements because they are required in such small amounts. Boron, manganese, copper, zinc and molybdenum are, in fact, toxic to plants except in minute quantities, and applications must be made with care.

Lack of sufficient boron slows down plant growth, distorts the stalks, curls the leaves or causes cracking and corky areas in fruits and vegetables. Excessive liming is one factor that reduces availability. Forty-five pounds of agricultural borax (11% boron) per acre, very evenly distributed once every three years, is sufficient to correct boron deficiency. That is approximately five pounds to an average-sized home garden.

Manganese deficiency also generally occurs under alkaline conditions, but since its availability to the plant is related closely to organic and bacterial processes, the deficiency symptoms are difficult to determine. Speckled yellow leaves and curling of the leaf margins are indications, and if recognized in the early stages can be halted by either broadcasting manganous sulphate at the rate of 40 lbs. per acre, or spraying with a solution of the same, 1 lb. to 50 gal. water. Excess manganese in the soil is definitely toxic, and sometimes occurs in very acid soils. This can be overcome by reducing the acidity.

The amount of copper required by plants is very small, but essential, and a deficiency can cause die-back of shoots and premature leaf fall. Although considerable copper is present in most soils, poor aeration and excess moisture tend to fix it in an insoluble form. Plants showing deficiency symptoms can be helped by spraying with a solution of not more than 0.2% copper sulphate.

Zinc appears to be necessary for synthesis of some of the important plant hormones, and the assimilation of carbon dioxide. Soils usually contain adequate amounts, but it becomes fixed and unavailable under alkaline conditions. "Little leaf" in apples and pears, a common symptom of zinc deficiency, can be corrected by spraying with a solution of 5% zinc sulphate during dormancy, or 0.2% at petal fall.

Deficiency symptoms of molybdenum (diffuse yellow mottling and rolling of leaf margins) usually occurs in over-acid soils. Failure of legumes in some soils has been found due, not only to lack of lime, but a lack of molybdenum required by nitrogen-fixing nodule bacteria. A spray solution of ½ lb. of sodium molyblate per 100 gals. of water is sufficient to make corrections.

Briefly, then, watch for deficiencies of magnesium, copper and molybdenum in acid soils, and deficiencies of iron, boron, manganese and zinc in alkaline soils.

We have dwelt at some length on organic and chemical fertilizers for two reasons, first to provide a fairly complete list of plant needs, secondly to provide a quick reference. Now let us, as briefly as possible, examine their application in a gardening fertilization program.

(6) Fertilizing the Vegetable Garden

Outside of a separate plot for acid-loving potatoes, the main vegetable garden should be limed often enough to maintain a pH average of around 6.5. If ground limestone is used, apply it in the fall, but since hydrated lime dissolves so readily, don't apply it until after the heaviest winter rains are over, around the end of January.

Vegetables respond more definitely to manure and compost than most other crops, but maximum results are obtained if the organics are supplemented with chemical fertilizers. Apply manure or compost in the late fall or early spring to allow rain and frost to break it up. Turn it into the soil as soon as the ground is workable after the end of January. If neither manure or compost are available, a crop of rye planted in October and turned under when it is around four inches high, will help provide some humus and keep the soil open.

Just before planting, broadcast a complete commercial fertilizer that suits your soil and crop requirements. With some compost or manure in the soil a 5-10-5 or 6-8-6 fertilizer, 3 lbs. to 100 sq. ft., should suffice. But if you find that leaf crops like lettuce and cabbage are not responding like they should, mix a booster solution of nitrate of soda, 5 tablespoons to a gallon of water, and use one gallon on each 16 feet of row. Some of the high nitrogen liquid fish fertilizers will produce the same result with less danger of burning foliage.

For potash lovers, like potatoes and root crops, a 4-10-10 fertilizer is generally most suitable in lighter soils, with 5-10-5 in the clays or clay loams. Some gardeners prefer to place fertilizer for potatoes below and each side of the seed piece, a practice which has proven worth the extra time and effort.

(7) Fertilizing the Orchard

The lime content of the orchard needn't be, in fact shouldn't be, as high as for vegetables. Strawberries, raspberries and loganberries will thrive in fairly acid soils (pH 5.5), though currants, gooseberries and fruit trees, especially the stone fruits, like it between pH 6.0 and pH 6.5 Generally speaking, underliming is safer than overliming.

Small fruits and fruit trees are humus lovers. Their root systems occupy the ground for years, and may become very extensive, so long-lasting fertilizers like manure, compost and bone meal are particularly valuable. For most soils a' dressing of 6-8-6 commercial fertilizer, 2 lbs. per 100 sq. ft. broadcast along the rows in the early spring will be satisfactory for cane fruits and currants, but strawberries should have an additional dressing of ammonium phosphate about the middle of August to strengthen the plants after cropping.

A general rule for fruit trees is a pound of 6-8-6 fertilizer per inch of diameter of the trunk, for each tree. It should be applied in a wide band around the foliage perimeter of the tree, where the feeder roots lie, during the last week in February or the first week in March. If the soil lacks nitrogen, a high nitrogen fertilizer like ammonium sulphate can be used, but care must be taken not to be too generous. Terminal growth on apples, cherries and plums should not exceed a foot a year on older trees and two feet on peaches and apricots. Too much nitrogen puts on wood at the expense of fruit.

(8) Fertilizing the Flower Border

Annual and perennial flowering plants, bulbs, and most deciduous shrubs, have lime requirements similar to vegetables, pH 6.0-6.5. A fall dressing of compost and 5 lbs. of bone meal per 100 sq. feet, will keep bulbs and roses happy. Quick-growing annuals may show need for a midsummer stimulant, and a booster solution of nitrate of soda, liquid fish, or seaweed concentrate will pay off in growth and bloom.

Where flowering trees are spaced along the perennial borders it is wise to give them individual treatment, as with fruit trees. If holes are punched with a crowbar in a band around each tree and the fertilizer placed in them, it will reach the roots away from the competition of flowers and bulbs.

(9) Fertilizing Evergreens

While coniferous evergreens are more lime tolerant than the broad-leafed group, all thrive in acid soils, pH 4.5 to pH 5.5, and many are definitely injured from overliming. When planting evergreens beside new house foundations, it's important to remove all plaster, cement or rubble from the soil.

All types of evergreens need good drainage, and most of them require lots of moisture. Unlike deciduous trees and shrubs, their moisture requirements are year round. Humus, therefore, is a must where evergreens are concerned and if rotted manure and compost are unavailable, use peat moss liberally with occasional applications of bone meal. Complementary feedings of chemical fertilizers must not be overlooked, especially if the foliage shows need of nitrogen. Sulphates like sulphate of ammonia are preferred because of their acid reaction, but care must be taken to make sure they are well watered in to prevent root burn. Most conifers have a mass of fibrous roots, which have become "balled" in the nurseries by progressive transplantings. Thus they are fairly shallow rooted and favor a surface mulch of leaf mold, peat moss, rotted pine needles, sawdust or what-have-you to keep the roots cool and moist. Special "acid mix" fertilizers are available for evergreens, and if you have fairly extensive evergreen plantings it would be well to have some on hand.

(10) Fertilizing the Lawn

Turf grasses like a slightly acid soil (around pH 6.0), so go easy with lime on your lawn. If you're certain the soil is too acid, dress it in the fall with slow-acting ground limestone at the rate of 50 lbs. per 1,000 sq. feet.

For healthy, vigorous growth, lawn grasses need regular feeding. Top dressings of screened compost in the spring, with bone meal and processed sewage added, are hard to beat for sustained, vigorous growth, and their cost is not as high as it might seem, over the long pull. The chemicals are cheaper, but leach out rapidly from heavy waterings. If you're using them, it's best to use them "little and often". The chief plant nutrient needed for lawn growth is nitrogen, so make certain the fertilizer you choose is high in that element. An application of 8-6-4, 20 lbs. per 1,000 sq. feet around the first of March, plus once a month sprinklings of nitroprills throughout the summer (well watered in), with another 8-6-4 treatment in mid-August, should keep your lawn like a billiard table. If this sounds like a lot of work, try one of the new urea compounds we mentioned previously. They release nitrogen at a slower, evener rate than the chemicals, without danger of burning. Twenty pounds of 20-5-5 mixed ureaform, or 33 lbs. of 12% ureaform per 1,000 sq. feet, applied in the fall will carry the grass through in fine shape until late spring, when another application at half the previous rate should be sufficient to maintain summer growth. Their only drawback is their very slow action in cold or wet soils.

In recent years, combination "weed-and-feed" lawn fertilizers have become popular, since, in one application they perform two jobs. For good results, care must be taken to follow manufacturer's instructions.

(11) Summary

Unless otherwise stated, packages of commercial fertilizers contain only the three major plant nutrients, nitrogen, phosphorus and potassium, in their various combinations. The minor elements, iron, magnesium and sulphur, and the trace elements, boron, manganese, copper, zinc and molybdenum, can either be purchased separately or in various combinations. Since these are very toxic used in excess, great care must be taken to follow the directions carefully. One of the easiest, cheapest and safest ways to apply many of the trace elements is by using a liquid seaweed fertilizer recently developed.

NOTE: An organic fertilizer, 'Steer Manure', processed to be weed and odor free, has become very popular in recent years, not only because of its reasonable price, but because it is rich in humus, with some fertilizing value, without the acidity of peat moss. It's an excellent soil conditioner and lawn dressing.

Planning and Planting

While a good deal of satisfaction may be derived from tilling and conditioning the soil, the real fun of gardening begins when you stand with your hand full of seed packets and your wheelbarrow loaded with bedding plants and shrubs. Planting can be an enjoyable, exciting experience indeed, but eagerness and zeal, without planning, often lead to confusion and disappointment.

(1) Planning and Planting the Vegetable Garden

Any average soil can be conditioned to produce vegetable crops, and we have outlined lime and fertilizer requirements. The site chosen should be one which receives as much sunlight as possible. Drainage, of course, is important and if this is a problem on your property you are faced with two alternatives—you can delay planting until late spring, when the ground begins to dry out, or you can build up planting beds six or eight inches above the general ground level. Whatever you do, never try to sow seeds and set out plants in soil .so wet that it sticks to the hoe.

The space available for vegetables, the size of your family and your personal preferences should determine what crops to grow. It will help considerably to put your plan on paper before planting. Rule off a square or rectangle, allowing one-half inch for each foot of actual garden space. Then list the vegetables you wish to grow. From the plant-ing table (page 24) estimate the row footage you require to supply your needs, and fit each vegetable into your plan, always remembering to keep the taller crops, like corn and pole beans, on the north or east side to avoid shading the remaining garden area. For easy cultivation and weeding it's advisable to plant crops in rows as long as possible.

Time to plant varies with different crops, different seasons and different localities, and in the planting table we have tried to strike an average for the Pacific Northwest region. It is important to remember that seed sown in cold wet soils will usually rot, or at best germinate unevenly. The minimum soil temperature for even the hardiest subjects is around 45 deg. F. So don't be too anxious to "rush the season" unless you are favored with light soil and a sheltered location.

There are over thirty vegetables grown in home gardens in this area, and while some may be considered more important than others, we will deal with them all, as briefly as possible, in the same order of planting shown in the table.

BROAD BEANS are one of the earliest and hardiest vegetables to grow. Sometimes they can be planted in October, sprouted, mulched with leaves or peat moss, and brought safely through the winter. But it's a gamble, and you're not too much behind by sowing them in mid-February. They should be planted in rows two feet apart, 8 inches apart in the row and 2 inches deep. Remember they grow

STARTING CUCUMBERS IN VENEER PLANT BANDS

tall and are heavy yielders. Pinch out the tops at the first sign of black aphis. Ten feet of row will provide 15 lbs. or more. Broad Windsor, 75 days to maturity, is one of the best varieties.

LEEKS are hardy, easily grown plants that thrive on most any soil, but favor the sandier loams. Plant the seed in mid-February, ½ inch deep in rows 18 inches apart, and transplant when they are 6 inches high. Set them 3 inches apart in trenches about 4 inches deep, and fill in gradually as they grow. In heavier soils they can be hilled up. This practice makes the stems white and succulent. Usually leeks can be left in the ground all winter without harm. London or American Flag are good varieties that mature in 150 days.

RADISHES germinate at 50 deg. F. and may be sown in mid-February. They like a loamy fertile soil and should be grown quickly for best flavor. Plant the seed ½ inch deep in rows 14 inches apart, and thin to 2 inches apart in the row. Scarlet Globe and Icicle both mature in 25 days under good conditions.

SHALLOTS, or multipliers, can usually be set out safely after the middle of February. They're useful as flavoring for soups and stews and really do "multiply". Fifty bulbs,

planted 3 inches apart, 2 inches deep, in rows a foot apart, will supply the average household with flavorings until fall onions are ripe.

PARSLEY is a hardy annual that grows in most any soil. Scatter a bit of seed along the border of the vegetable garden toward the end of February and you'll probably never have to sow again, as one plant at least is sure to go to seed that summer and replenish your supply. Moss Curled is a well known and satisfactory variety.

PARSNIPS are one root vegetable that will germinate around 50 deg. F. and can be sown outdoors during the last week in February. Percentage of seed germination is low, so it's better to sow fairly thickly, one inch deep, firmly pressed, in rows 18 inches apart. Thin young plants 4 inches apart. In heavier soils some gardeners make deep, cone-shaped holes with a crowbar, fill them with compost and sow three or four seeds in each hole, thinning to one. They are one root vegetable that can be left in the ground all winter and even improve in flavor after a few frosts, but don't use them after the tops begin to sprout in the spring. A ten-foot row should yield 15 lbs. Improved Guernsey Hollow Crown (120 days to maturity) is good for the lighter soils, and Short Thick (100 days to maturity) more suitable for heavier soil.

ONION SETS, unlike shallots, will develop into full-size onions. Set them out around the first of March. A pound of sets should yield 40 lbs. of onions. The small sets will yield just as big a crop as the larger ones and are less likely to divide or run to seed. Plant the same as shallots, being careful not to bury the sets too deep.

GREEN ONIONS for salads can be sown the same time as sets are planted. Plant the seed ½ inch deep in drills 12 inches apart, and make sure you press the seed firmly into the soil. Thin out the plants when three or four inches high. A 10-foot row will flavor a lot of salads, but if you're fond of them plant more. Evergreen Bunching is a variety that will mature in 60 days.

SPANISH ONIONS, globe onions and pickling types take longer to mature, 100 days or more from seed, and prefer light, fertile, well-drained soil, with lots of summer sun to ripen them properly. You can gain time by planting seedlings or growing your own under glass and transplanting. White Sweet Spanish or Riverside Spanish are two good Spanish varieties, Yellow Globe Danvers and Australian Brown two reliable cooking onions and White Portugal (Silverskin) an excellent variety for pickling. Plant the same as green onions, but thin out the larger varieties to 4 inches in the row.

EARLY POTATOES should be sprouted in flats in full light around February 1st for planting out a month later. If the sets are half buried in rotted sod and kept moist, roots develop that promote an earlier crop. The sets should be dipped in a solution of formaldehyde or Semesan Bel to avoid scab. Avoid planting potatoes in heavily limed soil. They prefer the mellow loams to the clays and insist on good drainage. Each set should contain 2 or 3 eyes and should be planted 4 inches deep in rows 30 inches apart, at least a foot apart in the row. Five pounds of seed potatoes should plant 50 feet of row and yield ten to one. Varieties like Warba or Early Epicure mature in 60 to 75 days, and often can be lifted in time to release the ground for late crops like squash or marrows.

PEAS are probably the favorite of all garden vegetables and grow in most soils, though they appreciate fertility. As we enter the first week of March in the Pacific Northwest, we can start thinking about planting the earlier varieties. Perhaps the best use of garden space results from planting two rows about 8 inches apart, spacing each set of double rows 3 feet apart. This is particularly useful with the tall varieties, as wire or other support can be placed between the 8-inch rows. Plant the seed about 2 inches deep and the same distance apart in the row. Some gardeners prefer to sow peas in a furrow, 4 inches deep, and gradually fill it in as the plants grow. Fifty feet of (single) row should yield 50 lbs., so unless you are growing quantities for freezing or canning, it's wise to space small plantings over as long a period as possible, either by planting successive crops of dwarf varieties (55 to 65 days maturity) or some dwarf and some tall varieties (75 days to maturity). But don't forget that peas are a cool weather crop and plantings that mature during midsummer are inferior in both yield and flavor to earlier harvests.

Round-seeded varieties are less likely to rot when planted early, but most are of poor flavor. Alaska (semi-dwarf) is one of the best, and matures in 55 days. Laxton's Progress is hard to beat for an early dwarf (16 inches), with the same maturity time as Thomas Laxton (60 days, 36 inches high). The latter is one of the best for freezing. An old-timer, but still a fine-flavored dwarf is Lincoln (Homesteader) with maturity in 62 days. For the taller higher-yielding varieties it's hard to beat Tall Telephone or Alderman, both maturing in 75 days and growing five feet or more in height.

CARROTS may be sown after the middle of March as a rule. Like most root crops they prefer the lighter loams. Seed should be sown thinly, 1/2 inch deep, firmly pressed, in drills 18 inches apart. When 2 inches high thin to 2 inches apart, or to 1 inch apart until they are pencil thickness, then remove every other one for early use. A ten-foot row should yield 15 lbs. when matured. For heavier soils plant stump-rooted varieties like Oxheart or Danvers Half Long (both mature in 75 days), or for average soils plant Imperator Long (77 days to maturity) or Chantenay Red Cored (70 days).

SPINACH is a cool-weather plant and must be grown quickly in a rich limed soil or it will run to seed. Plant the seed in early March, 1/2 inch deep in rows 15 inches apart, and thin plants to 4 inches apart in the row. A twenty-five-foot row will yield a bushel or more, so space your plantings to give successive crops. King of Denmark is a good small-leafed variety, while Bloomsdale and a new one called America are good long-standing savoy types.

SWISS CHARD is a useful vegetable often overlooked by gardeners. It can be sown in early March, 1/2 inch deep in rows 18 inches apart, and should be thinned to about a foot between plants. Ten plants will yield a terrific crop of crisp leaves and succulent, celery-like stalks. If planted in midsummer it will provide a crop for Christmas and often go through the winter. Lucullus is the best known variety and matures in 52 days.

LETTUCE, like spinach and other leaf vegetables, must be grown quickly in rich moist soil to yield crisp sweet leaves or heads. It doesn't germinate too well below 50 deg. F., so it isn't wise to sow the seed directly into the soil before the first of April. However, plants grown under glass and hardened off can be set out at the same time, to produce an early crop. Seed should be barely covered with fine soil, pressed down firmly, in rows 15 inches apart, and plants thinned to 12 inches in the row. Probably the best way to avoid a "feast or famine" with lettuce is to set out a dozen plants of head lettuce, like New York 12, about April 1st, followed in two weeks with another dozen, and at the same time sowing a 10-foot row of Grand Rapids leaf lettuce which matures in 45 days, and a 10-foot row of Tom Thumb head lettuce which matures in 55 days. A final planting of Oak Leaf lettuce around the middle of May will extend the supply through till July.

SPRING CABBAGE AND CAULIFLOWER must be sown under glass in late January to provide plants that will mature before the hot weather arrives, so, unless you have a cold frame to start them, you would be wise to purchase established plants around the first of April. Remember that they all mature at the same time, so don't plant more than you'll need, or space plantings over a thirty-day period. Plants should be set 18 inches apart, in rows 30 inches apart. Both cabbage and cauliflower are particularly susceptible to root maggots and disease (clubroot), so be sure to dip the plants in a fungicide solution and dust the soil around the roots with chlordane. Two reliable varieties of spring cabbage are Early Jersey Wakefield (65 days to maturity, conical) or Golden Acre (65 days to maturity, round). Early Snowball and Early Erfurt are two good varieties of cauliflower and both mature in 55 days.

BORECOLE OR KALE may be sown in early April for a spring crop, or in August for a fall and winter crop that often goes through until the following spring. Sow seed ½ inch deep in rows 18 inches apart and thin to a foot apart in the row. Dwarf Green Curled Scotch is a well-known variety that matures in 55 days.

BEETS like the soil a little warmer for germination than most root crops, and unless your soil is light, shouldn't be sown until the middle of April. Sow the seed in limed fertile soil, about ½ inch deep in rows 18 inches apart and thin gradually for greens or bunching beets until the plants are 4 inches apart. A ten-foot row will yield 20 lbs. of large beets, less if they are pulled before maturity. Since they mature quickly, successive crops may be grown in one season. Early Flat Egyptian (50 days to maturity) and Detroit Dark Red (58 days to maturity, globe) are two good time-tested varieties. Ruby Queen is an excellent newcomer.

SUMMER TURNIPS must be grown quickly to be sweet and tender, and favor a rich, sandy loam. Sow the seed thinly, ½ inch deep, pressed firmly, in rows 2 feet apart, and thin to 4 inches in the row. The thinnings may be used for greens. A ten-foot row will yield as high as 30 lbs. Early Purple Top Milan (yellow) or Early Snowball (white) both mature in 60 days.

NEW ZEALAND SPINACH is a valuable follow-up to the earlier varieties as it is a heat-resistant variety that can be cropped all summer. Do not plant seed until the end of April as it won't germinate in cold soil. Thin plants to 18 inches in the row. Half a dozen plants will provide an amazing yield of tender tips.

CORN is a warm-weather crop, and the seed will rot if the soil isn't 55-60 deg. F. Some of the hybrid varieties may be sown around the middle of April, but it's usually May before conditions are right. Plant seed 2 inches deep in rows 30 inches apart, and space plants a foot apart in the rows. For pollination reasons it's better to plant two parallel short rows than one long single row. Ten feet of row should yield 3 dozen good ears. There are numerous varieties available, but Spancross is a good early hybrid (60 days to maturity) and Golden Cross Bantam (84 days maturity) and Sugar King (76 days maturity) are two good main crop varieties. Corn is a heavy feeder, so fertilize generously.

BUSH BEANS are another vegetable that likes warm soil and May 1st is plenty early for the first sowing. Plant seed 2 inches deep in rows 2 feet apart and thin plants to 4 inches in the row. Ten feet of row should yield as many pounds. The wax butter beans, like Top Notch Golden Wax, mature in 50 days. They aren't as good for freezing as the green varieties like Tendergreen (52 days to maturity). Lima beans such as Improved Bush Lima are not any harder to grow, but like lots of heat and take 75 days to mature.

POLE BEANS will yield more from the same area than bush varieties, but are a little more trouble. The best way to plant them is in hills 2 feet apart, thinned to 3 or 4 plants to a hill. Tall poles should be placed in the centre of each hill before planting. Scarlet Runners are the hardiest and one of the most prolific, but unsuitable for freezing. They mature in 65 days. Kentucky Wonder, with the same maturity time, may have either golden pods or green pods, with the latter preferable for freezing.

TOMATOES are probably second only to peas in home garden popularity and have undergone more experimentation and controversy than any other vegetable. One thing is certain, they are heat lovers, and nothing is to be gained by planting them too early. Even during the first part of May, nights in the Pacific northwest area are often too cold for tomatoes unless they are protected by caps or cloches. It's possible to start them outdoors from seed, but they won't usually mature fruit and common practice is to set out established plants started under glass in March. There are staking and bush varieties, with arguments in favor of both, so it's just as well to plant a few of each. They like a loamy, rich moist soil on the acid side. Staked plants have the advantage of being off the ground, exposed to full sun for better ripening, but need constant pruning of side shoots for best results. Tops should be nipped off after the fifth or sixth fruiting truss. The non-staking or bush types don't require pruning and often yield heavier crops per plant, though the fruit may be smaller. The ground under this type should be mulched with straw or plastic to keep the fruits clean and free from mold. Plants should be set at least

18 inches apart for staked varieties and 3 feet for the other, with rows 3 feet apart for either type. A dozen plants will provide enough for table use for a small family, but for canning or juice you will need two or three times as many. By spraying with fruit-set hormones you can prevent early blossom drop to a large extent, thus increasing yield and bringing more fruits to early maturity.

There are many excellent varieties, acid and non-acid, with new ones being developed each year. For general use and reliability, however, it's hard to beat some of the time-tested ones. Early Chatham and Victor (both 60 days to maturity) are good quality bush varieties, and Sutton's Best of All, Stokesdale, Bonny Best and Scarlet Dawn (non-acid) are all reliable staking types with around 70 days maturity.

CUCUMBERS are plants that practically demand heavy fertilization, preferably with organics like manure or compost. They also need continuous warmth and moisture to mature quickly. In the Pacific northwest they are best set out as plants, 3 per hill, around the middle of May. If the ground isn't warm, caps should be placed over the hills. Seed planted under caps is often satisfactory and should be planted half an inch deep, half a dozen to a hill, and the best three plants kept. Remember that the vines spread rapidly and a space five feet square is not too much for each hill. Under good conditions, two or three hills will produce an amazing quantity of cucumbers. If you want some for pickling, and have the space, increase plantings accordingly. Burpee Hybrid (60 days to maturity), Straight Eight (70 days to maturity), and Improved Long Green (70 days to maturity) are three good slicing varieties. Chicago Pickling (58 days to maturity) and National Pickling (54 days to maturity) are two of the small types.

SQUASH are a favorite with many gardeners and are easy to grow in soil well supplied with humus, but they do take up space. They can be set out like cucumbers, as established plants, or planted directly in the ground, one inch deep, around the middle of May. The hills, three plants per hill, should be allowed a space of at least five square feet. Each hill should yield ten good-sized fruits, so avoid overplanting. For early use plant Table Queen Acorn (80 days to maturity), and for winter keepers, either Green or Golden Hubbard (105 days to maturity).

MARROWS can be treated the same as squash, and will yield sooner. Both White Bush and Green Bush varieties mature in 56 days.

PUMPKINS, too, are easily grown if the soil is moist and rich in humus. They are planted the same as squash or marrows, but need more space per hill if possible. Connecticut Field is the well-known large Hallowe'en pumpkin (115 days to maturity), and Small Sugar (110 days to maturity) a fine flavored smaller variety, excellent for pies.

MUSKMELONS AND WATERMELONS are a gamble in the Pacific Northwest because the summer nights aren't often warm enough to ripen the fruit. But if they're planted and treated like cucumbers (under caps), and your soil is light and rich in humus, you will likely succeed, especially if you choose early ripening varieties. Lake Champlain or Pennsweet are two orange-fleshed melons of good flavor that normally mature in 80 days. New Hampshire Midget and Early Canada are small watermelons that sometimes ripen in 70 days.

PEPPERS are tender plants and love heat, so should not be sown until well on into May. It's better to buy plants and set them out a foot apart in rows 18 inches apart when the ground is really warm, as they don't take long to mature. A dozen plants will produce a lot of peppers. Early Pimento is the earliest (55 days to maturity), Harris Early Giant (75 days to maturity) is a mild green type, and Long Red Cayenne (70 days to maturity) is very hot.

LATE POTATOES should be in the ground as we approach the first of June, though plantings until the middle of that month should mature satisfactorily. Plant an inch deeper than the earlier varieties, but with the same spacing. Choose varieties known to be suitable for your area and that store well. Netted Gem and Columbia Russett are two of the older varieties still widely grown.

CELERY is not the easiest plant for the amateur gardener to grow successfully. It requires deep, rich, well drained but moist loam, and consistent watering is essential to keep growth unchecked and succulent. It may be sown in the spring, but to avoid bolting during summer heat it is safer to set out plants at the beginning of July. They can be placed in a trench six inches deep, spaced 6 inches apart, rows 3 feet apart, and the earth filled in as they grow, or they can be hilled up like potatoes. Golden Plume is a quick maturing (85 days) white variety that doesn't bolt easily. Salt Lake Utah is a reliable green variety, but requires 130 days to mature.

RUTABAGAS or Swedish turnips are not usually sown until midsummer in the Pacific Northwest, partially to avoid root maggot, and because they mature best under cool moist September weather. Soil should be deep, moist, fertile, and not too heavy, although some clay is desirable. Seeds should be sown 1/2 inch deep in rows two feet apart, and the plants thinned 4 inches apart in the row. American Purple Top and Laurentian are two good varieties that mature in about 90 days.

FALL CABBAGE, BRUSSELS SPROUTS AND SPROUTING BROCCOLI, members of the Brassica family, all have a maturity period of around 120 days, and should be sown about the middle of August, 1/2 inch deep in rows 30 inches apart, and the plants thinned to 18 inches apart in the rows. Rich loam, well supplied with humus, neutral or slightly acid, is ideal for this group. Since these plants all stand a considerable amount of frost, they usually come through Pacific coast winters unharmed, and provide an early spring supply of fresh vegetables. Danish Ballhead and Penn State Ballhead are good fall cabbage varieties, Catskill a time-tested variety of sprouts, and Italian Green Sprouting (Calabrese) an excellent variety of broccoli that often matures in 90 days. The purple sprouting varieties take a month longer.

SUMMARY

All the vegetables mentioned so far are either annuals or biennials, but there is a small group of perennial plants, including some herbs, which hold some importance in the kitchen garden, and we should not conclude our survey without a brief description of some of them.

ASPARAGUS, for example, is a popular hardy perennial that will grow in any type of well-drained soil, though it prefers a fertile, limed loam that has been well manured. It should be planted at one side of the garden where it will not be disturbed. Though it may be grown from seed, the best plan for the novice is to obtain one-year-old roots, freshly dug, and set them out in a trench eight to ten inches deep, 16 inches apart. Cover these with 2 inches of topsoil, and as the plants reach a foot in height, fill in the trench to ground level. An occasional light dressing of common salt, and a winter mulch of manure or compost will help develop the young crowns, which should not be cropped until the second year from planting. Mary and Martha Washington are the two best-known varieties.

ARTICHOKES have been known to man since Biblical times, but haven't been too popular in North America partly because of a widespread confusion between the two species, the globe artichoke and the Jerusalem artichoke.

The edible portion of the former is the immature flower buds produced by the plant. The globe artichoke may be grown from seed, but planting suckers from high-producing plants is much preferred. Suckers planted in the spring, 4 feet apart, will bear a crop the first year. Green Globe is a good variety.

The edible portion of the Jerusalem artichoke is its tuberous root, which resembles a small potato and is utilized in the same way. Also, though it can be grown from seed, it is best planted like potatoes, in rows 3½ feet apart, 20 inches apart in the row, and about 4 inches deep. The storage life is very short. French White is one good variety.

CHIVES belongs to the onion group and is used mainly as a flavoring for soups, salads and stews. It grows in most any soil, and can be grown from seed, though it's much simpler to divide a clump. A little goes a long way and one or two clumps in the perennial border will be out of the way, and provide a bit of color from the violet blossoms.

HORSERADISH is a perennial belonging to the mustard family, although its fleshy white roots closely resemble the parsnip. It likes deep rich soil and is propagated through sets (side roots the size of a pencil), not seed. Plant the sets horizontally in a furrow four inches deep, 18 inches apart and cover with 3 inches of soil. Four to eight sprouts will start growing, but all but the strongest should be broken off. Half a dozen plants will provide plenty of horseradish for the average family.

SWEET MARJORAM is an herb that is much prized for its tender aromatic leaves, used for flavoring purposes. It is hard to start from seed, but easily propagated by root divisions, and not difficult to grow in any average soil. It may also be grown in pots. Three or four plants are enough for most families.

MINT, both peppermint and spearmint, may be easily grown in any garden. It should be planted in an isolated spot where it can't spread into the main vegetable garden, as it stools rapidly from the crown after planting. It can be grown from seed but is easily propagated from root divisions. A couple of plants will supply an abundance of tender tips to flavor green peas, or make sauce for lamb chops.

THYME belongs to the mint family and is used in much the same way. Plants may be started from seed or rooted layers from a large plant. It will grow in any fertile, well-drained soil. One or two plants in the rockery or planter will provide summer perfume as well as stems for drying and storing.

SAGE is another aromatic plant with leaves used for flavoring, especially in poultry dressing. It may be started from seed or root divisions, and will thrive in any well-drained soil. Plants should be kept cut back to prevent them from getting woody and to produce tender young side shoots. Two plants will supply ample fresh or dried leaves for the average family.

BASIL AND DILL are not perennial herbs like the others mentioned, but once seed has been sown somewhere along the edge of the garden, it nearly always provides a plant somewhere that reseeds for the following year. Basil is used for seasonings and dill for pickling.

(2) PACIFIC NORTHWEST VEGETABLE GARDEN PLANTING TABLE

Planting Date	Vegetable	Seed Depth	Row Width	Row Spacing	Yield per 10-ft. Row	Varieties
Feb. 15th	Broad Beans	2"	24"	8"	15 lbs.	Broad Windsor
" "	Leeks	3/4"	18"	3"	10 lbs.	Large Flag
" "	Radishes	3/4"	14"	2"	5 lbs.	Scarlet Globe, Icicle
" "	Shallots	1"	12"	3"	5 lbs.	Dutch
" "	Parsley	1"	18"	3"	5 lbs.	Moss Curled
Mar. 1st to 15th	Parsnips	1"	18"	4"	15 lbs.	Hollow Crown
" "	Onion sets	1"	12"	3"	10 lbs.	Dutch
" "	Onion seed (Greens)	1/2"	12"	Thin to use	5 lbs.	Evergreen Bunching
" "	(Spanish)	1/2"	12"	4"	10 lbs.	Riverside, White Sweet
" "	(Globe)	1/2"	12"	4"	10 lbs.	Danvers, Australian
" "	(Pickling)	1/2"	12"	1"	8 lbs.	White Portugal
" "	Potatoes (early)	4"	30"	12"	20 lbs.	Warba, Early Epicure
" "	Peas (early)	2"	Dble. 36"	2"	10 lbs.	Alaska, Laxton's Prog.
" "	Carrots	3/4"	18"	Thin to 2"	15 lbs.	Danvers, Imperator
" "	Spinach	3/4"	18"	4"	5 lbs.	Denmark, Bloomsdale
" "	Swiss Chard	1/2"	18"	12"	8 lbs.	Lucullus
April 1st to 15th	Lettuce plants		18"	12"	5 lbs.	New York 12
" "	Lettuce seed	1/2"	18"	Thin to 12"	5 lbs.	New York, Grand Rapids
" "	Spring cabbage plants		30"	18"	20 lbs.	Wakefield, Golden Acre
" "	Spring cauliflower		30"	18"	15 lbs.	Erfurt, Snowball
" "	Borecole (Kale)	1/2"	24"	18"	10 lbs.	Green, Curled Scotch
" "	Beets	1/2"	18"	4"	20 lbs.	Egyptian, Detroit Red
" "	Summer Turnip	3/4"	24"	2"	30 lbs.	Purple Top, Snowball
" "	Peas (main crop)	2"	Dble. 36"	2"	15 lbs.	Telephone, Alderman
" "	N.Z. Spinach	1/2"	18"	18"	5 lbs.	New Zealand
May 1st to 15th	Corn	2"	30"	12"	3 doz.	Spancross, Sugar King
" "	Bush Beans	2"	24"	4"	10 lbs.	Golden Wax, Tendergreen
" "	Pole Beans	2"	24"	Hills, 2 ft.	15 lbs.	Scarlet Runner, Kentucky Wonder
" "	Tomatoes (staked)		36"	36"	4 lbs. plant	Best of All, Stokesdale, Early Girl
" "	Tomatoes (bush)		36"	18"	5 lbs. plant	Early Chatham, Early Canada
" "	Cucumbers (plants)		5 ft.	Hills, 5 ft.	15 lbs. hill	Straight Eight, Chicago
" "	Cucumbers (seed)	1"	5 ft.	Hills, 5 ft.	15 lbs. hill	Straight Eight, Chicago
" "	Squash	1"	5 ft.	Hills, 5 ft.	25 lbs. hill	Acorn, Hubbard
" "	Marrows	1"	5 ft.	Hills, 5 ft.	25 lbs. hill	White Bush
" "	Pumpkins	1"	6 ft.	Hills, 6 ft.	25 lbs. hill	Connecticut, Small Sugar
" "	Muskmelons	1"	5 ft.	Hills, 5 ft.	25 lbs. hill	Pennsweet, Champlain
" "	Watermelons	1"	5 ft.	Hills, 5 ft.	10 lbs. hill	E. Canada, N. Hampshire
" "	Peppers	3/4"	15"	12"	10 lbs.	Early Pimento
" "	Potatoes (late)	5"	30"	12"	25 lbs.	Gem, Kennebec
June 15th to 30th	Celery plants		36"	6"	20 lbs.	Golden Plume, Utah
" "	Rutabaga	1/2"	24"	4"	30 lbs.	American Purple Top
July 15th to 30th	Fall cabbage plants		30"	18"	25 lbs.	Penn State, Ballhead
" "	Fall cauliflower plants		30"	18"	20 lbs.	Late Pearl, Igloo
" "	Brussels Sprouts plants		30"	18"	15 lbs.	Catskill, Long Island
" "	Sprouting Broccoli	1/2"	30"	18"	15 lbs.	Italian Green, Purple Sprouting

24

(3) Planning and Planting the Home Orchard

To those occupying a property less than half an acre in size, approximately 100 x 200 ft., the limitation of space is a curb on ambitions for an extensive orchard. Yet it is surprising what variety can be established in a fairly small area, with careful selection and layout.

One prime determining factor is drainage, and if you can't overcome a high winter water table you had best forget fruit trees, particularly the stone fruits, and settle for the shallower-rooted cane and bush fruits. If you insist on trying fruit trees under adverse conditions, keep to dwarf apples, pears and prunes.

Assuming drainage is no problem, your first step is to strike a balance of space allotment between the vegetable garden and the orchard. Here personal preference must decide. Do you want potatoes, OR strawberries, corn OR currants. Once you have settled such questions, you can determine the size of the orchard area.

We would point out at this juncture that you don't have to plant all your fruit trees at the back of your property. If you contemplate wide borders of ornamental trees and shrubs surrounding your lawn area, plan to intersperse a few dwarf or semi-dwarf fruit trees with the ornamentals. They are attractive in bloom, colorful in fruit, and though spraying and pruning might be easier if they were all together, the saving in space will more than compensate.

The number of fruit trees desired depends on personal preference, available space, and the choice and size of species. While you don't need to know all the methods used by nurseries to obtain dwarf, semi-dwarf or standard trees, it will help you when making purchases to be familiar with some of the most commonly used rootstocks. The East Malling Research Station in England has pioneered the development of special rootstocks, particularly for apples and pears. The two apple stocks used most extensively in the Pacific northwest are East Malling IX (E.M. IX), and East Malling VII (E.M. VII).

The number nine stock, as it is generally termed, is the most dwarfing of all apple stocks, producing earlier bearing, earlier ripening fruit than any other. It's ideal for city gardens, where space is at a premium, but has a shallow, brittle root system and requires staking. Trees on this stock grow about eight feet high, can be spaced 8-10 ft. apart, and with proper fertilization will yield up to 75 lbs. of fruit when fully grown.

The number seven rootstock is an excellent semi-dwarf for the home orchard where space isn't quite as important a matter. It has a stronger root system than E.M. IX, doesn't require staking, and is more adaptable to the heavier types of soils. Trees on this stock reach about 12 ft. in height, and should be spaced 12-15 ft. apart in most soils. You can expect a harvest of 125 lbs. from a mature tree.

Recent experiments to produce trees less subject to disease and insects, have resulted in the development of some new understocks called Malling Merton, and these are becoming available in semi-dwarfs (MM 104) and trees about 2/3 the size of standards (MM 106).

So-called standard apple trees are grafted either on seedling rootstocks or East Malling stocks that produce trees the same size. They grow 20 ft. or more in height, require a spacing of 25 ft. or more, and produce up to 250 lbs. per tree after ten years of growth.

Dwarf pears are grown on quince rootstocks, Malling types A, B and C. Quince A and B stocks produce trees a little larger than C, reaching a height of about 10 ft. and requiring to be spaced that far apart. Quince C stocks mature fruit at an early age, usually in their third year, and take the same space as number nine apples. They will produce 60 lbs. or more per tree when mature.

Standard pears, grafted on seedling pear stocks, grow about the same size as standard apples, a little more upright in habit, but should be spaced the same distance apart. A fully-grown standard pear tree will produce 300 lbs. or more of fruit.

Apricots and peaches are dwarfed on Yellow Kroos plum stocks, and others, which make bushy trees about 10 ft. in height, requiring a 10 x 10 ft. spacing. Yield varies so from season to season and variety to variety, it is difficult to estimate, but 50 lbs. of fruit could be expected in a good year. Standard peaches and apricots, on seedling rootstocks, will grow twice the size of dwarfs, take twice the space, and yield two or three times the crop.

Prunus Besseyi, St. Julien, and Yellow Kroos are used for dwarfing plums and prunes. Here again there are such wide variations between varieties that ultimate sizes and yields are hard to determine, but it would be wise to space dwarfed plums 15 ft. apart, and standards 20-25 ft. Plums and prunes normally produce heavy crops, from 75-300 lbs. per tree.

As yet sweet cherries have not been dwarfed too successfully, and on the usual Mazzard or Malaheb stocks require a 30 x 30 ft. spacing. Yields are often heavy, up to 300 lbs. or more on adult trees, provided pollination requirements have been met.

Sour cherries are normally fairly small trees, around 10 ft. in height, with a spread of 15-20 ft., and can be spaced accordingly.

Pollination demands will limit your choice of fruit trees to some extent. A single sweet cherry, for example, is not self fruitful, and there are several varieties of apples, pears, plums, peaches and apricots which require either companion trees or grafts of pollenizers placed upon them. In most suburban areas in the Pacific Northwest, where fruit trees are widely planted, pollenization isn't often a problem, but in new subdivisions it can be. It's wise for every gardener to protect himself, and the following chart of commonly planted varieties, with indicated pollenizers, will serve as a guide.

Varieties	Approx. Ripening Period	Suggested Pollenizers	Description and Use (Best use first named.)
SUMMER APPLES			
Crimson Beauty	Mid. July	None Required	Red—Cooking
Close	"	"	Red—Eating, Cooking
Yellow Transparent	Late July	"	Yellow—Cooking
Lodi	Early Aug.	"	Yellow—Eating, Cooking
Julyred	"	"	Red—Cooking, Eating
Melba	"	"	Red—Cooking, Eating
Early McIntosh	Mid. Aug.	"	Red—Eating, Cooking
EARLY FALL APPLES			
Wealthy	Early Sept.	"	Red—Eating, Cooking
Gravenstein	Mid. Sept.	Red Delicious	Red or Yellow—Eating
King	Early Oct.	Red Jonathan	Red Cheek—Eating, Cooking
Tydeman's Red	Mid. Oct.	None Required	Red—Eating, Cooking
Cox Orange	"	"	Russet—Eating
McIntosh Red	"	"	Red—Eating, Cooking
Fameuse (Snow)	Late Oct.	"	Red—Eating
Summered	Early Nov.	"	Red—Eating
Spartan	"	"	Red—Eating
LATE FALL AND WINTER APPLES			
Red Jonathan	Mid. Nov.	"	Red—Eating, Cooking
Baldwin	"	McIntosh Red	Blush—Eating, Cooking
Yellow Delicious	Late Nov.	None Required	Yellow—Eating, Cooking
Red Delicious	"	"	Red—Eating
Wagner	"	"	Blush—Eating, Cooking
Winter Banana	Early Dec.	"	Yellow—Eating
Melrose	Mid. Dec.	Yellow Delicious	Red—Cooking, Eating
Winesap	"	"	Red—Cooking, Eating
Rome Beauty	Late Dec.	None Required	Red—Cooking
Yellow Newton	"	"	Yellow—Cooking, Eating
Red Northern Spy	"	"	Red—Eating, Cooking
Vanderpool Red	"	"	Red—Eating, Cooking
SUMMER PEARS			
Bartlett	Late Aug.	Bosc or Conference	Yellow—Eating, Canning
Conference	Late Sept.	None Required	Green—Canning
Flemish Beauty	"	"	Green—Canning
FALL PEARS			
Winter Bartlett	Late Oct.	Bosc or Conference	Green—Eating, Canning
Anjou	"	None Required	Green—Eating, Canning
Winter Nelis	Early Nov.	"	Yellow—Eating, Canning
Comice	Mid. Nov.	"	Yellow—Eating, Canning
Bosc	Late Nov.	"	Russett—Eating
PEACHES			
Red Haven	Early Aug.	None Required	Red-Yellow—Canning, Eating
Pacific Gold	Mid. Aug.	"	Red, Yellow—Eating, Canning
Rochester	"	"	Red-Yellow—Eating
Golden Jubilee	Late Aug.	"	Yellow—Canning, Eating
J. H. Hale	Early Sept.	Rochester	Yellow—Eating, Canning
Veteran	"	None Required	Red-Yellow—Canning
Elberta	Mid. Sept.	"	Yellow—Canning
APRICOTS			
Tilton	Early Aug.	Moorpark	Canning
Perfection	"	"	Canning, Eating
Moorpark	Mid. Aug.	None Required	Canning, Eating
Wenatchee	"	"	Canning, Eating
SUMMER PLUMS			
Beauty	Early Aug.	Burbank	Blue—Eating
Burbank	"	Gold	Red—Eating
Gold	"	Burbank	Yellow—Eating
Peach Plum	Mid. Aug.	Gold	Blush—Eating, Canning
Santa Rosa	"	Gold	Purple—Eating
Mallard	"	Gold	Purple—Eating
FALL PLUMS			
Victoria	Early Sept.	None Required	Red—Eating, Canning
Bradshaw	Mid. Sept.	"	Blue—Eating, Canning
Yellow Egg	"	"	Yellow—Eating
Green Gage	"	"	Green—Canning, Jam
Early Italian Prune	"	"	Blue—Canning, Jam
Italian Prune	Late Sept.	"	Blue—Canning, Jam
SWEET CHERRIES			
Stella	Early July	Self Fertile	Red—Canning, Eating
Bing	"	Van or Deacon	Black—Eating, Canning
Deacon	"	Van or Bing	Red—Canning, Eating
Royal Anne	"	Van or Deacon	Yellow—Canning, Eating
Van	Mid. July	Bing or Deacon	Black—Eating, Canning
Lambert	Late July	Van or Deacon	Black—Eating, Canning
SOUR CHERRIES			
Montmorency	Mid. July	None Required	Red—Canning, Pies
Early Richmond	"	"	Red—Canning, Pies
Olivet	Late July	"	Red—Canning, Pies
English Morello	"	"	Dk. Red—Canning, Eating

NOTE: Ripening period indicated does not necessarily mean picking period, as pears and late varieties of apples are picked at maturity, and ripen later. See Chapter I (H) on Harvesting and Storage.
NOTE: Even though varieties indicated as not requiring pollinator are mainly self-fertile, there is usually a heavier set of fruit where two or more varieties are planted together. This is particularly true with pears.

(5) Planting Fruit Trees

In well-drained soils, fall planting is best as it gives the roots a good chance to settle in and even establish some growth before the sap starts to run in the spring. However, on heavier soils, where drainage might be a problem, planting should be delayed until February or March.

Setting out a fruit tree is a simple operation, but requires some care. Dig a hole at least 30 inches in diameter and 24 inches deep. Discard the bottom foot of subsoil and replace it with compost, rotted manure, or inverted sods. Even if the ground has been fertilized, a generous shovelful of bone meal mixed in with the soil won't be wasted, and won't harm the roots. While permanent staking is not necessary with standard or semi-dwarf trees, a stake helps establish the tree during the first year, and assists when planting. When the hole has been prepared, drive the stake firmly into the centre, then tie the tree temporarily to the stake. With standard trees the point of graft should be set slightly below ground level, but with dwarfs and semi-dwarfs it should be set a couple of inches above ground level. Make sure the roots are evenly spread, then carefully fill the hole, pressing the soil firmly around the roots to eliminate air pockets. If the ground is dry, fill the hole with water and let it drain away. Fill the last three inches with loose earth to form a mulch. Retie the tree properly to the stake, and avoid cutting the bark by using a tree-tie or by running a piece of wire through an old piece of rubber or plastic hose and twisting it around both tree and stake in a figure eight. For dwarf trees, which must have permanent stakes, galvanized iron pipe is ideal, though 2 x 2 cedar posts will last several years. (See Fig. 4.)

(6) Planting Cane and Bush Fruits

The trailing cane fruits, such as loganberry, boysenberry and blackberry, will grow in either light or fairly heavy soils, with a preference for the clay loams, provided drainage is adequate. They all have one drawback for the home gardener — they require considerable space.

They should be planted at least six feet apart in the row, with the rows the same distance apart. Probably the best way to save space with these plants is to train them along a side or back fence, provided they get sunlight, but if this can't be done you will have to set up posts with horizontal wires to tie the canes to. Two wires, $2\frac{1}{2}$ feet apart, with the bottom one $2\frac{1}{2}$ feet from the ground, will do the job satisfactorily.

Two-year-old plants are best for home planting, but one-year "tips" can be used. Care must be taken not to break off the new growth buds just above the roots. Canes produced during the current year will fruit the following year. When the plant has become well established, cut out all but eight or ten of the strongest canes. These should be left on the ground until late spring, to avoid any chance of freezing, then tied to the wires, four or five on each side. After fruiting, the old canes should be cut out and the new growth from the crown trained along the ground close to the rows to avoid damage from cultivation. Short wooden stakes every few feet will keep them within bounds.

The loganberry is fine for jam and preserves, and delicious out of hand. It is a heavy yielder (15 to 20 lbs. per plant) and can be obtained in a thornless variety that is easy to handle.

The boysenberry is also excellent for jam and preserves, and delicious eaten fresh, when fully ripe, but doesn't yield as heavily as the logan and is less hardy.

When we come to blackberries, there is a wide choice. The Himalaya is a well-known blackberry that has gone wild in many places in the Pacific Northwest, and is such a rampant, thorny grower that it is difficult to control in the home garden. The fruit is of medium size, sweet, and the plant is a heavy producer.

The Evergreen blackberry, with or without thorns, is similar in size and flavor to the Himalaya, but easier to handle. It crops well, is very sweet, but the seeds have a hard coating, which detracts somewhat from its value. This applies to the Olallie blackberry also, a very large fruit, slightly tart when eaten raw but delicious preserved.

The best flavored of all, for pies, preserves or jam, is the Cascade blackberry. It is a heavy yielder, hardy, and doesn't require quite as much room as the others mentioned.

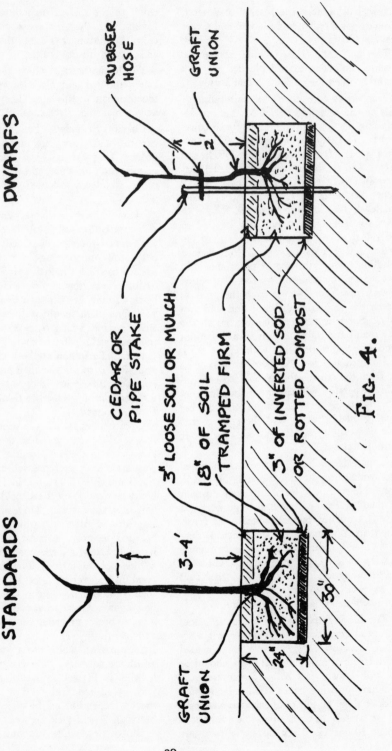

HOW TO PLANT FRUIT TREES

STANDARDS

DWARFS

RUBBER HOSE

GRAFT UNION

CEDAR OR PIPE STAKE

3" LOOSE SOIL OR MULCH

18" OF SOIL TRAMPED FIRM

3" OF INVERTED SOD OR ROTTED COMPOST

GRAFT UNION

3-4'

1"

2'

24"

30"

FIG. 4.

A new development, the Marion blackberry, is as large as a logan, fine flavored and a very heavy producer.

The bush cane fruits include raspberries, currants, gooseberries and blueberries, with the first named the leader in popularity.

Raspberries will grow in a wide range of soils on the acid side (pH 5.5), but are demanding in humus and moisture requirements, and fussy about drainage. There are three types of raspberries, red, black and purple. Red raspberries are planted from one-year-old "sucker" canes, cut back to 12 inches, set with the crown 3 inches below soil level, 18 inches apart in the row, with rows six feet apart. Canes may be tied to individual stakes, or to one wire strung between posts, but the most satisfactory way of handling them is to put in posts about 25 feet apart with crossarms two feet long nailed to each post about 4 feet from the ground. Notch the crossarms on each end and run galvanized wire between the notches all the way round and tighten firmly. Fruiting canes should be tied to the wires with tape or cord, and topped at 5 feet. As the new canes come up from the crowns they should be kept inside the parallel wires. Cut out the old canes after fruiting, keep sucker growth from becoming established beyond the crowns, and thin new cane growth to half a dozen strong canes per crown.

Latham is a reliable, hardy variety, suited to a wide range of climatic and soil conditions. Newburgh is less hardy, but superior in quality. Taylor is a fine large berry of excellent quality, but less suitable for freezing than Willamette or Washington. September and Indian Summer are two everbearing varieties, but their quality isn't quite up to the others mentioned. A dozen canes of any well-grown red raspberry should produce between 35 and 50 lbs. of fruit.

The black raspberry or "black cap" does not produce suckers, the canes rising only from the crown. New plants are obtained from layers or root divisions. They should be set with crowns just below the surface and the new growing canes should be headed back at about 30 inches to encourage laterals. These laterals, in turn, should be cut back to about 10 inches. Black raspberry roots are closer to the surface than those of the red variety, and thus more easily damaged by cultivation. Munger is one of the best known, and a good quality fruit.

Purple raspberries, which are a cross between the red and black varieties, are not too common in this area. They are planted and pruned like black caps.

Currants have always been a popular home garden bush fruit, are hardy and easily grown. They are heavy feeders, partial to manures and moisture, and will thrive in the cooler clay loam soils with a pH of around 6.0.

New plants should be set with the crowns 4 inches below soil level (Fig. 5), with a 5 x 5-foot spacing. Black currants, which bear fruit on one-year-old wood, must be pruned back heavily each year after fruiting, to force new growth. Two good varieties of black currants are Boskoop Giant and Baldwin. One plant should yield 5 lbs. of fruit. Red currants, which require the same spacing, will yield 8 lbs. or more per bush. Red Lake and Perfection are both excellent varieties. Red currants bear their fruit mainly on two and three-year-old wood, and require different pruning, chiefly a thinning of older fruiting canes.

Gooseberries are not everybody's dish, but if you like them, you like them, and they grow well in the cool, moist Pacific Northwest area. They prefer a well-drained silt or clay loam (pH 6.0) and, like currants, are heavy feeders. Plant the same depth and distance apart as currants. There are two strains, English and American, which have been hybridized to provide many varieties. Whinham's Industry, a large sweet red berry, and Whitesmith, a large yellow fruit, are two good English varieties, less subject to mildew than some others. Oregon Champion is the best known American variety in this region, a heavy bearer of green, medium-sized fruit, and very thorny. There are thornless varieties like Spinefree, which are a joy to pick but which are not heavy yielders. One of the best hybrids is Pixwell, a hardy, prolific plant with large red fruit and a minimum of thorns. Depending on the variety, one gooseberry plant will yield between 3 and 6 lbs.

Blueberries, while a popular and highly

HOW TO PLANT SMALL FRUITS

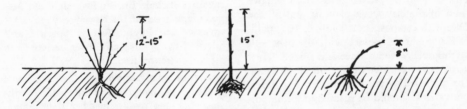

CROWN OF CURRANTS AND GOOSEBERRIES SET 4" BELOW SOIL LEVEL

CROWN OF RASPS SET 3" BELOW SOIL LEVEL

CROWN OF LOGANS, BOYSENS & BLACKBERRIES SET 1" BELOW SOIL LEVEL

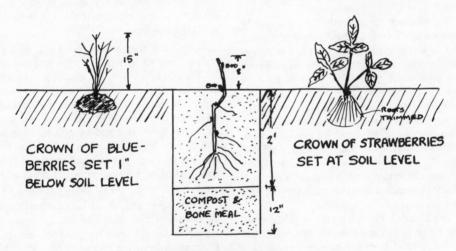

CROWN OF BLUE-BERRIES SET 1" BELOW SOIL LEVEL

COMPOST & BONE MEAL

CROWN OF STRAWBERRIES SET AT SOIL LEVEL

Roots Trimmed

GRAPES SET LEVEL WITH FIRST OF 2 BUDS

FIG. 5

desireable fruit, are not adaptable to many home gardens because of special soil and acidity requirements.. They are peat-loving plants, requiring very acid conditions (pH 4.5 to 5.0) and a constant supply of moisture and humus. In a fibrous loam you can create acidity by incorporating peat moss or sulphur, but if your soil is one of the heavier clay loams, the only way you can grow a blueberry plant satisfactorily is to remove most of the clay when planting and fill the hole with compost, peat and oak leaf mold. Plants should be set with the root ball slightly below the surface and spaced 5 feet apart each way. Don't expect much of a crop for the first few years. Two plants of different varieties should be planted to insure pollination. Some of the older varieties, like Rubel and Rancocas, are more foolproof for home gardens than newer crosses like Earliblue, Concord and Bluecrop, though the latter yield much larger berries. One mature blueberry plant will often yield 5 lbs. of fruit.

Strawberries are probably the most widely planted small fruit in the home garden, and the most neglected. Many gardeners forget that, unlike cane or bush fruits, strawberries are short-lived, with three years at most of bearing life. Yields from older plants diminish rapidly, so care must be taken to replant at regular intervals or you will be faced with disappointment. Strawberries prefer a well-drained sandy loam, slightly acid (pH 5.5 to 6.0) and, like all small fruits, need lots of organic material. They rotate well with potatoes, which enjoy the same type of soil and acidity.

Well-rooted runner plants should be set out 15-18 inches apart in the row, with rows 3 feet apart. Care must be taken to see that the crown of the plant is set just level with the soil surface. A dusting of chlordane powder in each hole before planting will help control root weevils and wireworms. During the first season, all blossoms and runners should be cut off. After the blossoming period in the second year, a mulch of grass, straw or sawdust should be laid down between the rows to keep the berries clean. Runners should be cut off if you want plants to yield a full crop. One pound of fruit per plant is a fair average, though this can be doubled under good conditions.

So many varieties have been established, with new ones arriving each year, it would be wise to check with your local agricultural agency for the latest information. Old-time favorites include British Sovereign and Magoon, and some of the newer, virus-resistant varieties are Puget Beauty, Sparkle and Siletz. Two good everbearing varieties are Streamliner and Red Rich.

Grapes are a fascinating subject for home garden experimentation in the Pacific Northwest, but one must remember their limitations. Where the average mean temperature is 55 degrees from April to June, and 65 degrees through July to September, some varieties will ripen satisfactorily, especially in the warm sandy loams. Low wet ground must be avoided, and a southern exposure against a wall or fence will aid materially in maturing the fruit.

Grapes are deep-rooted plants and an ample reservoir of humus and bonemeal should be placed in each hole, a couple of feet below the surface, before planting. Two-year-old, well-rooted plants are best, and should be cut back to two buds, with the lower bud set at soil level. It would be well to drive in a four-foot stake when planting, to tie up the first year's growth. Grapes require a special method of pruning which is dealt with later in a chapter on that subject. (Ch. I-F).

Varieties are of either European or American origin, with the latter the most adaptable for the coast region. Fredonia and Campbell's Early are two good blue concord types, Portland is an excellent green grape and Caco a high-quality red. Two European types that ripen in some districts are Pearl of Csaba, a green grape, and the well-known Thompson's Seedless, also green. One thrifty vine should yield 15-20 lbs. A seedless green grape named Himrod is one of the best new varieties for Pacific Coast planting.

Species	Soil & Acidity	Planting Period	Planting Depth	Row Width	Row Spacing	Yield p. Plant	Varieties
Loganberry	Clay Loams	Oct.-Mar.	Crown 1" below soil level.	6 ft.	6 ft.	15 lbs.	Regular or Thornless
Boysenberry	pH 5.5-	"		6 ft.	6 ft.	10 lbs.	Regular or Thornless
Blackberry	pH 6.0	"		6 ft.	6 ft.	10 lbs.	Himalaya, Evergreen, Olallie, Cascade, Marion
Raspberry (red)	Loams & Clay	"	Crown 3" below soil level.	6 ft.	18"	3 lbs.	Latham, Newburgh, Haida, Willamette, Washington,
Black Cap	Loams	"		6 ft.	30"	5 lbs.	September, Heritage, Munger
Purple Raspberry	pH 5.5	"	"	6 ft.	30"	6 lbs.	
Black Currants	Clay Loams	"	Crown 4" below soil level.	5 ft.	5 ft.	4 lbs.	Boskoop Giant, Baldwin
Red Currants	pH 6.0-	"		5 ft.	5 ft.	8 lbs.	Perfection, Red Lake
Gooseberries	pH 6.5	"		5 ft.	5 ft.	6 lbs.	Whinham's Industry, Whitesmith, Oregon, Champion, Pixwell
Blueberries	Peat Loam pH 4.5	"	Crown just below soil level.	5 ft.	5 ft.	5 lbs.	Rubel, Rancocas, Earliblue, Concord, Bluecrop
Strawberries	Sandy Loam pH 5.5	Mar.-Apr.	Crown at soil level.	3 ft.	18"	1-2 lbs.	Sovereign, Puget Beauty, Totem, Northwest, Quinault, Red Rich
Grapes	Sandy Loam pH 6.0	Nov.-Mar.	Bury stem to 2 buds above ground level.	6 ft.	7 ft.	15 lbs.	Fredonia, Campbell's Early Portland, Caco, Pearl of Csaba, Interlaken, Himrod
Rhubarb	Rich Loam pH 5.5	Oct.-Mar.	Crown at soil level.	4 ft.	4 ft.	10 lbs.	McDonald Canada Red

PLANTING ORNAMENTALS

Deciduous flowering or shade trees should be planted the same as fruit trees (see Fig. 4) but evergreens require somewhat different treatment. When purchased at a nursery, all but very small sizes of evergreens are in metal or fibre containers, or wrapped in burlap (Balled and Burlapped). In either case the roots are protected by, and are growing in, a ball of soil which must not be broken or disturbed when transplanting. Shrubs in containers should be well moistened before any attempt is made to remove them. A sharp rap on the bottom of the container will usually loosen a shrub sufficiently to slip it out. If not, the can or fibre pot should be cut. Mix some good compost and peat moss (no chemicals) to fill the hole, which should be deep enough to be able to set the shrub to the same depth as the soil mark, and wide enough to be able to tamp the soil mix firmly around the root ball. A slight depression should be left to facilitate watering, which should follow planting immediately. Some B1 solution mixed with the water will help counteract any transplanting shock.

Burlapped shrubs may be planted the same way, but with the burlap on. When the shrub is set in the hole the burlap may be folded back and covered with earth, when it will rot quickly. Do not attempt to break the root ball or spread out the roots. Water both roots and foliage often, especially in dry weather, as most evergreens are shallow-rooted. Don't plant deeper than the soil mark shows. A peat moss mulch will help conserve moisture and maintain the acid condition most evergreens favor.

Propagation

While the reproduction of plants is mainly the concern of the nurseryman or plant hybridist, there is bound to come a time with every home gardener when he wants more of some plant he already has, or a neighbor offers him a "piece" of a particularly fine subject he has been eyeing and envying for years. In either case he should know what to do about it.

Previously we described the structure of a plant—roots, stems, leaves, flowers and fruit —and its classification as an annual, biennial or perennial. All plants in all classes are reproduced either by seed (sexual reproduction) or by the use of vegetative plant parts (asexual reproduction).

(1) Seeds

Seeds are composed of three parts, the embryo or "germ", which is actually a living plant whose growth has been restricted, the endosperm or food storage unit, and the testa or protective seed covering.

To produce a seed, it's obvious we must first have a flower, and this may be either "perfect" or "imperfect," botanically speaking. A perfect flower is one complete with pistil (ovary) and a stamen (pollen), and therefore is capable of self pollination. Most of the common fruit and vegetable plants belong in this category. Imperfect flowers have *either* a stamen *or* a pistil, but not both. Plants like walnuts and filberts, which bear long (staminate) catkins and terminal (pistillate) flowers, or cucumbers, squash and sweet corn, with both male and female flowers on the same plant, are a few examples. Sometimes, as with asparagus, stamens and pistils are on different plants.

Where pollen is transferred from the stamen to the pistil in the same flower, or from one flower to another on the same plant, we say the plant is "self pollinating." Where such pollen is transferred from one plant to another, it is "cross pollinated."

We all know the value of insects, particularly bees, in both self pollination and cross pollination. Wind is another important pollinating agency, especially with plants like filbert nuts and corn, and that is why they receive better pollination when planted in squares or blocks, rather than long single rows.

Of course flowers must be fertilized in order to set fruit or mature seed, but pollination does not necessarily insure fruit or seed maturity. Incompatibility may exist between pollen and pistils of the same plant, a condition known as "self sterility." The Hale peach, Bartlett pear and Burbank plum are some examples.

Where similar incompatibility exists between pollen and pistils of different varieties or species, they are said to be "intersterile." For example, Bing, Lambert or Royal Anne cherries are intersterile, one with another, but a single pollenizer such as Van or Deacon will pollinate all three, and itself be pollinated.

Defective pollen and flower parts, as well as environmental and nutritive factors such as frost damage to bloom and lack of sufficient nourishment, also result in sterility.

Seed is considered alive or 'viable,' if it is capable of germinating and this capability may be affected by the strength of the plant it comes from, the age of the seed before planting, and the conditions of seed storage.

In order for seed to germinate properly, moisture, temperature and oxygen must be properly interrelated. The amount of water necessary for the saturation necessary to promote germination varies with different seeds. Corn, for example, is saturated by 43% of its weight in water, but peas require 107%. The same wide differences apply with regard to temperature. Seeds of cool season crops like peas and spinach, will germinate fairly readily as low as 45 Deg. F, more readily as you approach 70 Deg. F, but over 80 Deg. F. germination declines rapidly. On the other hand, warm season crops such as muskmelons require a minimum of 60 Deg. F. and the higher the temperature the quicker they germinate. It is obvious, therefore, why it's important not to plant certain seeds in the open ground until conditions are right.

The seed is a living structure and the embryo requires oxygen for the initiation of growth, so when seeds are planted too deep or in compact, wet seed beds, germination may be prevented. Even when environmental conditions are favorable, certain seeds may not germinate without delay or without some prior treatment. Hard seed coats may prevent admission of water and may have to be made more pervious by scratching or cracking. Sweet pea seed is one in which germination can be assisted by such treatment. Sometimes dilute sulphuric acid, acetic acid or hot water are employed, and some seeds require to be frozen or stratified. Fortunately for the home gardener, most vegetable and flower seeds germinate without difficulty.

Before closing this discussion on seeds, it would be well to remember that many diseases are transmitted either from the seed surface or from within the seed coat. Corn smut, cabbage rot, and "damping off" of many kinds of seedlings may result if seed is not treated before planting. Various or-

TRANSPLANTING SEEDLINGS

ganic mercury compounds have been manufactured for this purpose and are sold as dust or liquid, under various trade names.

(2) Asexual Propagation

The methods by which plants can be produced asexually are bulb propagation, layerage, cuttage and graftage. Certain plants favor certain methods, as we shall see by examining each method briefly.

Herbaceous plants that persist through the winter by means of subterranean buds may be divided into four groups: *bulbs* (layered or scaly), *corms* (solid bulbs), *rootstocks* (rhizomes or pips), and *tubers* (stem or root). See Fig. 6.

In some bulbs, like tulips, narcissus and hyacinths, the scales are continuous around the axis, forming a series of layers, hence the term "layered" bulbs. With tulips the old structure is consumed in growth of the plant, and a new large bulb, with three or four small ones, reproduced each year. These smaller bulbs require one or two years of additional growth before they, in turn, bloom and produce bulbs. With narcissus (which includes daffodils, jonquils, paperwhites and Chinese lilies) new bulbs are produced laterally, but the old bulb continues to grow. These laterals or "splits" can be separated easily from the mother bulb and after three years will flower and produce laterals of their own. With hyacinths the old bulb itself splits up into several rather large ones, and a ring of small, flat bulbs forms around the basal plate. Some of these young bulbs will reach maturity in two years, most of them will take four. All these types of bulbs

ASEXUAL PROPAGATION

LAYERED BULBS

MOTHER TULIP BULB
& 3 SPLITS

MOTHER DAFFODIL BULB
& 4 SLABS

SCALY BULBS

MOTHER LILY BULB & SCALES

CORMS

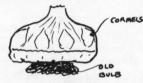

CORMELS

OLD BULB

GLADIOLUS BULB

RHIZOMES

GERMAN IRIS

STEM TUBERS

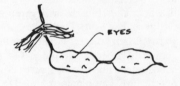

EYES

POTATOES

ROOT TUBERS

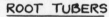

EYES

ROOT CAP

DAHLIA TUBERS

LAYERAGE

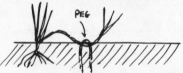

PEG

A CARNATION PEGGED FOR LAYERING

CUTTINGS

SOFTWOOD
CUTTING

HARDWOOD
CUTTING

LEAF
CUTTING

GRAFTAGE

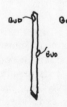
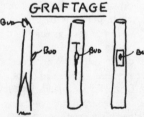

BUD

BUD

BUD

BUD

BUD

FRUIT TREE
SCION

SADDLE
GRAFT

SHIELD
BUDDING

PATCH
BUDDING

FIG. 6

can be propagated from seed, but sometimes take as long as seven years to reach a flowering stage.

In other types of bulbs, like lilies, the scales are not continuous around the axis, but are narrow and fleshy and may be removed singly from the outer edges of the bulb, hence the term "scaly" bulb. For propagation, scales are removed from the bulb in the late flowering stage, a dozen or more from one bulb without damage. The scales are covered immediately with a couple of inches of soil and by the following spring will have produced bulblets on the concave sides, usually two to a scale. They can be removed and planted, or left for another season. It's at least two years before they will produce flowers. Seeds are produced by almost all lilies, which has made possible considerable hybridization and development of new varieties.

A corm, or solid bulb, is actually not a true bulb, though it produces roots from the lower surface, as bulbs do. Buds are formed on the upper surface which produce small corms for reproduction. Corms are produced by gladiolus, crocus, and some species of iris. The larger corms, in addition to blooming, will be replaced by new bulbs on top of the old ones, which will bloom the following year. The small cormels, when planted for two years, will flower and repeat the performance of their parents. Gladiolus, like lilies, tulips, etc. can be hybridized and grown from seed, and every year dozens of new varieties come on the market.

A rhizome rootstock is really just a stem growing horizontally, slightly below the soil surface. The German iris (flag) is a typical example. The plants spread rapidly and after flowering, pieces of rooted rhizome may be severed from the parent plant and set out on their own. The banana is one of the most important fruit plants to be propagated in this way.

A pip, as produced by Lily of the Valley, is an upright part produced upon a horizontal rootstock, and is actually a rhizome with a different name.

Tubers may be classified as stem tubers (potatoes) or root tubers (dahlias). A stem tuber is simply a shortened, thickened underground stem, with scale-like scars subtending the eyes. Propagation is effected by cutting up the tuber in pieces, each of which must contain one or more "eyes" and sufficient food to start up the new plant. Potatoes have been planted so long in this way that they rarely bloom any more, though development of new varieties must come from cross pollination and seed.

Root tubers such as dahlias and sweet potatoes produce fleshy roots resembling the stem tubers, but possess a rootcap not found in the other group and don't have eyes on the roots themselves, but on the rootcap. This cap or crown may be divided with a sharp knife, but care must be taken to make sure that each part of the crown has at least one eye and a good-sized piece of tuber attached.

Thus far, in our discussion of asexual propagation, we have dealt mainly with bulbs and herbaceous material. When we seek propagation of woody material, such as trees and shrubs, the problem becomes a little more complicated.

One of the easiest and most reliable methods for the home gardener, on a wide range of subjects, is layerage. Stems that form roots while still attached to the parent plant are called "layers," hence "layerage." Many plants, like strawberries, produce natural layers freely by runners, others like blackberries or loganberries arch over and contact the earth where the tips root. Some plants, like chrysanthemums, produce natural layers from the crown of the plant.

Where branches form roots at one point only, at the tips for example, they are called simple layers, and where long shoots are alternatively covered and exposed over their entire length, they are termed compound layers. Tip layering is usually done in the early spring. With the cane fruits, like loganberries, tips are covered with a couple of inches of soil, when they root readily. With bushy plants, like filberts or lilacs, branches are bent in a wide arc, pegged to the ground a few inches below the tip in a U shape, leaving the tip exposed. Some species root quickly and may be transplanted the same season while others require two seasons to develop a good root system.

A method of compound layering known as trench or continuous layering, where a branch is covered for its entire length, will stimulate growth from nearly all the buds, thus providing many more plants than by the tip layering method. Low branches of lauristinus, forsythia, cotoneaster and many other plants can be pegged down and treated in this way. As shoots arise they should be covered gradually with soil to encourage more roots. Sometimes a whole plant is cut back to within a foot of the ground and the earth hilled up to cover all the branches within a few inches of the top. This is called mound or stool layerage. If the soil is kept moist throughout the season, roots will form along the covered branches and when the plants become dormant in the fall, the soil is scraped away and the rooted branches cut off and transplanted. Gooseberries and currants are adaptable to this method of propagation and it is used extensively for rooting dwarf apple or quince stocks.

There is one other method of layerage developed long ago by the Chinese to root branches of stiff growing plants that don't sprout or sucker readily. Called air layerage, it involves notching or girdling the stem of the plant and wrapping it with a suitable medium for rooting. Sphagnum moss, wrapped with plastic to keep air out and moisture in, will do the trick. When roots become established, simply cut off the stem below the root and transplant.

Cuttage as a propagative process differs from layerage inasmuch as the parts used are detached from the parent plant before they have a chance to develop roots. This method is used extensively by nurserymen in propagation of ornamental plants, deciduous and evergreen, and where plants strike roots readily is a cheap and convenient means of rapid increase.

Plant parts used in making cuttings may be roots, leaves or stems. Sweet potato and horse radish are propagated commercially from root cuttings, and blackberries, raspberries, etc., can be increased in this way without difficulty. The technique of taking cuttings varies with different species, but pieces of root not less than 1/4 inch in diameter and from two inches to six inches long,

taken in early winter, stored in moist sand for callusing, and planted out in spring, will usually root satisfactorily.

Leaf cuttings are used mainly in the propagation of house plants such as African violets, gloxinias, etc., but may be taken from chrysanthemums, camellias and many others. Leaves are cut with a vein in the centre and a portion of the petiole or leaf stalk at the base. Roots and the new shoot will develop at the base of the cutting when set in moist sand under proper temperature and humidity.

Stem cuttings are by far the most important and commonly used method of propagation by cuttage. They may be made from herbaceous plants, like geraniums, or from woody plants of all kinds. Soft, succulent cuttings of herbaceous material require special attention regarding temperature and moisture, but root quickly under favorable conditions.

Cuttings of trees and shrubs that are made from current season shoots are known as semi-hardwood, or softwood, cuttings. Shoots that snap clean when bent are considered right for semi-hardwood cuttings. All but the terminal leaves are removed. Cool temperatures to prevent wilting, high humidity, plus bottom heat from either manure or electric heating elements, are essential for best results with many subjects. On a small scale, cuttings may be planted in flats placed in a shaded location and sprayed often, or placed under a bell jar or plastic covered pot to keep up the humidity. (See Fig. 7.)

Hardwood cuttings are taken from ripened wood, usually one year old. Cuttings of deciduous plants like roses, currants, or hydrangeas, are taken during the dormant season, and either stored in a moist material like sand or sawdust and planted out in early spring, or cut and planted directly into the ground in late winter, just before the new growth starts. Cuttings from four inches to 12 inches long, depending on the plant, are removed with a sharp knife or secateurs. Cuttings of conifers, two inches to six inches long, require foliage to be removed from the lower portion of the stem. They may be taken during spring, summer or fall, if perfect rooting conditions are provided. Some

PROPAGATING SOFTWOOD CUTTINGS

METHOD 1.

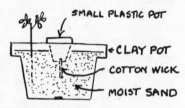

SMALL PLASTIC POT
CLAY POT
COTTON WICK
MOIST SAND

PLUNGE CUTTINGS IN
COARSE SAND - FILL SMALL
POT WITH WATER.

HIGH HUMIDITY SUSTAINED
BY ENCLOSING POT WITH
POLYETHYLENE.

METHOD 2.

METHOD 3.

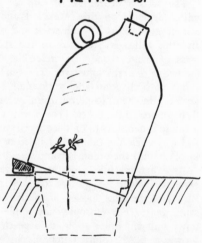

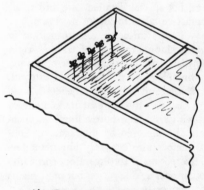

WHITEWASH COLD FRAME
GLASS - SPREAD SAND 4" DEEP,
MOISTEN, & INSERT CUTTINGS.
SPRAY DAILY.

BELL JAR MADE FROM GALLON
GLASS JUG WITH BOTTOM REMOVED.
PLUNGE POT OF CUTTINGS INTO GROUND.
TILT JAR SLIGHTLY FOR VENTILATION.
KEEP IN SHADE.

FIG. 7.

TYPICAL CHRYSANTHEMUM CUTTINGS

root within a couple of months, others take six months or longer.

Several broad leafed evergreens, like holly and camellias, are grown from hardwood cuttings, but special detailed care and treatment must be taken to insure success.

Many factors influence root formation in cuttings, including the time of taking, origin on the plant, rooting medium, temperature, light, humidity a n d chemical treatment. Clean, sharp sand is the most generally used rooting material, though peat moss alone or mixed with sand, and horticultural vermiculite, are all employed by propagators. Control of temperature is a very important factor in the rooting of cuttings. Root formation may occur over a wide range, but most plants favor a temperature between 55 and 70 Deg. F., with bottom heat preferred. High humidity should be maintained to prevent drying or wilting, and this is often difficult for the home gardener unless he provides himself with a hot bed, small greenhouse, or heating cable under a plastic covering. Many kinds of chemicals have been used to induce root formation, from potassium permanganate, vinegar, or sugar solutions, to the latest hormones and gases. In many cases, such as holly, they have proved effective, but in other hard to root items they have had little or no effect.

Graftage, or the art of inserting a part of one plant into another with continued growth, is one of the oldest of horticultural practices. Parts cut from any plant to be used for grafting are termed scions. They are usually obtained from dormant, one-year wood, and kept under cool moist storage until ready for use, which is just before growth begins in the spring. Sizes of scions vary for different methods, but a typical scion for grafting on an apple tree, for example, should be five inches or six inches long, with at least three plump buds.

Wood used for budding, which is really just another term for grafting, may be taken during the current season, when it has ripened, and used immediately, or stored at a temperature of between 32 deg. F. and 36 deg. F. for use the following spring. Buds are simply sliced off with a sharp knife and inserted into a T slot on the stock to be budded, or cut in a square patch and placed where a similar patch has been cut out of the stock.

The success or failure of bud or graft union depends on the formation and comingling of callus by both stock and scion, and this callus is produced by the spongy mass of white tissue just under the bark, known as the cambium layer. The cambium layers of both scion and stock must be in perfect alignment, to permit the flow of sap through one to the other. That is why a firm pressure is necessary to produce a graft union, and why a scion or bud must be tied or held in place until the union is completed.

As a general rule a horticultural variety may be budded or grafted on any other variety of the same species, or species of the same genus. For example, any apple will unite with any other apple, or a peach will grow on peach, plum, almond, cherry or apricot rootstocks. But a pome fruit (apple) will not unite with a stone fruit (peach, etc). The fact that stock and scion will unite isn't always assurance that the union will be enduring, for there are many cases of physiological uncongeniality.

There are many methods of grafting, all of which require considerable skill, and many types of rootstocks for different purposes, and if the reader is interested in pursuing this subject in detail, or any other phase of propagation, he would be wise to obtain special textbooks on the subject.

Watering and Cultivation

These seem like simple enough operations, on the face of it, and they are, yet it's surprising how easily they can be done wrong, and very important that they be done right.

After the heavy winter rains in the Pacific Northwest, moist soils are saturated deep into the subsoil, providing a generous reservoir of moisture. The gardener's concern at this time is more often how to get rid of water than to apply it. However, when the warm spring winds begin to blow, the land dries out quickly. A thin crust forms on the soil surface, cracks open up, and the sun and wind suck moisture from the earth at an amazing rate. If nothing is done to check this process, the gardener is reaching for his hose weeks sooner than necessary.

(1) The Time for Tillage

There is an optimum moment, both for soil tilth and moisture conservation, when the soil crust should be broken and the soil stirred. If it's done too soon, lumps form, particularly in the clay soils, that will take the rest of the summer to break up. If done too late, the earth may be hard and the moisture reservoir gone.

A simple test to determine the right time for tillage is to pick up a handful of soil and squeeze it. If it balls up and moisture oozes forth, it is too wet. If it crumbles easily but still holds together, it is just about right. This condition will not last long, so don't delay tillage an hour longer than you have to.

Right after tillage is an excellent time to plant, provided temperature conditions are favorable. The damp, aerated soil will germinate seeds quickly, often without any watering from the hose. Once germination

has taken place, the gardener without experience is apt to keep sprinkling the soil surface every day or so. It should be remembered, however, that, once rooted, the water requirement of young plants is low. Their root system, however, will be developing and pushing down into the earth to make use of available plant nutrients. Frequent shallow watering induces root growth close to the surface, prevents deep feeding, and makes plants unable to withstand any period of drought later on. This early season sprinkling is particularly harmful to deep rooted plants, like tomatoes. Plant development is overstimulated and when fruits begin to swell and the normal demand for moisture increases to fill the fruit, plants will suffer, producing blossom-end rot, unless the increasing water requirements are met.

(2) The Time for Watering

Turn over a spadeful of soil and see how far the moisture is from the surface. If need is indicated, make certain the ground is saturated to the full depth of the plant roots. It takes five gallons of water per square yard to provide the equivalent of one inch of rainfall which, under average conditions, will penetrate about a foot. Thorough soakings every ten days or two weeks should be sufficient in average soil under average temperature conditions.

(3) Rules for Watering

In the vegetable garden it will be obvious that moisture requirements of some plants will be greater than others, so that particular attention may have to be given certain subjects .Onions, for example, are less demanding than squash or cucumbers. It will be equally obvious that plants require more moisture than usual while filling or maturing than at the beginning of the season. For example, care must be taken to assure ample moisture when pea pods are starting to fill, or corn cobs swelling. On the other hand, once the crop is assured and ripening, damage may result from an over supply. Tomatoes will split their skins, onions rot, and potatoes get watery and subject to disease if they get too much water late in the season.

The same conditions apply with small fruits. Strawberries need considerable moisture to develop and set their fruit, but too much when the fruit is ripening will produce watery, poorly flavored berries, subject to quick spoilage. Raspberries are notably demanding in their moisture requirements, but an overabundance will produce crumbly berries lacking in sweetness and keeping qualities.

Tree fruits in the Pacific northwest are more likely to suffer from a lack of summer moisture than an over supply, unless the home gardener has been particularly generous. Trees, with their abundance of leaves, consume huge quantities of water. Even a dwarf tree, with a heavy set of fruit, needs the equivalent of six or seven inches of rainfall during the summer months. In the home orchard one is likely to water fruit trees like vegetables, which is a mistake. Tree roots penetrate far deeper into the soil and watering must be thorough to reach them.

Ornamental trees along the lawn or flower borders usually obtain enough moisture from the watering of other subjects, but if the trees are large, occasional extra doses won't go amiss. Those hose attachments that plunge two feet or more into the ground are useful for this purpose, and put the water right where it is needed.

Generally speaking, the watering of flowers and shrubs should be treated the same as vegetables, infrequently during the earlier part of the season, deeply when occasion requires it during the hot dry summer. There are so many special requirements, however, that it is difficult to generalize. Some plants, like roses, don't like their foliage wetted more than necessary, while others, like camellias, rhododendrons, and most conifers,

suffer in dry warm weather if their foliage isn't sprayed regularly. Some subjects, like begonias and clematis, like their roots kept cool and moist at all times, while broom and geraniums, to mention a couple, prefer conditions on the hot dry side. Such differences are somewhat confusing and make watering a problem unless minimized by proper landscaping, a subject we will deal with later.

While the lawn will require more water, oftener, than any other part of the garden, the principle of watering deeply at intervals rather than frequent sprinklings, applies just as emphatically as elsewhere. Grass roots penetrate at least six inches and if they are forced to the surface to seek required moisture, will be subject to quick destruction should watering be withheld suddenly. Overwatering, on the other hand, tends to make the soil sour and compact, promoting mosses and fungous diseases.

(4) Methods of Watering

There has been a long standing controversy between two schools of thought on the best way to water, by ground irrigation or by sprinkling. While this is of more concern to the commercial grower than the home gardener, it is, nevertheless, of some interest. Irrigation by the furrow method has the advantage of placing the water where you want it with a minimum of loss through evaporation. To be effective, however, the ground must have the right slope in the right direction, and should be absorbent enough to take water at a reasonable rate without flooding. Sometimes, when the ground has dried out considerably, water running along furrows doesn't have much lateral movement and may not reach all the area intended. For the home gardener, ground irrigation would be most effective in the orchard. If it's possible to employ it in the rose garden or chrysanthemum bed, so much the better.

Sprinkling, in spite of considerable loss from evaporation, has the advantage of covering a complete area, and in a manner that can be regulated according to the absorptive ability of the soil. Sprinklers can be adapted to a 10 foot or a 50 foot space, moved anywhere, left as long as required, even adjusted to a small or large output. For lawns they are the most feasible method of coverage. Their flow, however, can often be deceptive. Make certain when you move a sprinkler or sprinkler hose, that satisfactory penetration has been accomplished.

(5) Cultivation

Cultivation and moisture control go hand in hand, for several reasons. Weeds, as we all know, are moisture robbers, and surface cultivation that destroys them not only prevents further loss from weed competition, but provides a dust mulch that prevents some loss from natural evaporation. Surface cultivation with a Dutch hoe should take place after every watering, as soon as the soil begins to dry out, after every rain, and as often as necessary to control weed growth. Deeper cultivation, with a hand cultivator or roto-tiller, should take place only when the ground has been compacted after winter rains or heavy watering, because too much tillage of this sort destroys organic matter and prevents bacterial action so necessary for plant growth.

(6) Mulching

Mulching is an integral part of cultivation practice, weed control, and moisture conservation. Also, if the mulch is organic it will increase the humus content and fertility of the soil.

We have mentioned the dust mulch caused by surface cultivation, but mulching by application of various materials to the soil surface can become even more effective. What you use depends on cost, availability, and resultant appearance. Manure, straw, grass clippings, leaves, peat moss, sawdust and shavings are some types of material that may be used, with varying results. Some of these decay fairly rapidly under moist conditions, and, even without cultivation into the soil, will soon become incorporated with it and lose part of their mulching effect.

Sawdust has been proven a very satisfactory, cheap material for conserving moisture over a continuing period, provided a depth of at least three inches has been applied. In the home garden, however, it should be used with restraint. If soil is heavy, a sawdust mulch tends to retain water too long, and excludes oxygen to such an extent that plants will suffer, even die. Under such conditions planer shavings would be better. Sawdust isn't particularly attractive in flower or shrub borders, especially after it has weathered, and when used in the vegetable garden care must be taken not to mix it with the soil unless nitrogen fertilizer has been applied previously to offset the nitrogen taken from the soil as the sawdust cellulose decomposes. As much as 10 pounds per 100 square feet of ammonium nitrate the first year, and half that much the following year, should be applied. Sawdust and shavings will do a good job in the orchard, around fruit trees, between rows of cane or bush fruits, and even in the strawberry patch. Gradual decay of the material will provide humus, even good fertilizer, over the years, especially where steady applications of chemical nitrates have been added. This means that additional sawdust must be spread every couple of years to keep the mulch effective. Contrary to popular belief, it doesn't make the soil acid, but if anything has the opposite effect.

For a mulch around evergreens and acid loving plants, it's hard to beat peat moss or the peat moss compounds now on the market everywhere. The latter, plus a sprinkling of bone meal, also make an ideal mulch for the rose bed or flower borders, where the earthy dark brown color blends harmoniously with soil or foliage. Since it is very slow to deteriorate, its effect on the nitrogen content of the soil is negligible and it is not necessary to add extra nitrogen as with sawdust.

Hay or straw provides an excellent loose spring covering between rows of vegetables and can be dug or tilled into the soil at the end of the growing season to provide humus for the following year.

Mulching paper, black plastic and aluminum foil are becoming more popular every year, especially in the vegetable garden where they retain warmth and moisture and eliminate weed growth. Of course they add nothing to the condition or fertility of the soil.

Whatever you use, the saving in your water bill will probably pay for the cost of the materials as well as release valuable hours of watering and cultivating time for other more interesting activities.

Pruning

Contrary to popular conception, pruning is not one of the occult sciences. It is partly a science, of course, but it is an art as well, the art of making a shrub or tree grow the way you want it to. This is not as difficult as it seems when you understand some of the purposes and principles involved.

(1) Purpose and General Rules

Pruning plants is done to increase their flowering or fruiting capacity, to improve their appearance, and, or, to make them stronger and long lived. It is practised widely on deciduous plants, to a lesser extent on evergreens. Pruning on all subjects, particularly trees, should begin early in their life, preferably at planting time. Ten minutes spent training the young tree to a good framework is worth ten hours pruning after the tree is blossoming or bearing. Though pruning doesn't change a tree's natural habit of growth, it can be used to alter that growth to some extent. "As the twig is bent, so the tree inclines," the old saying goes, and it is true.

(2) Pruning Ornamental and Fruit Trees

The first step is selecting the shape. There are four fundamental shapes, with which most of us are familiar: the main leader or pyramidal shape, the open centre or vase shape, the umbrella shape, or the modified leader shape. (See Fig. 8.)

The main leader type is most suitable for shade trees, like silver birch, copper beech, maples, mountain ash, and the like. Once you have established the height you want the first branch from the ground, and a framework of well placed branches around the trunk, there is little pruning to be done in subsequent years except the occasional removal of crossing or broken branches.

The open centre or vase shape is used for flowering plums, crabapples, hawthornes, etc., trees that normally don't reach a great height. To accomplish this shape on a young tree, simply select four or five strong branches spaced around the trunk, and instead of heading back the lower ones hard, try to keep them more or less the same height, at the same time remembering to take out the main leader to a strong upright lateral. As years go by, keep a main leader from establishing itself, keep the centre free from cross branches, thin lightly where crowding is obvious, and let the natural habit of the tree do the rest.

The umbrella shaped tree is found mainly with weeping varieties of cherries, crabapples, dwarf maples, etc. Considerable skill is required to establish the framework in these, and so they are usually sold in the nurseries with the main branching already set. The average gardener would be well advised to buy them that way. Little pruning, except removal of cross branches, is required to maintain them.

44

FOUR BASIC SHAPES TO PRUNE TREES

MAIN LEADER TYPE   OPEN CENTRE OR VASE TYPE   UMBRELLA TYPE   MODIFIED LEADER TYPE

PRUNING APPLES AND PEARS

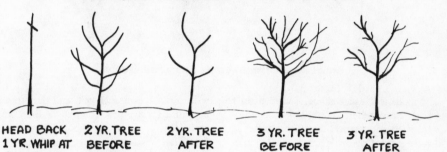

HEAD BACK 1 YR. WHIP AT PLANTING   2 YR. TREE BEFORE PRUNING   2 YR. TREE AFTER PRUNING   3 YR. TREE BEFORE PRUNING   3 YR. TREE AFTER PRUNING

PRUNING PEACHES - CHERRIES & PLUMS

DE SHOOTING 1 YR. PEACH   AFTER 3 WEEKS GROWTH   ALL BUT 4 BRANCHES REMOVED   END OF SEASON AFTER DESHOOTING   2 YR. TREE BEFORE PRUNING   2 YR. TREE AFTER PRUNING

FIG. 8

TWO-YEAR PEACH TREE—BEFORE AND AFTER PRUNING

The modified leader shape is used mainly for fruit trees, where strength is more important than appearance. Any breakdown in a mature fruit tree will occur usually at a crotch, so it's important to choose framework branches with wide angles to the main trunk. Also two branches mustn't grow at the same level as the leader, or in time the leader will be forced out.

Though fruit trees are sold in nurseries as two or three-year-old branched stock, sometimes only one year "whips" are available. In planting a whip there is only one thing to remember: head back the top to promote branching, three or four feet from the ground on standard trees, two to three feet for dwarfs. After the first season's growth you should have half a dozen or more side branches, some of which will be stronger and better angled from the trunk than others. Select the best three to five of these, careful to locate them at different positions around the trunk, and if the laterals have made two to three feet of new growth, cut back a third of this growth to buds facing outward. After another year's growth the scaffold branches

will themselves branch out, and these should be pruned back just enough so they won't outbalance their parent shoots. Further scaffold branches may be chosen at this time, if needed, and any thinning necessary to keep the tree open to air and sunlight. At the end of the third season the framework of the tree should be set, and henceforth pruning should consist of cutting any strong ingrowing or crossing branches, heading back limbs that are getting out of proportion, and a general light thinning to promote circulation. Remember that too heavy pruning results in dwarfing the tree, and delays bearing. Little and often should be the rule on older trees, and let common sense be your guide.

Generally speaking this treatment applies to apples, pears, cherries and plums, but a relatively new method of training young trees has become popular, and we will outline it. Peaches are generally sold by nurseries as yearlings, and as a rule are heavily branched. After heading back the top to between three and four feet from the crown, all lateral shoots should be cut back to one bud. When growth starts, shoots will develop

46

from these buds, and when they are four or five inches long select the best four or five for scaffold branches, remembering to space them around the trunk at least six inches apart. Cut out all the others. You should end up with a modified leader tree, similar to what we have described for apples, and from then on treat it the same, remembering that growth in peaches is usually heavy and requires considerable thinning out.

Pruning dwarfs is essentially the same as pruning standards, only on a smaller scale, except where it is desirable to train them along wires or fences as espalier or cordon trees (See Fig. 9.) We will deal, briefly, with each of these types, as they are becoming more and more popular with the home gardener as a means of saving valuable space.

An espalier is a tree with one to six branches, all grown horizontally. To start a double espalier, which is simply a long-armed T shape, select a strong one-year "whip" from the nursery and head it back two feet from the ground. If you aren't going to plant it against a fence or wall, set up a horizontal support of heavy galvanized wire or pipe two feet high and, for each tree, about six feet long. When branching takes place, choose the two strongest side shoots near the top of the trunk, one on each side, and train them horizontally along the support. Remove all other branches. It will take two seasons of growth for these two arms to reach the length you want. Meanwhile lateral growth will occur and this should be cut back within four inches of the parent branch. This is accomplished by summer pruning, which is simply pinching out the tip of each shoot when it has produced six or eight leaves. If further growth occurs after this has been done, pinch out the tips again. Only the terminals of the main branches are left unpruned during the summer season and when the tree becomes dormant these can be headed back, if necessary, to stay within the space allotted. At the same time, the summer pruned laterals should be cut back to the first or second bud of that season's growth. The reduction of leaf surface by this summer and winter pruning controls the tree's capacity to produce food, thus controlling its growth,

and at the same time encourages formation of fruit buds, or spurs. Two-tiered, or even three-tiered espaliers can be established by heading the young whip higher and training another pair or two pair of arms at right angles to the main trunk.

A cordon differs from an espalier only in the position it is trained to hold, obliquely or vertically, instead of horizontally. A single oblique cordon can be started either by planting the young whip at an angle of 45 degrees or by heading it 18 inches from the ground and training one strong branch at that angle. Planting trees in this manner slows up the flow of sap and induces the lateral buds to break and form spurs. Where they don't do this they must be summer pruned as previously described. Single oblique cordons can be planted two feet apart, and will require some support. A wooden or wire framework with horizontals spaced every 18 inches from the ground to a height of six feet will be found necessary to accommodate full growth. Modified forms of the single upright or oblique types of cordons can be grown, such as the U-shaped double cordon, or the fan combination. While both the cordon and espalier forms are suitable for growing both apples and pears, and to a limited extent, plums, most growers prefer the cordon form for dwarf apples and the espalier for dwarf pears. The fan shape is suitable for peaches against a wall.

Before closing our discussion on pruning trees, there are a few general observations that may be useful. It is important to remember that the distance from the ground to the first branch never alters. Many people are under the mistaken impression that as a tree grows upwards, branches extend with it and new ones break out below. As the girth of the trunk expands, the diameter of the branches increases also, but the position of the framework branching remains unchanged.

Where old trees are sound and merely suffering from neglect, they may be brought back to controlled growth if you remember to do it gradually. Your first impulse may be to de-head or de-horn such a tree in one operation, to give it a fresh start. If you do this, you will promote a forest of "water

METHODS OF TRAINING DWARF FRUIT TREES

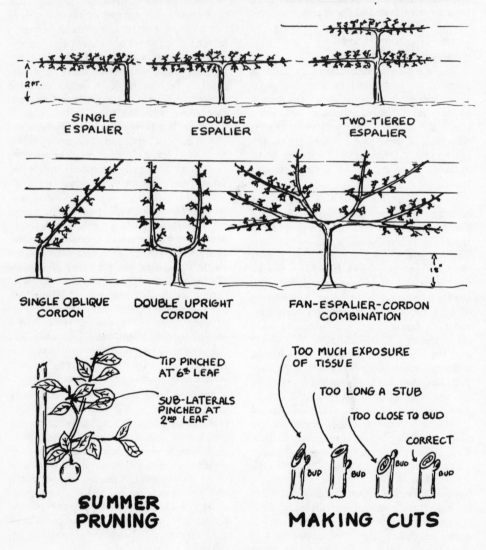

2 FT.

SINGLE ESPALIER

DOUBLE ESPALIER

TWO-TIERED ESPALIER

SINGLE OBLIQUE CORDON

DOUBLE UPRIGHT CORDON

FAN-ESPALIER-CORDON COMBINATION

18"

TIP PINCHED AT 6ᵗʰ LEAF

SUB-LATERALS PINCHED AT 2ⁿᵈ LEAF

SUMMER PRUNING

TOO MUCH EXPOSURE OF TISSUE

TOO LONG A STUB

TOO CLOSE TO BUD

CORRECT

BUD   BUD   BUD   BUD

MAKING CUTS

FIG. 9

sprouts," soft, sterile shoots that will provide leaves to sustain the tree, but little if any flowering or fruiting wood.

The best way to treat a long neglected tree is to space pruning operations over a three-year period, removing a few of the larger limbs each year, thinning out gradually, and at the same time cutting a few strong roots. Root pruning is a shock to the tree and shouldn't be overdone, but will help prevent quick compensatory growth forced by removal of large limbs. Heavy branches which grow out from the trunk at a sharp angle should be cabled. Where there are two the same size, growing in a Y shape, one should be cut back part way to maintain an unequal balance and avoid an eventual splitting. Long limbs that end in numerous branches should have the mass of branches thinned to lighten the load. Large cuts should be slanted, and coated with tree paint or emulsified asphalt to keep out moisture and insects until the wounds heal. Branches should be cut flush with other main branches without leaving stubs. If a limb has broken off leaving a ragged scar and torn bark, the injured area should be cleaned up and smoothed with a sharp knife or chisel, and the margin of the wound cut back to sound bark. Trees partly blown over by storms should be pulled upright and wired to stakes until the roots take new hold. If a tree is heavily infected with disease or rot, and you wish to save it, you would be wise to consult a tree expert before taking steps. There is an old jingle that says: "There is somethin' very final about the cuttin' of a limb, for no amount of sighin' will put it back ag'in."

(3) Pruning Small Fruits

In a previous chapter on planting small fruits we mentioned some of the pruning practices necessary to sustain production, but a brief repetition might fix them in mind more sharply.

With strawberries, pruning is merely a matter of keeping the runners cut off as they grow, and also the blossoms during the first year, and shearing the summer's growth of leaves in the fall.

Old raspberry canes should be cut out immediately after fruiting, and sucker growth away from the crowns should be removed be-

FORMING AN ESPALIER FRUIT TREE ALONG A WIRE FENCE

fore it becomes established. Weak canes from the crowns should be cut out, leaving half a dozen strong canes. When new canes have reached the horizontal wire supports (four feet from ground), they should be tied and, if over six feet, topped to five. Laterals, if any, should be cut back to six inches.

Old fruiting wood on loganberries, boysenberries and blackberry vines should be removed as soon as possible after fruiting, and the new cane growth kept on the ground parallel to the rows to avoid damage. This should be left until late spring before tying up to wires, to avoid any chance of late frost or wind damage. If laterals weren't shortened during the summer, they can be cut back before the canes are tied. Thin canes should be removed, leaving no more than eight strong canes per plant.

Black currants, which fruit on one-year-old wood, often send out a foot or more of new growth each season. A third of this should be cut back during the late fall or early spring, and cross branches removed. Old wood that is choking the centre of the bush may be removed right after fruiting, when it will help force new growth.

Red currants and gooseberries not only bear some fruit on one-year wood but on spurs on two and three-year-old wood as well. It's sound practice to remove each year

PRUNING FLOWERING SHRUBS

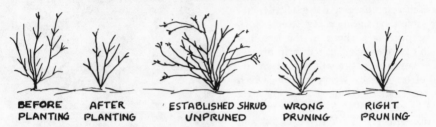

BEFORE PLANTING   AFTER PLANTING   ESTABLISHED SHRUB UNPRUNED   WRONG PRUNING   RIGHT PRUNING

PRUNING ROSES

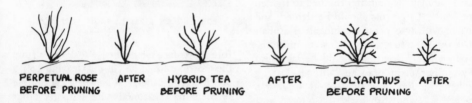

PERPETUAL ROSE BEFORE PRUNING   AFTER   HYBRID TEA BEFORE PRUNING   AFTER   POLYANTHUS BEFORE PRUNING   AFTER

PRUNING SMALL FRUITS

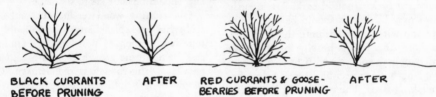

BLACK CURRANTS BEFORE PRUNING   AFTER   RED CURRANTS & GOOSE-BERRIES BEFORE PRUNING   AFTER

PRUNING GRAPES

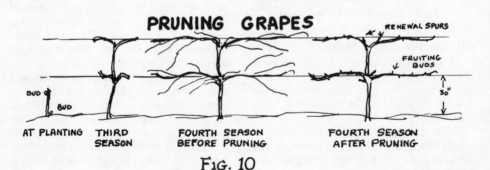

RENEWAL SPURS

FRUITING BUDS

30"

BUD

BUD

AT PLANTING   THIRD SEASON   FOURTH SEASON BEFORE PRUNING   FOURTH SEASON AFTER PRUNING

FIG. 10

a third of all wood that has borne two crops. Gooseberries, in particular, have a lot of spindly shoots that must be cut out.

Blueberries tend to overbear by producing a lot of twiggy laterals on two-year-old producing wood. To keep the fruit up to size, many of these laterals must be thinned out, as well as old, non-productive canes and any canes that show dieback from canker. Thin, one-year growth should be removed also, and long shoots of current growth shortened.

There are several approved systems of grape pruning, all based on the fact that fruit is borne on canes of current season's growth which have arisen from buds that grew the year before. It's necessary therefore, to maintain a good supply of one-year-old wood, and when the vine is bearing care must be taken to see that too many fruit clusters aren't allowed to mature, or the plant will be weakened.

Probably the simplest method of pruning grapes for the home garden is the four-arm Kniffen system. (See Fig. 10.) At planting time the vine is cut to two buds and the shoots which arise tied to a stake. At the end of the first season the best of these canes is again cut to two buds. Now the roots are strong enough to send up heavy growth and at the end of the second season the strongest and straightest of the canes is saved to form the main trunk. It is cut back to five feet and tied to the stake. By the end of the third season there should be many canes along both sides of this trunk. If the vine isn't planted against a wall or fence, two horizontal wires will have to be set up 2½ feet from each other, the bottom one the same distance from the ground. All growth should be cut away except two canes originating near each wire, one on either side of the trunk. These are the four "arms" for the permanent framework. The two at the top wire should be cut back to five buds each, those at the lower wire to four buds each. Only growth on one bud on each arm is allowed to extend (about four feet), the others left for renewal spurs for the next year. Each year four canes are extended and tied to the wires and four are spurred for renewal. Each of the four foot extended canes will have

seven or eight buds that will produce fruit clusters.

It's important to remember that grapes shouldn't be pruned too late in the spring when the sap is rising, or they will bleed badly. Also, when making cuts, a stub of about one inch should be left above the beds. This is contrary to other pruning practice, but grapes have such a pithy wood that there is a certain amount of dieback when a cut is made.

(4) Pruning Deciduous Shrubs

With a few exceptions, flowering shrubs and vines should be pruned as little as possible, allowing them to take their natural, graceful shapes. The practice of pruning to confine shrubs to restricted areas is bad, and an indication of poor landscaping. However, pruning may be helpful in shaping young plants, and is sometimes necessary for removal of decayed or damaged growth. With some species, like Buddleia and roses, annual pruning and shortening of shoots is necessary to obtain larger blooms, and it is practical to prune certain carpeting shrubs to keep them from getting too rampant, but the vast majority only require a light thinning that won't mar their natural branching habit. Where pruning is indicated, unwanted shoots or branches should be removed flush with the junction of an older branch or stem and weak growth should be removed at the base. Whatever you do, don't trim off the lower branches and young shoots and round off the top like a crew cut.

Pruning of flowering shrubs should be adjusted to the plant's blooming habit. Shrubs like forsythia, flowering currant, mock orange and lilac, whose flowers develop in spring or early summer from buds formed the previous summer, should be pruned immediately after the blooming period. With shrubs like abelia, buddleia, hydrangea and tamarix, that flower in mid or late summer on wood produced that season, pruning may be done that fall, or delayed until the end of the dormant period in early spring, when the extent of any winter injury may be determined. For quick reference, here is a list of some of the better known deciduous flowering shrubs found in the Pacific northwest, and their flowering habits.

51

Spring blooming deciduous shrubs, to be pruned promptly after flowering:

Amelanchier (Shadblow)
Azalea Mollis
Berberis Thunbergi (Barberry)
Chaenomeles (Flowering quince)
Cotoneaster (Horizontalis, etc.)
Daphne Mezereum
Deutzia
Exochorda (Pearlbush)
Forsythia (Goldenbell)
Enkianthus
Fothergilla
Kerria
Lonicera (Bush honeysuckle)
Magnolia soulangeana
Potentilla (Cinquefoil)
Ribes (Flowering currant)
Spirea (Van Houttei, thunbergi, etc.)
Syringa (Lilac)
Viburnum opulis sterile (Snowball)

Summer blooming deciduous shrubs that may be pruned from late summer to spring:

Abelia
Amorpha (Indigo Bush)
Buddleia (Butterfly Bush)
Caryopteris (Bluebeard)
Ceanothus
Hamamelis (Witch Hazel)
Hibiscus (Rose-of-Sharon)
Hydrangea
Hypericum (St. Johnswort)
Euonymus
Fuchsia Riccartonii
Kolkwitzia (Beauty Bush)
Lavender
Ligustrum (Privet)
Rhus (Sumac)
Rhus Cotinus (Smoke tree)
Spiraea (Anthony Waterer, Froebelli, etc.)
Tamarix
Weigela

(5) Pruning Roses

Because of their widespread popularity, roses merit extra attention when it comes to pruning. Though there are differences of opinion on how they should be pruned, there is unanimity on the reasons why it is necessary to encourage bloom, to shape for pictorial effect, to restrain excessive growth. The methods used to accomplish these ob-

jectives vary to some extent with the different rose groups.

One group which includes the so-called species roses (rugosas) and the large flowered climbers, needs comparatively little regular pruning. Rugosas and rugosa hybrids should be treated like flowering shrubs, with pruning restricted to the removal of dead wood and crowded centre canes, and a light cutting back where necessary for confinement. This should be done as soon after the blooming period as possible.

The same practice applies to the large flowered climbers—a thinning out of old canes after blooming, cutting back main stems where necessary to conform to an arbor or trellis, and a shortening of laterals.

Another group, including the small flowered climbers, the ramblers and their relations, should never be touched until after blooming. They give one spring burst of bloom on one-year-old wood, and as soon as the blossoms fade this should be cut back to the ground. New growth will arise from the crown, providing the canes for the following year's bloom.

The third and largest group includes the bush and bedding roses—teas, hybrid teas, hybrid perpetuals, floribundas and polyanthas. All these are grown mainly for flower effect rather than for size or foliage, and therefore are pruned back severely to throw their strength into blooms.

Its a good idea to partially head back high growing plants in the fall to prevent the winter winds from whipping them back and fourth, breaking canes and loosening roots, but the main pruning must be left until spring, usually around the middle of March. How much to cut back depends on the type of rose, its position and purpose in the garden, and the strength and habit of the individual variety. However there is one general rule that should be remembered: roses of weak, straggly growth should be cut back more severely than those of tall vigorous habit.

When hybrid teas are planted it is wise to cut out all but three or four of the strongest stems and head these back to four or five buds, but recent experiments have shown that severe cutting back on older plants weakens them and prevents normal flower growth. From 10 inches to 18 inches, depending on the subject's vigor, is about right for established plants. When making the cuts, care must be taken not to cut too close or too far from the bud. Buds that face outward from the centre of the plant should be chosen, and canes should not be all cut the same height so they won't all come into bloom at the same time.

The floribundas and polyanthas may be divided into two classes, for pruning purposes, the larger-flowered types with growing habits like hybrid teas, which should be pruned the same way, and the smaller-flowered varieties which should be pruned according to the purpose for which they are being used. If used as a hedge, the dead wood and interfering canes are removed, but the main shoots are retained and the side shoots merely shortened. When planted in beds they should be cut to within 10 inches or 12 inches of the ground. As border specimens they should be pruned to conform in height, width and diameter to the area they are supposed to occupy.

With all varieties of teas, floribundas, etc., removal of faded blooms not only keeps up a tidy appearance but encourages the growth of new wood for later flowering. When cutting roses for the house during the early part of the blooming season, they should be cut with short stems, leaving two or three eyes on the new wood above the main stem. Removal of too much foliage in the spring weakens the plant and reduces the size of subsequent bloom. Toward midsummer, as foliage develops, longer stems may be taken.

(6) Pruning Evergreens

Except where used as hedging, evergreens should be pruned as little as possible. For one thing, much of their beauty lies in their individual form. For another, since new growth is rarely produced from mature wood, the removal of a sizeable branch usually leaves a gaping hole that may never be filled. If young, vigorous spruces, pines and cedars tend to become unbalanced, branches making excessive wood can be held back to some degree by a careful cutting back of their tips to the extent of one or two year's growth. Dwarf types in foundation plantings like-

wise can be kept dense and somewhat restricted by shearing or pinching the end buds as new growth begins in the spring. But the necessity for this can be avoided by predetermining the ultimate size before planting, or by using soft foliage evergreens such as yews, better adapted to shearing than the stiff-needled sorts.

Spreading forms of juniper or yew may be cut back to lusty side shoots if they are intruding upon lawns or pathways, but broadleafed evergreens like rhododendrons, camellias, etc., grow so slowly that they rarely need pruning for years after planting, except for shaping the plant. If they do obstruct windows or views eventually, select the tallest branches and cut them back to strong side branches, being careful not to remove too many at one time. Rhododendrons are one subject that will recover from hard pruning, but if such is done you must expect to sacrifice bloom for a year or so.

Spring blooming flowering evergreens that may be pruned after flowering:

Andromeda (Lily of the Valley shrub)
Aucuba (Spotted laurel)
Azalea Kurume
Berberis (Buxifolia, Darwini, Julianae)
Camellia japonica
Choisya ternata (Mexican orange)
Cytisus (Broom, such as praecox)
Cotoneaster (Microphylla, Dammeri, conspicua decora)
Daphne (Cneorum, odora, retusa)
Erica Carnea (Spring blooming heathers like King George, Spring Beauty, Springwood and Vivelli)
Eleagnus (Oleaster)
Hedera (Ivy)
Kalmia (Mountain laurel)
Leucothoe Catesbaé
Mahonia Aquifolium
Osmanthus
Rhododendron
Skimmia
Viburnum rhytidophyllum
Viburnum Tinus (Lauristinus)

Summer blooming evergreens that may be pruned in the fall:

Calluna Vulgaris (Fall flowering heathers like Alba Plena, H. E. Beale, Cuprea)
Carpenteria (California mock orange)

Cistus (Rock rose)

Erica Cinerea (Fall flowering heathers like Coccinea, C. D. Easson, Victoria)

Erica Vagans (Lyonesse, Mrs. Maxwell)

Ericaceae (The tree heaths)

Escallonia

Holly

Prunus lusitanica (Portugal laurel)

Pyracantha (Firethorn)

Spartium Junceum (Spanish broom)

Stranvaesia

Veronica (Buxifolia, pageana, etc.)

(7) Pruning Hedges

Hedges present pruning problems to many home gardeners. There are not only two kinds of hedges according to the material used (deciduous or evergreen), but two kinds according to the manner in which it is used (clipped and formal, or natural and informal).

The clipped hedge should consist of plants that take kindly to persistent shearing, like privet, barberry, boxwood, yew and lonicera. Unless they are very dwarf varieties they should be cut back when planted to between six and 12 inches. When there is six or eight inches of new growth, half of this should be cut back, either the same season or just before growth starts the following spring. Repeat this cutting back, both on top and sides, until the plants have grown solidly together, remembering always to keep the base of the hedge wider than the top. (See Fig. 11). After the hedge is a solid wall of green, two seasonal prunings are enough for most subjects, one after growth has become well started in the spring, and the second in midsummer. Late pruning tends to stimulate growth that may not ripen before winter and thus stand a chance of dieback.

If you have a good eye, hedge trimming may be done free hand, but it's safer to use a measuring stick and a horizontal line.

The hedgerow, or informal type, where shrubs or trees are planted in a row where the spacing allows them to retain their individuality, calls for only enough pruning to keep the plants vigorous and within bounds. A light shaping rather than a shearing is all that is necessary. Such a hedgerow may be all deciduous material, all evergreen, or a combination of both.

PLANTS SUITABLE FOR FORMAL HEDGES

A. DECIDUOUS	Planting distance	Best pruned ht.
Berberis thunbergi nana (Dwarf green barberry)	12"	18"
B. atropurpurea nana (Dwarf purple barberry)	12"	18"
Cotoneaster acutifolia	12"	3-4'
Caragana	12"	3-4'
Rosa multiflora japonica	15"	5-6'
Berberis erecta (Upright barberry)	18"	6-8'
Ligustrum (Privet)	18"	6-8'

B. EVERGREEN		
Berberis buxifolia nana	15"	18"
Buxus suffruticosa (Dwarf	8"	8-12"
Buxus sempervirens (Regular boxwood)	12"	18-24"
Lonicera nitida (Evergreen honeysuckle)	12"	3'
Ligustrum ionandrum (Evergreen privet)	15"	4-5'
Taxus baccata (Eng. yew)	18"	4-5'
Prunus laurocerasus (English laurel)	24"	6-8'
Chamaecyparis arizonica	30"	6-8'
Chamaecyparis lawsoniana Lawson's cypress)	30"	6-8'
Thuya pyramidalis	24"	8-10'

PLANTS SUITABLE FOR INFORMAL HEDGES

A. DECIDUOUS	Best pruned height
Ribes alpinum (Fl. currant)	6'
Spirea Van Houttei, thunbergi	6'
Philadelphus (Mock orange)	7'
Cotoneaster Simonsi	7'
Syringa (Lilac)	8'
Ulmus pumila (Chinese elm)	10-15'

B. EVERGREEN	
Picea excelsa (Norway spruce)	8-10'
Chamaecyparis elwoodi	6'
Chamaecyparis fletcheri	8'
Chamaecyparis alumi	8-10'
Pinus mugho (Mugho pine)	8'
Thuya rosenthali	10'
Thuya plicata aurea	10-15'
Cupressus arizonica (Arizona cypress)	12-15'

PRUNING FORMAL HEDGES

A - DECIDUOUS

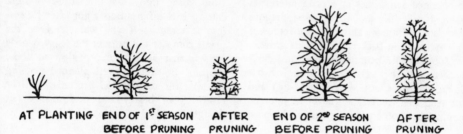

AT PLANTING   END OF 1ˢᵗ SEASON   AFTER   END OF 2ⁿᵈ SEASON   AFTER
             BEFORE PRUNING   PRUNING   BEFORE PRUNING   PRUNING

B - EVERGREEN

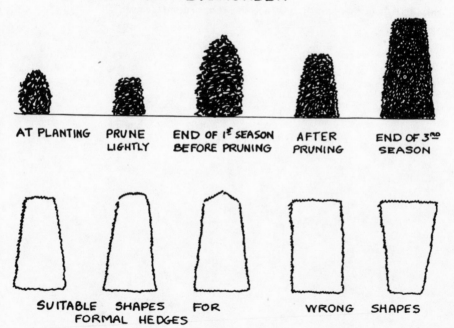

AT PLANTING   PRUNE   END OF 1ˢᵗ SEASON   AFTER   END OF 3ʳᵈ
            LIGHTLY   BEFORE PRUNING   PRUNING   SEASON

SUITABLE   SHAPES   FOR   WRONG   SHAPES
   FORMAL   HEDGES

FIG. 11

Picea pungens (Colorado spruce)	15'
Chamaecyparis lawsoniana (Lawson's cypress)	15'
Ilex pyramidalis (Holly)	15'

(8) Pruning Annuals and Perennials

The pruning of flowers is often overlooked by gardeners, but exciting results may be obtained sometimes if a little interest is taken. Plants like sweet peas, snapdragons and petunias grow far more floriferous if they are pinched back early in their growth. On subjects like peonies, dahlias and chrysanthemums, the practice of snipping out all subordinate side buds (disbudding) and throwing the strength of the plant into the terminal bud, will yield extra large blooms.

Root division of iris, phlox and other perennials that clump up quickly, will greatly improve performance if practised every two years. Others, like delphiniums, if cut back promptly after their first flowering, will often flower again later in the season. The shearing of rockery plants like aubretia, alyssum and pinks, right after blooming, not only keeps plants tidy but prevents their strength from going into seed formation. A light cutting back of heathers right after flowering, is essential if you want to keep the plants compact and prevent the leggy, woody growth that accompanies neglect of these subjects. In short, a well planned pruning program for annuals and perennials will be rewarded by beauty and performance not thought possible.

NOTE: Pruning of conifers like spruce, pine and fir, is best done in the spring, after the trees have made a few inches of new, soft growth. By cutting back a third to half of this growth, new side shoots are encouraged.

Spraying

"To spray or not to spray, that is the question."

Probably no other phase of gardening has become more puzzling, confusing and annoying to the home gardener. At every garden centre, shelves and counters overflow with chemicals of every imaginable sort for combatting garden pests and diseases, and each year the manufacturers add something new. We have little doubt that they do the job for which they were developed, but are they all really necessary, and if so, why?

(1) Purposes

Chemical spraying is done mainly to control plant diseases, kill insects and exterminate weed growth. To a lesser extent it is done to set or thin fruit blossom, prevent fruit drop, and in recent years to fertilize plants through their foliage.

(a) Plant Diseases

Diseases in plants may be caused by one or more of three types of organisms, fungi, bacteria, or viruses, with the first named the worst offender. Humidity encourages the growth of fungi, and the damp mild climate of the Pacific northwest provides ideal conditions for such fungus enemies as mildew, leaf spot, rust, wilt, black and brown rot, etc. Bacterial diseases and viruses, while perhaps not directly encouraged by humidity, are spread to a great degree by insects, and this same climate has pampered as large an assortment of plant-devouring "bugs" as there are plant species to feed upon.

We can combat disease in the garden to a considerable degree by prevention methods, sanitation, and the selection of disease immune or disease resistant plant varieties. Proper cultivation, pruning, fertilization, etc., to keep plants in a thrifty, vigorous condition, will leave them less subject to attack. Use of the best seed, properly treated before planting, and the quick roguing out of weak or diseased transplants, careful collection of crop refuse and the burning of any suspected disease carriers, will all help.

A careful, systematic inspection of growth, to catch and control disease before it spreads is also important. Some diseases can be controlled or prevented by spraying plants during their dormant season, and a winter or "clean-up" spray is essential in any garden with woody, deciduous plants like fruit trees and shrubs. At this time sprays can generally be made strong enough to kill all spores with which they come in contact, without causing any damage to the plant. There are many fungicides on the market for this purpose, lime-sulphur solution, bordeaux mixture, etc., and all are effective when properly applied. With all sprays the correct time of application is important, as well as a thorough drenching of the subject and the ground beneath it. Weather should be dry enough to allow at least four hours for the spray to set and do its work.

Many diseases have to be controlled on the growing plant, and in such cases the spray material must be diluted considerably to avoid damage to soft green tissue. Thus summer sprays are preventative only, forming a thin layer over the leaf or stem surface which will kill spores or bacteria attempting to gain entrance. It's obvious, therefore, as new growth arises, that it becomes necessary to repeat spraying at intervals if full protection is to be assured.

For reference purposes, we will list the most important plant diseases commonly found in the Pacific northwest, with controls briefly indicated.

PLANT DISEASES COMMON TO THE PACIFIC NORTHWEST AREA

DISEASE	SYMPTOMS	PLANTS AFFECTED	CONTROL MEASURES
Powdery mildew	White or purple mold on leaves	Roses, apples, grapes, onions	Sulphur dust or liquid phaltan on appearance.
Leaf spot	Brown or black spots on leaves	Roses, cane fruits, cherries, strawberries, cucumbers, tomatoes, beets	Bordeaux or phaltan every 10 days until checked.
Rust	Brown or orange spores on leaves	Raspberries, asparagus, snapdragons, asters	Ferbam dust or spray, also Zineb. Burn affected canes or material.
Smut	Black spores on leaves or stems	Corn, onions	Treat seed before planting. Destroy affected plants.
Damping-off	Rotting ot seed or seedling	All vegetables and flowers	Treat seed, fumigate soil, avoid overwatering.
Fungus wilt	Wilting and dying of plant	Cucumbers, melons, etc.	Treat seed, destroy affected plants.
Brown rot	Blighted leaves, rotted fruit	Plums, cherries	Captan spray every two weeks from pre-pink stage.
Black rot	Black or brown veins in leaves	Cabbage, cauliflower	Treat seed, destroy affected plants.
Ring rot	Yellow leaves, cheesy tubers	Potatoes	Use certified, treated seed.
Cornyeum blight	Red spots on leaves or fruit	Apricots, cherries, peaches	Bordeaux 10 days after petal fall and in September.
Botrytis	Leaf burn. Rotting of stem or bulb	Bulbs, peonies	Destroy affected plants, or spray with zineb in mild cases.
Club root	Swollen, knobby roots. Wilting	Cabbage, cauliflower, sprouts, turnips	Lime soil, dip transplants in corrosive sublimate.
Potato blight	Dry, brown spots on leaves and stems	Potatoes	Spray with bordeaux every 10 days after plants are eight inches high.
Bacterial blight	Defoliation, brown spots	Beans, peas, celery, willows.	Cultivate when dry. Spray with bordeaux.
Spur and cane blight	Brown lesions	Raspberries, logans, blackberries, etc.	Burn canes after harvest. Dormant spray with fungicide.
Leaf curl	Blisters on leaves	Peaches	Use fungicide, mid-December. Repeat mid-January.
Fire blight	Exudation, cankers	Pears	Cut out and burn cankers in winter.
Anthracnose	Cankers on limbs	Apples	Cut out cankers, dormant spray.
Black knot	Black warts on twigs	Plums	Cut out knots, dormant spray.

We haven't listed virus diseases, such as red stele in strawberries, mottle leaf or little cherry in cherry trees, stony pit in pears, etc., because there are no known correctives at present. Affected plants should be destroyed and the ground replanted with disease resistant varieties or other plant species. Diseases like corky core and die back in fruit trees, caused by boron deficiency, or gummosis in cherries, caused by over-fertilization or excessive irrigation, cannot be controlled by chemical sprays but by cultural methods.

(b) Insects

Damage from insects, like that from disease, can be minimized to some extent by good horticultural practice. It is a proven fact that insects first attack the weaker plants. However, they have to eat, and there are so many of them, that even the thriftiest subjects are not immune. There are at least fifty named insects that do major plant damage in the Pacific northwest region, and as many more of lesser concern. It would be a boon to the home gardener if all these appeared at one time and all could be exterminated by one insecticide in one application, but of course such is far from the case.

This battalion of plant enemies is divided into two platoons, those that attack the roots, and those that attack the leaves, stems and fruits. The soil insects are in the minority, the main ones being cutworms, root maggots, wireworms, weevils and nematodes. All but the last named can be pretty well controlled by stirring 5% granular diazinon into the soil before transplanting or treating established plants with the same chemicals in liquid form. Rootlesion or "meadow" nematodes are parasites that feed on root cells of many garden plants, with varying degrees of injury indicated by slow growth, pale foliage and reduced production. Young roots that should normally be white may show brownish spots or "lesions." Experiments for treating nematode infected plants are being carried out constantly at research stations but so far no practical method for the home gardener has been found.

The large group of insects that function above ground includes sucking insects like aphis, thrips, spiders, mites and scale, and chewing insects like beetles, earwigs, slugs, worms, borers, flies, grasshoppers and ants. Since all of these directly attack the leaves of plants, they must be combatted with foliage sprays or dusts containing such insecticides as sevin, diazinon, methoxychlor or malathion. Some, like slugs or earwigs, are best controlled by the use of specially treated baits.

Recent research has developed a group of chemicals called "systemics." When any of these chemicals are sprayed on the foliage, or in some cases even painted on the bark of trees, they enter the sap and provide enough toxidity to prove fatal to sucking insects like aphids over a period of weeks, even months. Much experimentation, such as residual effect on fruit crops, must be completed before these chemicals will become available for general use, but the possibility of controlling even one group of insects throughout a growing season with a single chemical application, is intriguing indeed.

Meanwhile, we will have to carry on our battle against insects with proven material. For reference purposes, we will list some of the most important pests and their modus operandi. For exact timing and measurement of control materials mentioned, we suggest you follow directions outlined on manufacturer's containers or those on spray charts obtainable from garden centres and agricultural agencies.

NOTE

Long before the hue and cry about chemical pollution, scientists had been researching other methods of pest control, and still are, throughout Canada and the U.S. Biological controls, sterilizing male insects with gamma rays etc. will, hopefully, greatly reduce the need for chemical pesticides. Until they are established and widespread the home gardener should use prescribed controls in moderation, and only when absolutely necessary.

COMMON INSECT PESTS FOUND IN THE PACIFIC NORTHWEST

INSECT	DESCRIPTION	PLANTS PREFERRED	ACTIVE PERIOD	CONTROL
(A) SOIL INSECTS				
Slugs	Grey, fat, slimy, feed at night	Leaf vegetables and flowers	April, May	Metaldehyde bait or spray.
Cutworms	Grey, flat, ¾-inch curled worm	Leaf vegetables and flowers	April to June	Stir 5% granular diazinon into soil.
Cabbage and onion maggots	White maggot, ¼-inch, attacks stems, roots	Cabbage, onions, turnips	April to June	Stir 5% granular diazinon into soil.
Carrot fly maggot	Thread maggot, ½-inch, tunnels roots	Carrots, parsnips, celery	Mid-June-mid-Aug.	Stir 5% granular diazinon into soil.
Wireworms	Brownish larvae, one inch, hard-shelled	Potatoes, cabbage, gladiolus	May to Aug.	Stir 5% granular diazinon into soil.
Strawberry root weevil	Beetle larvae, ½-inch, white, legless	Strawberries, primulas	April to June	Stir 5% granular diazinon into soil.
White grub	June beetle larvae, fat, white, curled	Strawberries, vegetables	May and June	Stir 5% granular diazinon into soil.
Root weevils	Small white grubs, parents chew leaves	Azaleas, camellias, rhododendrons	April to June	Stir 5% granular diazinon into soil.
(B) FOLIAGE INSECTS				
(1) SUCKING INSECTS				
Aphids	Soft green, grey, or black lice on new growth	Nearly all plants	All season, worse in spring	Malathion, diazinon, rotenone on vegetables.
Red spiders	Almost invisible, suck leaf chlorophyll	Roses, flowers, evergreens	Early June	Malathion, diazinon or kelthane spray.
Mites	Invisible without microscope	Fruit trees, shrubs, evergreens	April to Sept.	Malathion, diazinon or kelthane spray.
Scale	Tiny, white or brown, on twigs or bark	Fruit trees, evergreens	April to Sept.	Dormant fungicide, and diazinon spray in May.
Thrips	Minute, slim, black or brown fly	Gladiolus	March to May	Dust corms in storage, and malathion summer spray.
(2) CHEWING INSECTS				
Earwigs	Brown, beetle-like, ½-inch long, pincers	Vegetables, flowers, trees and shrubs	May to July	Sevin spray, poisoned baits, traps.
Flea beetles	Tiny, jumping, black, grey, blue	Potatoes, tomatoes, turnips, radishes	May to July	Methoxychlor, sevin spray or rotenone dust.
Potato beetles	Black and yellow beetle, red larvae	Potatoes, tomatoes	May to July	Methoxychlor or sevin spray.

COMMON INSECT PESTS FOUND IN THE PACIFIC NORTHWEST—(Cont'd)

INSECT	DESCRIPTION	PLANTS PREFERRED	ACTIVE PERIOD	CONTROL
CHEWING INSECTS—(Cont'd)				
Blister beetles	Large, soft, grey or black	Potatoes, beans, flowers	June-July	Methoxychlor dust or spray.
Cucumber beetles	Small, yellow stripes or spots	Vine vegetables, some flowers	Early June	Methoxychlor dust or rotenone.
Cankerworms or inchworms	Slim, long, grey-green	Deciduous trees and shrubs	June to Aug.	Methoxychlor or sevin spray.
Black beetles	Larvae a white grub, ½-inch long	Lawn grasses	May to Aug.	Diazinon drench.
Japanese beetles	Small, copper, dotted	Roses, grapes	June to Aug.	Methoxychlor spray or dust.
Rose chafers	Small, hairy, tan	Roses	June to Aug.	Methoxychlor spray or dust.
Cabbage worms	Green, ¾-inch caterpillars	Cabbage, cauliflower, turnips	April to June	Methoxychlor or rotenone dust.
Tent caterpillar	Brown, ¾-inch, hairy	Fruit trees, ornamentals	May-June	Methoxychlor spray or dust.
Currant worm	White worm, ¼-inch, from fruit fly	Currants and gooseberries	May-June	Methoxychlor spray or dust at petal fall.
Raspberry fruit worm	White worm, ½-inch, from sawfly	Raspberries	May-June	Methoxychlor spray or dust before bloom.
Leaf roller	Green worm, ½-inch, seals leaf edges	Strawberries, fruit trees	May-June	Methoxychlor spray or dust.
Sod webworm	Larvae of lawn moth	Lawn grasses	May-Aug.	Diazinon drench.
Juniper webworm or bagworm	Tiny larvae	Evergreens	June-July	Malathion or sevin spray.
Cherry fruit fly	Small, with white bands	Cherries	June-July	Malathion or diazinon spray. (Twice)
Codling moth	Brown moth, ¾-inch, pink caterpillar	Apples, pears	May to July	Diazinon, three sprays.
Bud moth	Greenish-white caterpillars, ½-inch	Apples, pears, holly	May to July	Diazinon.
Narcissus fly	Tiny brown fly	Daffodils, tulips	June-July	Methoxychlor dust in soil.
Leaf miners	Tiny maggots	Holly, azaleas	May-July	Diazinon or malathion spray.
Leaf slugs	Black or brown	Roses, cherries, pears.	Aug.	Diazinon or malathion spray.
Leaf hoppers	Tiny, green, white	Vegetables, flowers	May-June	Malathion spray, rotenone.
Ants	Black	Vegetables, fruits	Apr.-Sept.	Diazinon, 5% granular in nests.

61

If this long list of insect pests seems a bit frightening, please remember that it's highly unlikely that you will run across all of them, or even a high percentage, in a small home garden. Many of them, like gladiolus thrips or currant fruit worms, specialize on one or two plant species, others, like tent caterpillars, are not found every year. Still you may depend upon it that you will encounter a good many, no matter how small your garden may be, and it would be well to remember the chief offenders and plan a spray program to keep them in check.

To assist with such a plan, it might help to examine each garden area separately and pinpoint its particular pest problems and controls.

(2) In the Vegetable Garden

In the vegetable garden half your battle will be won if you remember to treat your soil with 5% granular diazinon dust at the rate of one pound to 200 square feet, before planting seeds. With tar paper squares around cabbage or tomato plants for extra protection, cutworms, root maggots and wireworms should be taken care of. For slugs and earwigs you will have to use specially prepared baits. Flea beetles, aphis and caterpillars are persistent enemies in the vegetable plot, and at the first sign of any of them grab your diazinon, methoxychlor or rotenone. Remember also to dust your young carrots when they are about an inch high to insure against attack by the carrot rust fly. If you are planting cucumbers, melons or squash, keep them dusted with methoxychlor until they are well established.

(3) In the Home Orchard

In the home orchard you will face special problems. If you have only small fruits, your main worries will be the strawberry root weevil and the currant worm. 5% diazinon granular worked around the strawberry plants, or, better, in the soil before planting, will give good control for a year or more. Control of the currant worm, which is hatched from eggs laid by the currant fruit fly, requires careful timing. The fly lays its eggs on the flower calyx just after petal fall and methoxychlor spray or dust must be applied at that time.

If you have fruit trees your worst enemies will be the codling moth and the cherry fruit fly. Here again timing is important. Brownish gray codling moths appear soon after apple blossom time and lay their eggs on leaves, usually close to the fruit. The white, round eggs are about the size of a pin and easily visible. They hatch between five and 20 days, depending on temperatures, and quickly make their way into the centre of the small green fruit. To catch this first brood, you must spray within a week after petal fall, usually between May 1st and 15th. It's wise to follow this up with another spray in a couple of weeks, and to catch a possible later brood, a final spray during the latter part of July. Diazinon spray is generally effective, and this will control any aphis or leaf rollers present at the time of application.

The cherry fruit fly is almost as large as a housefly, with dark bands on the wings and white bands on the abdomen. Flies begin to appear early in June and start laying their eggs under the skin of the under-ripe cherries. At least two sprays should be applied, the first between June 5th and 10th, another a week later. For years lead arsenate has been widely used for fruit fly control, but new combination sprays with malathion or diazinon, have been substituted, mainly because they have the advantage of controlling other pests like mites at the same time.

(4) In the Flower Garden

In the flower garden and shrub border, roses are probably the most susceptible to insect attack and require special attention. Following up the dormant fungicide spray which kills many insect eggs and larvae, roses should be sprayed shortly after new tender growth commences, around the first of April. Diazinon spray will check aphis, leaf rollers, weevils, thrips and hoppers. As the season progresses and mites and slugs appear, plus mildew and black spot diseases, a combination spray is best, one including malathion, and a fungicide like captan. Roses should be sprayed or dusted about every three weeks during the summer if you want clean foliage and good bloom. Where mildew is a special problem, regular applications of sulphur or karathane may be found necessary.

Outside of roses a general three-spray program will take care of average trouble in the flower garden. The first can be an extension of the first rose spray, a general application of diazinon to protect the new growth of shrubs, perennials, and newly planted annuals. About the middle of May, when growth is rampant and there is an abundance of new tender terminal leaves on most plants, another application of a good combination insecticide should be made. Warm weather always activates insects and between the middle of July and the first of August is a good time for a third treatment. Careful surveillance of foliage throughout the season will indicate need, or otherwise, for special requirements.

(5) Evergreens

Evergreens, with their tough foliage, are not as vulnerable to insect attack as deciduous plants, but they do have their enemies. One of the worst are the weevils that attack the roots of azaleas, camellias and rhododendrons, then, after changing to beetles, come up and feed on the leaves. Diazinon dust or emulsion worked into the soil before planting, or around the roots of established plants, will ward off the root attack. and spraying with malathion or diazinon emulsion from mid-April to mid-June will keep the leaves clean.

To control weevils, leaf miner, and bud moth on holly, it should be sprayed with malathion emulsion around the latter part of April before new growth starts, then again two or three weeks later, when growth is about half an inch long.

Conifers, especially junipers, are particularly susceptible to mites, spiders, scale insects and webworms, and should be sprayed with malathion 50 per cent emulsifiable when new growth first begins in April and again in mid-July. Heavy shedding of needles, or webs filled with dead foliage indicate the need for immediate action.

(6) Spraying Lawns

Lawns are considered by many to be more or less free of insect trouble, but sometimes

SPRAYING LAWN WEEDS WITH HOSE ATTACHMENT SPRAYER

those brown spots or patches you may attribute to fungus diseases may be caused by white grubs, the sod webworm, or just ordinary cutworms. White grubs are the larvae of the black beetle and operate deep down at the grass roots, sometimes causing whole patches of dead turf. If you see whitish colored moths flitting over your grass at dusk and settling occasionally, they are probably lawn moths laying their eggs. These eggs hatch into small white larvae called sod webworms that feed at the base of grass blades. Cutworms feed the same way.

In new lawns damage can be prevented for one season or more by stirring 5% granular diazinon into the top three inches of soil before planting (1 lb. per 200 sq. ft.), but in old lawns control must be achieved by mowing the grass, watering, then applying diazinon solution. The prewatering assists the chemical to drain down to the root areas where the insects feed.

(7) Weed Control

Weed control by the use of chemical sprays is not new, but each year improvements are being made on the effectiveness and selectivity of materials. A number of pre-emergence weed killing sprays have been developed for commercial bulb and vegetable growers, but their use in the small vegetable plot is not always practicable. One useful herbicide for controlling unwanted grasses has been tested successfully and put on the market. It contains dalapon, and will kill grasses, including couch, along fence lines, around trees, lawn edgings, etc. Another, called amino triazole, will kill difficult subjects like Canada thistle and morning glory. Neither of these leave residual toxidity in the soil for more than three or four weeks. (See footnote, p. 65.)

Most gardeners are familiar with the brush killer spray combining the hormones 2-4-D and 2-4-5-T. This is used to control woody growth like brambles and wild roses, and is quite effective, though careful application is necessary to avoid damage to nearby garden subjects from spray drift. This can be lessened somewhat by spraying in the green bud stage, about the last week in March, before garden crops or flowers have been planted or established much growth.

The most important area for weed control in the home garden is the lawn. Of course, the most effective weapon against lawn weeds is a vigorous turf. Proper fertilization, aerating, mowing and watering will promote a grass growth that will crowd many weeds to death.

Lawn weeds are of two types: broadleafed weeds such as daisy, dandelion and plantain, and narrowleaf or weedy grasses, such as velvet grass or crabgrass. The hormone 2-4-D will eradicate the broadleafed weeds. It is available in a variety of formulations, but the "amine" or low volatile "ester" formulations should be used in the home garden where there is danger of vapor drifting to sensitive plants like roses or annual flowers. Time of application is important. Results are better when the weeds are growing quickly, and when growth is young and sensitive, as it is during early spring. But it must be remembered that temperatures should be over sixty degrees F., preferably seventy, to secure best results. So be prepared to act on the first calm warm day in May. For old lawns follow the directions on the container, but for recently seeded lawns reduce the strength. Avoid watering and mowing for several days after planting.

To answer the problem of vapor drift, manufacturers have come up with a paraffin bar, impregnated with 2-4-D, that is dragged back and forth across the lawn. Wherever it touches a weed it does its work. It can't

reach all the small growth, but by continued treatments as the weeds grow, can do an effective job. Where weeds are few and scattered, they can be treated quickly by using one of the cane type applicators.

Mouse-ear chickweed has not been effectively controlled in lawns by 2-4-D, but a new chemical called neburon has been found satisfactory. Particular care must be taken to follow directions when applying, or lawn damage may result.

Crab grass is an annual grass that sometimes becomes a nuisance. Since it is an annual, one way or eradicating it is by preventing it from seeding, which can be done by frequent mowing. It can't stand to be shut off from light, even for short periods, so another control measure where there are isolated patches is to cover these for a week or ten days with tarpaper or black plastic. The other lawn grasses will yellow, of course, but will quickly recover and the crab grass won't. There is a selective herbicide for crab grass, containing potassium cyanate, which is similar in action to 2-4-D. Used as directed it won't harm other lawn grasses.

(8) Foliar Sprays

Feeding plants by spraying their leaves is a fairly recent development. Except for treating lawn grasses, it hasn't become commonplace in the home garden yet. In commercial fruit orchards, compounds containing 40 per cent or more of nitrogen in the form or urea have been used successfully. The nitrogen present in foliage sprays is quickly absorbed by the leaves and provides nourishment immediately, regardless of weather-soil conditions. Foliage application of nitrogen may be combined with pest-control sprays, thus doing two jobs at once.

(9) Hormone Sprays

We have mentioned the hormone sprays like 2-4-D that kill weeds. Others have been developed for setting and thinning fruit and for preventing premature fruit drop. It is well known that the first blossoms on tomato plants often drop from lack of pollination or cool night temperatures. This can be prevented to a great extent by spraying with a fruit set hormone. Early flowering fruit trees like peaches, apricots, and some plum varieties can be helped in the same way, provided they are self-fertile and don't require another type of pollen.

The thinning of fruit, particularly apples, by spraying the bloom with napthaleneacetic acid, a hormone-like chemical, has been done with good results in commercial orchards, but it requires perfect timing and some experimentation, and it is safer for the home gardener with only a few trees to thin by hand in the time-honored way.

Premature fruit drop, while not a serious problem in the small home orchard, can be controlled to some extent by hormone sprays. Certain varieties that are slow in reaching full color, can be held on the tree for days, even weeks, beyond their normal drop period, and where early fall winds are a problem the hormone treated trees won't shed nearly as heavily as those untreated.

Holly growers and even the home gardener with a few holly trees, may keep their cut holly from shedding leaves and berries by dipping it in a hormone solution.

The potentialities of hormones for growth stimulation or inhibition have been barely touched. Experimentation is going on continuously at research centres and agricultural stations throughout the country, and anyone interested in experimenting on his own, even as a hobby, should visit his nearest experimental station and find out the latest developments.

(10) A Word of Warning

Following the publication of Rachel Carson's sensational book on pesticides, "Silent Spring," there has been a spate of publicity, pro and con, on the dangers and values of spray applications generally. While it is undoubtedly true that many mistakes have been made, and present policing may not be fully adequate, it is equally true that without the use of modern pesticides and herbicides, growers on this continent could not have attained the highest per capita agricultural production in the world.

Whether we like it or not, chemical controls are here to stay, and the important thing is to maintain vigilance, from manufacturer to consumer, in order to minimize excesses and abuses. From the standpoint of the home gardener, two points should be emphasized. Firstly, he should follow exactly the directions given on the container. The manufacturer and government researchers have spent considerable time and money to determine the correct application of these products. If the manufacturer says one teaspoonful to a gallon, take his word for it. Don't impose your snap judgment that two teaspoonsful should be twice as effective. Secondly, take adequate precautions to protect your body from the effects of any sprays labelled toxic. A two-dollar mask might save your life, or at least an uncomfortable trip to the hospital, and a dollar pair of rubber gloves might save your hands from serious burns or blisters.

It follows, almost without saying, that similar precautions should be followed to protect bees, birds, wildlife and pets. For instance, you wouldn't spray a fruit tree in full bloom, when the bees are working it, or scatter arsenical baits indiscriminately near a bird bath. And common sense should warn you to keep all chemicals, toxic or otherwise, out of the reach of dogs and children.

NOTE:
The chemical dalapon should not be applied at the base of stone fruits, ornamental plums or flowering cherries, or any trees in light sandy soil.

A new chemical, paraquat, has been proven an effective grass and weed killer around the base of established trees, without subsequent foliar or root damage.

Handle carefully, avoid breathing spray mists. No known antidote.

Harvesting and Storage

Gardening is filled with pleasureable moments, and for many home gardeners some of the most exciting and satisfying are the moments of harvest. Yet it is a common occurrence to find a beginner, after hours of labor and dollars of expenditure, grow a wonderful crop of vegetables or fruit, only to lose half of it through bad timing in harvesting or improper storage afterwards.

(1) The Time Element

As every housewife knows, there is an optimum moment when a fruit or vegetable reaches the peak of its flavor and succulence. Commercial growers know this, of course, but for various reasons don't always harvest their crops when they should. For the home gardener there is no excuse. One of the main reasons he grows a crop is to obtain that extra freshness and perfection rarely found in commercially grown crops, a perfection that can result only from ideal maturity.

(2) Vegetables

It is not difficult to determine the "moment of truth" with leafy vegetables like lettuce, spinach and chard. They have a lush, green, crisp condition that is unmistakeable. They also have a very brief storage life. It must be remembered that all vegetables and fruits remain alive after harvest, giving off both carbon dioxide and heat. Highly perishable crops like the leaf vegetables respire very rapidly, and should be consumed as soon after harvest as possible. By lowering the temperature they are kept under, respiration can be slowed down and storage life increased, but not without loss of flavor and value.

Premature picking of peas and beans is better than picking too late, but a little experience will determine the right period. Pea pods should be full, but not tight, and show no signs of wrinkling or yellowing. Beans should snap easily between the fingers. If they bend or tear, they are overripe. Harvesting sweet corn takes a little practice. Before removing the cob from the plant, strip back the end an inch or so to determine whether or not the kernels are well filled. Cut a kernel with your thumbnail and if the milk spurts forth freely you may proceed with assurance.

Peas, beans and corn have a very brief storage life, not so much because of high respiration as the fact that sugars in these crops turn quickly into starches. We all know how sweet peas or corn taste when cooked and eaten immediately after picking, compared to flavor of the same vegetables a day later, even if stored in the refrigerator. Just a few hours makes the difference, so if you are going to freeze any of these crops, process and freeze them as quickly as possible after harvest.

The brassicas, which include cabbage, cauliflower, and Brussels sprouts, take longer to mature than the leaf vegetables and legumes, but are just as quick to over-ripen, especially during the warm days of summer. Constant surveillance is necessary to make sure the cabbage heads are cut while still firm and green, before there is any evidence of sun scald or splitting. Once cauliflower start heading, they develop rapidly, and must be used while the crowns are tight and white. If you have overplanted cabbage or cauliflower (a common occurrence) you can delay maturity briefly by cutting the roots on one side of the plant and bending the head over.

The drumhead varieties of cabbage may be kept for several months at temperatures just above freezing, provided the humidity is high, but cauliflower and sprouts lose flavor quickly, even at low temperatures. Broccoli, likewise, is highly perishable, but better than the others for freezing.

Green onions may be used at any time after they reach pencil thickness, but the globe varieties require a long ripening period in warm weather before they are matured properly. The tops must die down naturally, and then if the bulbs are lifted and cured in the sun for a few days they will keep in cool storage with moderate humidity for six months.

Tomatoes are ripe when fully red, and that is when they should be picked, but if the season is late and there are still a lot of greenish white, but mature, tomatoes on the vines, these will ripen in a few weeks storage at house temperatures, provided they haven't been chilled (45 deg. F.) for more than a day or two before harvest. If heavy rains occur during late August, when there is still a good chance of ripening weather, tomatoes may split unless the vines are pulled from the ground immediately, with just one or two roots still attached to the soil. In this way they may ripen up for a long time without injury. Tomatoes cannot be preserved by freezing, but of course may be bottled or canned.

Cucumbers should be picked green, the moment they have reached normal size. When they start yellowing, the crisp, tangy flavor will disappear and then much of their value is gone, even for pickling. On the other hand, melons, squash, marrows or pumpkin should be left to ripen on the vine, or they will be tasteless. Size and color are determining factors in the harvest date. If you contemplate storing such vegetables as winter squash and pumpkin, remember that a succession of cool nights (under 50 deg. F.), even though no frost occurs, will chill them sufficiently to cause damage and reduce storage life. Therefore they should be harvested as soon as maturity will permit, and held in a warm room for a week or ten days to cure. Extra storage life can be attained by washing the skins of squash or pumpkin with a solution of formaldehyde (one tablespoon to a quart of water). Thus treated they may be kept for three to six months at a temperature of around 50 deg. F.

Young beets, carrots and turnips are delicious when quite small, and may be harvested as "thinnings" over a long period, while the main storage crop increases in size. But by the end of September it is wise to dig these crops to avoid splitting from fall rains, or damage from slugs or worms. The only root vegetable that may be left in the ground all winter without harm is the parsnip, which actually improves after a few frosts. It's important, though, to lift parsnips in early spring before any top growth, as they turn toxic when this occurs. Root crops may be kept in storage for four or five months under 35 deg. F. temperatures and humidity around 90 per cent. One way to achieve this is to bury them outside in a large, shaded, box of damp sand, peat or sawdust, preferably the former. If you have room in your refrigerator for a few carrots, put them in perforated plastic bags and they'll keep well for weeks.

Potatoes may be dug for immediate use when the tops are still green, but if you intend to store them any length of time, don't dig them until the tops have ripened naturally. When storing potatoes, remember that they will become sweet if kept too long at low temperatures (40 deg. F.) and subsequently darken when cooked. They will keep for four or five months at 45 to 50 deg. F., under high humidity, but at these temperatures will start to sprout, particularly towards spring. These sprouts should be rubbed off before they reach any size or the tubers will shrivel. By spraying the foliage of root crops while still green, but just prior to harvest time, with a very dilute solution of maleic hydrazide, subsequent sprouting and root growth are inhibited. Also shrivelling and breakdown are eliminated for a much longer period than the usual storage term. Onions respond to the same treatment. It is interesting to note, in this connection, that gases given off by ripened apples will prevent sprouting of potatoes when stored in the same room.

(3) Small Fruits

Size, color and taste are the three most important factors in determining the maturity of berry fruits, with taste the final arbiter. When a berry is plump, glossy, and sugar sweet, you don't need to be told it's ripe, but if you have any doubt, watch the birds. They'll tell you when the first berry is edible, even if you can't see it, or are color blind.

We all know how perishable berries are, so full enjoyment can be attained only when they are consumed right after picking. No matter how they try, commercial growers and distributors can't hold that peak of freshness more than a day or so, and sometimes only a few hours. The sheen of strawberries for example, is affected even between the time of picking and cool storage. Berries picked and placed in an open, shaded shed, will begin to dull in color within a few hours. The only way the color can be held is to place them immediately after picking into storage at around 55 deg. F. Therefore when you contemplate freezing strawberries, or, indeed, any other berry, get them into containers and into the deep freeze or frozen food locker as quickly as possible.

Strawberries are picked with the hulls on, except for jam, but raspberries, logans, boysens and blackberries are picked free of their stems and the ease with which they come clean from the stem is an indication of their maturity. If you have to tug on a berry to free it, it isn't ripe, even if the color indicates it should be. The fruits on most berry plants ripen in different stages, requiring several pickings, and in none is this more evident than with blueberries. These berries ripen at the terminals of the clusters first, gradually ripening back along the stem, so care must be taken not to detach green or unripe fruit. The storage period is longer with blueberries than with most berry fruits, but like all the rest they are superior in every way when consumed fresh.

Picking black currants is somewhat of a chore, especially if the fruit is undersized. Like blueberries, the currants don't ripen on the clusters all at once and require successive pickings. Unless fully ripe they tend to hold tightly to the stem, and if they tear at the stem when you're picking, you had best wait a while longer. With red currants picking may be delayed sometimes until all the berries in a cluster have ripened, when the whole cluster may be severed from the branch like a bunch of grapes. Usually one or two pickings are all that are necessary to remove this crop. Since they are used chiefly to make jelly, all currants may be held in cool storage for several days without suffering much loss.

The color test doesn't always apply when picking gooseberries. The commercial varieties used for pies or jam are picked when green and the main indications of maturity are size and the ease with which they can be detached. With the large English varieties, bearing red or amber fruit, the color and taste tests both apply, for they are not ripe until quite sweet. Green varieties may be kept in cool storage for a week or more, but the English dessert types should be used immediately after picking.

Grapes are one fruit that must not be picked before maturity, under any consideration, for the sugar content will never increase in the fruit once it has been harvested. Size, color, and above all, taste, will tell you when the right moment has arrived. Storage of grapes is difficult, even for brief periods. Since they must be fully ripe when picked, they become overripe very soon afterwards, despite cool temperatures. They can't be frozen successfully but make excellent jam and jelly and, it goes without saying, wine.

(4) Tree Fruits and Nuts

Harvesting tree fruits properly is somewhat more complicated than the harvesting of vegetables or berries, but easily accomplished with a little practice and observation. First of all it is well to remember that both quality and storage life may be seriously injured by careless handling that results in bruising or such subsequent neglect as leaving picked fruit exposed for hours to the hot sun. Secondly, we should realize that while tree fruits are ripe when they reach best eating quality, they are often mature enough for harvesting long before they are ripe. This means, of course, that for high quality and long storage life, the fruit must be picked when mature, not necessarily when it is ripe.

This state of maturity is sometimes difficult to determine. It varies from district to district and from season to season. By and large, however, it is restricted within certain limits by the species variety, and from correlated statistics over a period of years your local agricultural agency can tell you with surprising accuracy the correct date to harvest various varieties.

With cherries, maturity and ripeness almost coincide, as with the berry fruits. Size, color and taste are the criteria for judgment, plus ease of picking. When you lift up the fruit and pull gently against the spur, it should detach at once. Cherries should be picked with the stems on, unless you are eating them directly from the tree. When the stem is pulled out, juice escapes and rot sets in quickly. Cherries may be stored under refrigeration for several weeks after picking. The sweet varieties are not suitable for freezing, but the sour varieties, when pitted, freeze quite well.

Peaches and apricots are usually up to size and color a week or ten days before they are ripe, and commercial growers harvest them at that time. But the flavor never quite equals fruit left on the tree until it is fully ripe. When slight pressure of the thumb leaves an indention on a peach or apricot you may feel certain it has reached perfection. If left too long on the tree, fully ripe, the skin softens and ants or wasps may ruin the fruit, or it will fall to the ground

and bruise. The storage period of fresh peaches is short, but their flavor can be captured by freezing.

With the possible exception of prunes, plums shouldn't be harvested until a few days prior to full ripeness, a condition that taste and condition of firmness will quickly determine. They are one of the most perishable of tree fruits and don't even hold up under refrigeration. Neither do they freeze well, unless the pits are removed.

Harvesting of pears probably causes more difficulty to the home gardener than any other fruit. Maturity in pears is often weeks prior to ripeness, and the tendency for the tyro is to wait too long before picking. A pear may look just right for size and color and be rotten at the core. It is wise to check closely with local authorities for the right time to pick different varieties. Generally speaking, when they are up to size and detach easily from the fruit spur when lifted against it, they are ready to harvest. They should be kept in storage at around 50 deg. F. and checked often. The earlier varieties cannot be kept more than a few days, but later varieties may be held for weeks with correct care. Unfortunately pears do not freeze well, but are one of the best of all fruits for canning.

The apple is unquestionably the most important tree fruit, both from the standpoint of popularity and adaptability for storage. As with pears, maturity is not always easy to determine. Size is an indication, of course, but color may be deceptive. Color is developed by weather conditions and often apples may mature in weather not conducive to color. If the so called "red" varieties are left on the trees after maturity to attain color, their storage life may be shortened considerably. Taste, too, may be a deceptive factor, especially with late varieties, for the flavor of an apple doesn't reach perfection until it is fully ripe. When, then, is the right time to pick?

One clue is indicated when the first few full size apples fall from the tree. If this date corresponds fairly closely with the variety date suggested by your local agricultural agency, you may proceed safely, especially if you find that the fruit detaches easily when you lift it against the spur.

The earlier the variety, the shorter its storage life, so don't attempt to keep the summer varieties more than a week or ten days after harvest or you will be disappointed. When you come to the fall or mid-season varieties you may expect (under 35-40 deg. F.) to hold fruit firm and edible for a month or six weeks, while with the winter varieties stored at the same temperature, with high humidity, you may be able to enjoy crisp firm apples for six months. Remember that mice and rats like apples, too, so they must be protected from vermin, and if they are stored in an outside garage or shed where the temperature might fall more than a few degrees below freezing, they may have to be rushed to warmer quarters occasionally.

Those fortunate enough to have walnut or filbert trees will discover by experience how to harvest and store the nuts, but we will offer a few observations to the uninitiated. The husks inside which walnuts grow and mature, will split open when ripe and the nuts will fall to the ground where they can be gathered easily. Sometimes, especially during wet weather, the husks don't shed the nuts cleanly and then they are liable to become badly stained. In either case, to clean up the shells and avoid mold forming, it is advisable to wash the nuts in a mild chlorine solution before drying them. Some varieties of filberts shed the nuts cleanly from the husks, while with other varieties the husks and nuts fall together and must be separated. In either case the nuts are ripe when they fall, although still soapy to the taste until they have been dried. Commercial growers subject both walnuts and filberts to drying temperatures of around 100 deg. F. for a twenty-four hour period, but they may be dried satisfactorily for home use by hanging them up in mesh bags in the kitchen for a few days, or spreading them out in trays in the sun room or porch. By sampling them occasionally you can tell when they have reached the right "nutty" flavor. Properly dried nuts may be kept in dry cool storage for a year, or longer, in perfect condition.

(5) Flower Bulbs and Tubers

In the average home garden, harvesting and storage are not confined to fruit and vegetables alone. Most gardeners have plantings, small or large, of flower bulbs, corms or tubers, which require certain care and treatment if they are to be preserved.

Commercial bulb growers, for purposes of reproduction or sale, make it a general practice to dig their crops every year, but the home gardener doesn't always do this, nor is it necessary. Daffodils, crocus, snowdrops, lillies, iris and hyacinth bulbs may be left in the ground for several seasons without much harm, but if the quality of the blooms is to be maintained they should be lifted, divided and disinfected at least every third year. Tulips are an exception. On account of their susceptibility to disease, they should be dug and replanted annually.

The best time to dig tulips or daffodils is when the tops have lost all trace of green, but before they become brittle. If you have to dig bulbs prematurely, to make room for plantings of annuals, don't remove the green tops but lay them out in a shallow trench and cover the bulbs with soil until the tops have yellowed. When the tops have been removed, place the bulbs in slatted trays to dry, or if you have only a small quantity, hang them up, properly labelled, in discarded nylon stockings. Dry them for a week or two in temperatures of 65-70 deg. F. away from direct sunlight or drafts, and store them in a cool, airy place until mid-August or early September, when you are ready to replant. Before replanting be sure to dip them in a cold solution of Semesan Bel (half lb. to five gals. of water) for five minutes, and plant at once in soil that has been treated for pests with aldrin, dieldrin, or chlordane. This procedure can be followed when digging most of the early bulbs, except lilies.

Lily bulbs are never completely dormant, and when dug for division or treatment, should be replanted without delay. Lilies are subject to more diseases than most bulbs and a study of these is essential if the home gardener is to succeed in growing them. Also there are so many varieties, with different habits and blooming periods, that no

GLADIOLA CORM WITH OLD CORM REMOVED, AND NEW BULBLETS

general procedure can be outlined for digging and replanting.

The gladiolus, one of the most popular and adaptable of all flowers for the home garden, should be dug and replanted annually. In most gardens the corms haven't ripened before the first of November, but they may be lifted at any time from four to six weeks after flowering provided the corms are cured as soon as they are dug. Cut the tops off a few inches from the bulbs and place them in trays to dry in a warm (75-80 deg. F.) well-ventilated place. After two or three weeks, clean them up by pulling out the remaining stubs of top growth and removing the old withered corm and root from the base of the new one. To prevent thrips from overwintering, and to avoid possible storage diseases, dust the corms immediately after cleaning with a mixture of captan and sulphur (half and half by volume). Cure the corms for another week at around 70 deg. F. and then store them in a dry, cool (38-45 deg. F.) well ventilated place where there will be no danger from frost.

Tuberous begonias are becoming more and more popular each year as the home gardener discovers that they offer no real problems. In the Pacific northwest they will continue blooming until quite late in the fall, and for large mature tubers plants shouldn't be disturbed until the first November frost blackens the foliage. Actually, while the plant is actively engaged in growth there is little development in the tuber. It is only during the last few weeks of the growing season that the tuber makes its greatest gain. The ideal time to dig is when the plant stalk breaks easily from the tuber at ground level. If it doesn't break easily, and you have to lift the tuber, be sure to leave a couple of inches of stalk, since injury to the tuber's growth ring will cause decay. Store plants with a ball of soil on the roots until the green growth cures. Afterwards, wash the soil away and place the tubers in full sun for four or five days, turning them over occasionally, until they are thoroughly dry and firm. This curing is important for successful wintering, as soft, watery tubers will rot quickly. Take care that the last vestige of current growth is removed before storing. They should be stored in a dry place at around 50 deg. F. but to keep them from shrivelling it is wise to put them in perforated plastic bags. Check them occasionally to make certain no mold develops.

Peonies should be left undisturbed for several years after planting. If they should "clump" eventually, they may be dug up, divided, and replanted the same day. The tubers can be stored in plastic bags or sand, if necessary, but unless there is good reason they should be returned to the soil without delay.

While dahlias will often survive from one year to another if left in the ground, they are tender, easily killed by frost, and tend to rot quickly in cold wet soils. Since they are late bloomers, they may be left to flower until the first frost. Then the tops should be cut off three or four inches from the crowns, and the plants dug and washed. The common habit of storing dahlias in open boxes in a warm basement is not good, for the tubers lose strength from shrinkage, and premature soft top growth occurs in early spring, which is almost certain to be damaged when they are replanted. To prevent this, store the tubers in damp peat moss, sawdust, sand or vermiculite in a cool place where there is no danger of freezing.

(6) Summary

Remember that the purpose of storing fruit and vegetables is not necessarily to determine how long a product will keep, but to maintain it in the best possible condition until it is required for use.

Careful selection of choice, undamaged specimens for storage will pay off in length of storage life and the prevention of storage diseases.

Occasional examination of stored produce will forestal any possibility of heavy loss.

An annual diary, recording ripening and harvesting dates, storage temperatures, product life, etc., will become invaluable as a reference.

(7) Harvesting Seed

For those who wish to produce their own vegetable or flower seeds there are a few points to remember.

Seeds saved from particular named plant varieties may not come true to parent unless they have grown in isolation from others of the same species. Cross pollination may take place with less desirable relatives and the results could be disappointing.

Also seeds saved from new hybrid crosses (corn, tomatoes, etc.) may not even germinate.

However seed from long established varieties of self-pollinating annuals or perennials will come true and may be saved from year to year, provided it has been ripened fully before harvest.

Many plants such as beets, carrots and parsnips will not flower in one season, unless planted early in the spring and even if they do the seed may not mature before frost. By denying such plants their full moisture requirements they can sometimes be brought to flower prematurely.

After thorough drying all seeds must be stored in moisture-proof and vermin-proof containers, and should be treated with a fungicide to prevent disease.

Landscaping

(A)   PRINCIPLES

(1) Purpose

It might be said that landscaping glamorizes a home like stylish clothes and jewels add charm to a pretty woman. Artistically done, it can change a plain, unnoticed property into an enchanting picture. On the other hand, the hasty, careless or inexperienced touch can create the opposite effect, and often does.

Some people doubtless would be happier if landscaping plans were included with their property at the time of purchase, and this would avoid many errors. But it would restrict the scope of imaginative gardeners eager to imprint their homes and grounds with their own personality, and after all, in this world of standardization, there should be some room left for individual creativity.

(2) Approach

The first thing the amateur landscaper should do, even before laying out a plan of any kind, is determine personal preferences. Do you like evergreens, deciduous material, or a combination of the two? Are you partial to broad-leafed evergreens, or conifers? Do you want lots of color in your garden, or are you on the conservative side? Are you a real garden enthusiast, willing to spend considerable time pruning, spraying, and coddling rare and tender plants, or are you the sort that can take gardening or leave it, and actually prefer fishing or golf? When you have answered all such questions you are ready for the next step, a study of plant material that satisfies your requirements.

It's fundamental that one must learn his ABCs before he can read or write, and it's just as basic for the would-be landscaper to familiarize himself with the plants he intends to use. He should visit nurseries and parks, to see the subjects in their youth and their maturity. He should drive around the city and study gardens where these subjects are attractively placed, or otherwise. He should pre-determine their soil likes and dislikes, their preference for sun or shade, their tolerance to frost, salt spray, wind or insects. He should know their type of root system, their ultimate size, their life span, speed of growth—in short, everything he can possibly find out about them. This knowledge may lead to many changes and substitutions, which is all to the good, for the time to make alterations is before planting begins, not five years later.

(3) General Rules

Once armed with familiarity of his chosen plant material, the home landscaper is ready to construct a plan that will blend it properly into his surroundings. If he has purchased a property that has been established for some time, where the grading and walks, the patios and lawns, are already laid out, there is little he can do to alter the basic plan without incurring considerable expense, so he must make the best of it. However, if he is fortunate enough to have a house built to his own plans, he can and should try to

LANDSCAPING HINTS

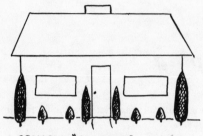

CONICAL, "SOLDIER" EFFECT.
– WRONG –

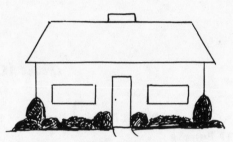

CURVED, FLOWING EFFECT.
– RIGHT –

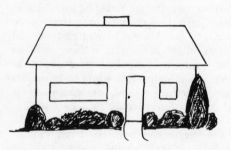

BALANCE WITH DOOR OFF CENTRE

DOOR OFF CENTRE WITH DRIVEWAY

BALANCE WITH L-SHAPE

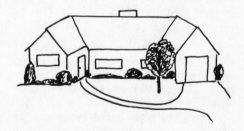

BALANCE WITH T-SHAPE

FIG. 12.

visualize how all the various aspects of the exterior features will combine to make the most pleasing effect at the homesite.

If possible, the house should be on a knoll or elevation, not only to provide a better view, but to assure good drainage. It should be placed reasonably close to the street for convenience, but far enough back to provide a sense of roominess. Drives and walks should be laid out as directly as possible from street to house, without cutting up the front area into small segments. Patios should be placed where they will provide the most privacy, shade and convenience, and rockeries where they will appear most natural.

When it comes to the actual landscaping, it will become evident that, although grounds and home must be tied together as a unit on the same property, each requires somewhat different landscaping treatment. For purposes of discussion, therefore, let us separate them temporarily into the "house area" and the "lawn area," and examine their special problems.

(B)   THE HOUSE AREA

(1) Foundation Planting

Since one of the main purposes of landscaping is to highlight the home's best points and tone down those least attractive, one important function is to hide the unsightly concrete foundations upon which the house stands.

Where a house sits close to the ground, as many without basements do, it is not wise to have solid plantings along the base. Group plantings at the corners will suffice. Where there is a narrow foundation it is just common sense to use dwarf plants except at the corners, or perhaps in large blank spaces between windows. A common practice is to string a miscellaneous assortment of evergreens (usually conical) along narrow beds beside the house, and when the plants are small the effect is sometimes pleasing. But it is likely to be short lived, and it is much better practice whenever possible to make wide beds, with taller plants at the back and a succession of lower plants in front, gradually sloping toward the lawn area. The whole planting should have a

curved, flowing effect. Base plantings on the corners, too, should add to this blending effect to soften the hard vertical lines of the building. (See Fig. 12.)

A good place to start your landscaping is at the front entrance. If this happens to be in the centre of the house, you will be able to use a balanced planting on either side. Start with a round or egg-shaped dwarf plant on each side of the front steps. Then accent both front corners with full bodied shrubs (or small trees) that won't grow higher than about two thirds the distance to the eaves. Between the entrance and the corners your choice will depend on the windows and the space between them, but at no point should there be shrubs that, ultimately, will interfere with visibility from the windows, or exceed the height of those planted at the corners. Avoid breaking the line from entrance to corner with tall, conical plants. Variation between evergreen and deciduous material is permissable, often desirable, and here let your personal preference prevail.

When the entrance is off centre, as many are, it is wise to extend the planting beyond the shorter side, to preserve a balance. If a driveway prevents this, accent the corner with as large an evergreen as space will permit, at any rate larger than anything used at the opposite corner. With an L-shaped property that has the entrance at the corner of the L, carry out the same idea of balance by planting a large evergreen or tree at the corner opposite the wing. If there should be two wings, with one of them a carport or garage, plant the large evergreen or tree as before, but on the inside of the carport.

There are so many variations in house plans that it's impossible to generalize, but once you get the idea of balance and streamlining in your mind's eye, you will be able to discover many other fundamentals about foundation planting. You will see that a narrow house can be made to appear wider by simply extending plantings beyond the corners, or a wide ranch-style home may be squeezed in, figuratively speaking, by planting heavily between windows and corners. You will notice how projections may be

SOME EVERGREENS ᶠᴼᴿ FOUNDATION PLANTING

CONICAL OR VERTICAL

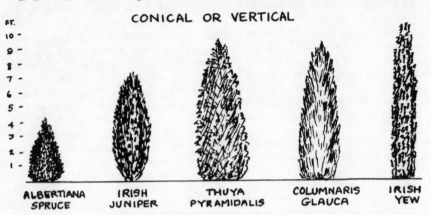

FT.
10 -
9 -
8 -
7 -
6 -
5 -
4 -
3 -
2 -
1 -

ALBERTIANA SPRUCE   IRISH JUNIPER   THUYA PYRAMIDALIS   COLUMNARIS GLAUCA   IRISH YEW

SEMI-PROSTRATE OR GLOBULAR

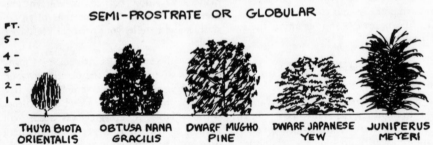

FT.
5 -
4 -
3 -
2 -
1 -

THUYA BIOTA ORIENTALIS   OBTUSA NANA GRACILIS   DWARF MUGHO PINE   DWARF JAPANESE YEW   JUNIPERUS MEYERI

PROSTRATE AND SPREADING

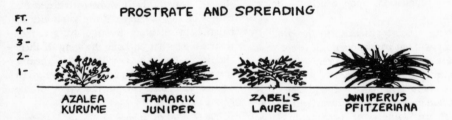

FT.
4 -
3 -
2 -
1 -

AZALEA KURUME   TAMARIX JUNIPER   ZABEL'S LAUREL   JUNIPERUS PFITZERIANA

FIG. 13.

softened by shrubs set against them, and how a loose informal shrub at the corner of a house will break the hard lines better than one more regular in outline.

There are no hard and fast rules, requiring a certain shrub here, another one there, on account of the wide choice available. To assist in a selection of material suitable for foundation planting, we will list a few of the many subjects that may be used with success in the Pacific northwest area. Fuller detail on any of these, and others, will be found in the alphabetical p l a n t guide (Ch. 9).

(2) Ten Good Dwarf Shrubs, Under Four Feet
(a) Deciduous:
SPIRAEA ANTHONY WATERER — Compact habit, red flowers, midsummer.

AZALEA MOLLIS — Small or large flowers in brilliant colors, spring.

CHINESE FLOWERING A L M O N D (*Prunus triloba plena*) — D o u b l e pink bloom, spring.

DWARF PURPLE - LEAFED BAR-BERRY (*Berberis thunbergi atropurpurea nana*)

(b) Evergreen:
AZALEA KURUME — Small or large flowers in brilliant colors, spring.

PERNETTYA MUCRONATA "BELL'S SEEDLING" — White summer bloom, deep pink berries in winter, small prickly leaves.

BERKMAN'S GOLDEN ARBORVITAE (*Thuya orientalis aurea nana*) — Globe or egg-shaped with gold-tipped foliage in flat, compact sprays.

DWARF HINOKI CYPRESS (*C. obtusa nana gracilis*)—Emerald green foliage in attractive, informal whorls.

DWARF JAPANESE CEDAR (*C. japonica vilmoriniana*) — A green globe in summer, turning bronzy in winter.

RHODODENDRON SPECIES — Blue, pink or purple bloom in spring, with varied attractive foliage.

(3) Ten Good Semi-dwarf Shrubs (Four to Eight Feet)
(a) Deciduous:
JAPANESE RED - LEAFED MAPLE (*Acer palmatum atropurpureum*) — Bright red foliage.

"BRIDAL WREATH" SPIRAEA (*Spiraea prunifolia flore plena*)—Early white bloom.

VARIEGATED WEIGELA (*Weigela rosea variegata nana*) — Green and gold leaves, pink bloom, early summer.

HYDRANGEA HORTENSIS — Large pink or blue flowers, late summer.

(b) Evergreen:
LILY-OF-THE-VALLEY SHRUB (*Pieris japonica*)—White bloom, early spring.

BROOM HYBRIDS—Cream, gold, pink or red bloom, spring to summer.

FIRETHORN (*Pyracantha*) — White bloom in summer, orange, red or yellow berries in winter.

RHODODENDRON H Y B R I D S — Broad, green leaves, flower clusters in many brilliant colors, spring.

HIMALAYAN BLUE JUNIPER (*Juniperus squamata meyeri*)—Good blue, informal.

DWARF ALBERTA SPRUCE (*Picea glauca albertiana conica*)—Compact, conical.

(4) Ten Good Upright Shrubs (Over Eight Feet)
(a) Deciduous:
FRENCH HYBRID LILACS (*Syringa vulgaris*) — White, mauve, blue or red bloom in early summer.

BEAUTY BUSH (*Kolkwitzia amabilis*) —Pink bloom in summer, gray-green foliage.

STAR MAGNOLIA (*Magnolia stellata*) —Large white bloom, fragrant, spring.

PEEGEE HYDRANGEA (*H. paniculata grandiflora*)—White flowers, turning pink, late summer.

(b) Evergreen:
CAMELLIA JAPONICA — G l o s s y green leaves, white, pink, red or variegated bloom, early spring.

LAURISTINUS (*Viburnum Tinus*) — Pink and white bloom, fragrant, winter into early spring.

IRISH JUNIPER (*J. communis hibernica*) — Silver-green foliage, stands clipping. Erect habit.

IRISH YEW (*Taxus fastigiata*)—Compact, upright, with dark green or gold-edged foliage and red berries.

UPRIGHT ARBORVITAE (*Thuya occidentalis pyramidalis compacta*) — Bright green, cedar-like foliage, compact and upright.

BLUE COLUMN (*Cham. lawsoniana columnaris glauca*) — Blue-green foliage.

These thirty shrubs, briefly described, are among the most popular, time-tested species used for foundation planting, but there are many others equally suitable, and it would be wise to make a study of them before making your final selection.

(C)   THE LAWN AREA

Once you have completed your landscaping plan for the house area, you are ready to tie it in with a plan to landscape the grounds. This plan should include not only the shape and grade of the lawn itself, but any borders adjoining it, rockeries imposed upon it, or hedges framing it.

(1) The Lawn Picture

Since the lawn is the central feature of the landscape picture you are trying to create, great care should be given to its layout. The size, slope and shape you give it, can greatly enhance or detract from the foundation planting, and in fact, either make or mar the whole home picture.

Naturally the size, and to some extent the shape, will be determined by the size of your property and the house upon it, as well as areas reserved for special use, or those unusable (rock outcrop). But unless you have an exceptionally large piece of property, the rule should be to use as much space as possible, in one piece, for grass.

This doesn't mean you must eliminate borders altogether, unless your property is very narrow, but it does mean it is better to sacrifice border space than lawn space, if you have to choose. Nothing looks less attractive than heavy border plantings surrounding a postage stamp lawn, unless perhaps it is the same size lawn cut up into circles and squares for shrubs and flower beds.

A fine lawn does not come by accident. Several things must combine to perfect it

—the grade, the soil, the degree of preparation, and the choice of seed.

If you are fortunate enough to have your house sitting upon an elevation, your lawn grading and drainage problems are more than half solved. A slope of one foot in a hundred (more is better) will provide surface drainage away from the foundation and keep the lawn from becoming winter waterlogged. If the house sits on a property that's absolutely level, you would be well advised to backfill against the foundation as high as possible, four or five feet out, grade down gradually to a slight depression, rising again to the property line. This will shed surface water away from the foundation and give the lawn a rolling effect that will create a sense of space. Should you be located on a high elevation, with steep slopes away from the house, you'll probably have to plan on terracing, for it is almost impossible to water or mow a lawn on an incline that drops more than one foot in three. Terraces are not advisable on small properties unless there is no alternative, in which case you should remember not to make the terrace wider than the remaining property between it and the property line. A sloping rockery, if well made, is sometimes better than a retaining wall or hedge, but the general topography will determine your choice.

(2) Preparing and Planting the Lawn

Once the basic grade has been established, you must deal with the soil. Chances are that topsoil and subsoil have become hopelessly mixed, and compacted from constant traffic, particularly close to the house foundation. The first step is to break this up thoroughly by rototilling to a depth of eight or ten inches. If the subsoil is preponderantly clay it will pay you to incorporate a generous amount of sand and peat into it, when rototilling, and if it is light and gravelly, plenty of peat to retain moisture. All stones and rocks of any size should be removed, and if there are areas where old turf is still alive, or patches of couch grass, you must delay your planting until this sod or couch has been killed completely, either by continuous cultivation or chemical treatment. A fine new turf may be spoiled completely in a very short time by a resurgence of wild grasses for there is no way of eradicating them.

Unless the contractor has been unusually careful in removing topsoil and spreading it afterwards, you will need to purchase additional soil to give you the depth necessary for a good turf. A minimum of four inches, (six inches is better) is required to sustain grass. This soil should be screened to remove all debris and bits of couch grass or thistle root that might be concealed in it, and if the humus content appears low, it's a good idea to add peat moss gradually as you are screening.

When the topsoil has been spread and roughly levelled, add your lime and fertilizer. If the soil is highly acid, you should add a hundred pounds of ground limestone to every thousand square feet, and half that amount to moderately acid soil. A mixed commercial fertilizer, 10-6-4, is satisfactory, but an organic like blood and bone or processed sewage will provide longer lasting effects. Two or three pounds per 100 square feet, thoroughly raked into the top three inches, will get the grass off to a good start.

Another item it will pay you to add to the topsoil before seeding is an insecticide to control Japanese beetle grubs, cutworms, wireworms, etc. By treating the soil with 5% granular diazinon at the rate of one pound per 100 square feet you will assure protection to the young grass for some time.

When the lime, fertilizer and insecticides have been thoroughly mixed into the topsoil, you are ready for the final rolling, raking and seeding. No matter how carefully you try to level the surface by raking, you will observe a number of humps and hollows the first time you go over it with a roller. You can gradually work these out by additional raking, but a simpler way is to tie a rope to each end of a ten-foot ladder weighted with stones, and drag this back and forth, lengthwise and crosswise, until the ground is perfectly smooth. After rolling a second time, the surface should be firm enough so your footprints barely show. Scarify this rolled surface lightly with the

tines of a rake, and the ground is ready for the seed.

It should be obvious that, after all the work and expense of preparing the soil properly, you shouldn't try to economize by purchasing cheap seed. The few cents a pound spread between ordinary seed and the choicest mixtures can make all the difference between an average lawn and a superior one.

Lawn grasses have two distinct types of root systems, one with runner roots branching out beneath the soil, sending up new tops, the other with runner roots that creep on top of the surface and make new roots at the joints. The former are most suitable for home lawns, the latter for golf putting greens and bowling greens.

There aren't many varieties suitable for making a good lawn. Kentucky blue grass has long been considered the best all around lawn grass, but it needs a well drained soil. Recently a new and superior variety of Kentucky blue, called Merion, has been developed. It will withstand closer cutting and is more disease resistant, but is slow to become established and by itself is rather coarse for a really first class lawn. Chewing's Fescue is a grass highly recommended for home lawns, is fine leafed, dark green, wears well, and will grow especially well in light soils. It will also tolerate some shade. Creeping red fescue should not be used as the sod becomes open and subject to weed invasion. The bent grasses are usually preferred for the heavier soils, and Colonial bent is one of the best, producing a beautiful, fine-textured turf. A mixture of Merion blue, Chewing's fescue, and Colonial bent, is hard to beat, and the mixture may be varied in accordance with your type of soil. For example, a good five-pound mixture for light, sandy soils would be three pounds Chewing's to one pound each of Merion and Colonial, and in the heavier soils, two pounds Chewing's to 1½ pounds each of the others.

Perennial rye grass will make a quick lawn, but is coarse and won't stand up well for more than two or three years. Red top is a similar grass that is used in some mixtures as a nurse grass, growing quickly and holding the soil until the more permanent grasses take hold. Neither of these, however, should be included in a mixture where you want a real good lawn.

The ideal time to sow grass seed is in the fall, from the middle of August until the middle of September. The soil is warm, seed germinates quickly, weed competition is at a minimum, there are usually soft rains, and day temperatures are not too high to damage the young grass. If it isn't possible to sow your lawn at this time, the next period is in April, as soon as the soil is workable.

Choose a calm day for seeding and sow when the soil is moist underneath but dry enough on top so it won't cling to the roller. You can either broadcast the seed by hand, half one direction, half the other, or rent a mechanical seeder. One pound of seed to 200 square feet is sufficient if properly sown. You may cover the seed by raking lightly to work it just below the surface, but a better way is to sprinkle about quarter of an inch of peat moss over the whole area. This must be rolled immediately, before any wind arises to blow the peat and seed away, then sprinkled with a fine spray. From then on never let the soil become dry. Many lawns are spoiled at the start by people neglecting to keep the seed moist. Once germinated, then suddenly dried out, seed quickly dies.

As soon as the lawn is well established, thorough waterings are needed to stimulate deep rooting, but care must be taken not to saturate the soil to a point where it becomes stagnant. When the grass has reached a couple of inches in height, start mowing. While the lawn is young, clippings should be removed to prevent any chance of matting and smothering the new turf. Later, when the lawn has thickened, short clippings may be left to provide humus, nitrogen, and a thin mulch at the soil surface.

(3) Lawn Maintenance

Usually the first problem to be faced after establishing a new lawn is weed control. No matter where topsoil comes from, it seems to contain a generous supply of annual and perennial weed seeds. If you allow these to germinate before sowing your lawn and cut them off with a Dutch hoe, you will eliminate considerable weed trouble. Those that do appear may be removed by hand or

easily controlled by hormone weed killers. (See Ch. I. (G))

During the spring and early summer, when grass is making its most vigorous growth, it should be cut at least once a week. There is some difference of opinion as to the best height to leave the grass, but it is generally agreed that too close cutting during hot weather exposes the roots and weakens the turf. One inch is a good height during spring months, with the mower raised another half an inch during July and August.

An annual fertilization program is necessary to maintain a lawn in healthy condition, for no other area is subject to such continuous leaching away of plant nutrients. In Chapter I (B) we outlined lawn fertilizer requirements, but they will bear brief repetition at this point.

As soon as the soil is reasonably dry in late February or early March, rake the lawn to remove any accumulation of winter rubbish, and go over it with an aerifier. Then apply 15 to 20 pounds per 1000 square feet of a complete 8-6-4 commercial fertilizer. If there should be moss in the lawn, caused usually by low soil fertility, sprinkle ammonium sulphate on the surface at the rate of 10 pounds per 1000 square feet, but don't wash it in. It will burn out the moss and although it will burn the grass to some extent, too, the latter will recover within two or three weeks.

Fertilizer requirements throughout the season depend on the general fertility of the soil and the amount of watering and rainfall, but may be determined easily by the color of the grass. Whenever it starts to turn light green, fertilizer should be applied. Usually, however, the March application, plus another of about half the spring rate in June, and a third full application in mid-August, will keep the turf in prime condition. Recent experience with the new urea compounds indicates that 33 pounds of 12% ureaform per 1000 square feet, applied during the latter part of August, plus another application of about half that rate in March, will maintain the lawn throughout the whole season.

Go easy with lime on your lawn. Turf

grasses like a slightly acid soil of about pH 6.0 If the soil is strongly acid you may add ground limestone at the rate of 50 pounds per 1000 square feet, but it would be well to test first, either with your own soil testing kit or by sending away a sample.

Renovation or rejuvenation of turf should be done in the fall, for the same reasons as a new lawn should be planted at that time. If brown spots have developed during the summer, they've likely been caused by compaction that has prevented penetration of moisture. Remove any heavy growth in such places and break up the soil with a digging fork or aerifier. With proper irrigation and fertilization these dry brown spots should quickly become green. Where the grass is thin or has become killed, you may have to reseed, but before doing so loosen up the soil and add a good dressing of compost. Be sure to use the same seed mixture as that in the original planting.

To maintain good turf under shallow-rooted trees is often a problem. For one thing, grass planted in such areas should be a shade tolerant variety like Chewing's fescue. You must fertilize under trees at twice the amount used elsewhere, and at the same time fertilize the trees by punching holes a couple of feet deep around the perimeter of the feeding roots and placing the fertilizer in these holes. Prune low branches to allow as much light as possible upon the grass, remove fallen leaves frequently, and leave the grass two inches high. When watering, be sure it penetrates at least six inches in the grassed area, and check soil occasionally for over-acidity, particularly around evergreens.

Damage to lawns by insects or disease can usually be corrected by the application of chemicals. We have mentioned a pre-seeding dieldrin treatment to control soil insects, and this can be carried out in established lawns by using dieldrin solution according to manufacturer's instructions.

There are certain fungus diseases to watch for in the humid Pacific northwest area, especially in poorly drained soils. Snow mould fungus attacks grass during mild periods in the winter, appearing as circular spots of whitish grey color, from a few inches to several feet in diameter. The fungus usually does not kill the grass, but should be kept from spreading by applying a mixture of dry corrosive sublimate and calomel. To cover 1000 square feet, mix four ounces of the powder (half of each substance), with 10 quarts of dry sand and spread it uniformly over the diseased area. Use care in handling as both these are deadly poisons.

Red thread disease is a fungus even more widespread than snow mould. Individual round straw-colored patches about four or five inches in diameter appear, then join together as the disease spreads. The area takes on a pinkish tinge caused by red or pink threadlike fungus growths that pin dead leaves and stems together. Treat the same as for snow mould.

If a lawn has been planted properly, is drained adequately, cut regularly at the right height, fertilized and watered according to a few simple rules, there isn't much likelihood of either a weed problem or a disease problem.

(D)   FRAMING THE PICTURE

With your foundation planting either accomplished or planned, your lawn established or laid out, your vegetable garden and orchard area set aside, all that remains to complete the landscaping picture is to provide the frame.

(1) Observations

If your property is small and your frontage narrow, this framing may be already accomplished by your neighbor's fences or hedges, or partially by your own driveway. If such is the case, don't squeeze yourself in by attempting elaborate border plantings of trees or shrubs. But if you have the space, much beauty can be added by the proper placement of shade or flowering trees, and the judicious use of shrubs, both evergreen and deciduous. Careful study, however, should preface any plan.

Is your house the low, ranch style so popular these days? If so, break the predominantly horizontal lines with some pyramidal material like the European White Birch or the Pacific Dogwood. If yours is a two-storey house on the Colonial style, try to reduce the perpendicular appearance by using spreading material like the Norway Maple or Persian Walnut.

It isn't necessary, or even desirable, to place such trees exactly opposite the ends of the house. Plant either in front of the foundation line or back of the rear corner, whichever sets the house off to best advantage and provides shade when and where you want it.

If your lawn is large enough to accommodate a few specimen trees, use low-branched, graceful material like the Japanese flowering crabapples, saucer magnolia, or Deodar cedar, and whatever you do don't plant them in straight lines, like soldiers on parade.

In border plantings, a combination of trees and shrubs is better than shrubs alone, as the latter tend to maintain a flat, regular appearance. Even if the borders are fairly narrow there should be room for a Japanese red-leafed maple, a smoke tree, or a weeping flowering cherry, and where there is room for trees to be spaced 20 or 30 feet apart, there are many beautiful subjects from which to choose.

Though it is often better to keep evergreen material grouped together, the pyramidal types of cypress, arborvitae and juniper, make an excellent background for most deciduous shrubs and add a pleasing variety to the overall picture.

Spacing is very important. Tall shrubs like lilac or mock orange should be at least six feet apart, and even dwarfer items like abelia or Anthony Waterer spirea need three to four feet. Consideration must be given also to shade tolerance, flowering time, habit and color, so there will be no disharmony of bloom or foliage.

Clumps of bulbs or perennials may be planted between shrubs, particularly while they are small, and edgings of annuals may be used to provide continuous color, provided they don't conflict with the show of the larger subjects.

There are many combinations that will produce a pleasing and long-lasting effect, if four things are kept in mind: harmony, balance, simplicity and practicality.

To assist in choice of material we will list a few of the best all-around trees, shrubs and perennials, suitable for framing the landscaping picture.

(2) Five Good Deciduous Shade Trees

EUROPEAN WHITE BIRCH (*Betula pendula alba*)—A quick growing, graceful tree with white bark, drooping branches and small-leafed foliage. Ultimate height about 50 feet with a spread of 30 feet.

COPPER BEECH (*Fagus sylvatica purpurea*)—An informal, open-branching tree with shiny purple foliage. It grows about the same size as the white birch.

PIN OAK (*Quercus palustris*)—A picturesque, pyramidal tree with beautiful fall coloration. A fairly slow grower with an ultimate height of 50 feet and a spread of 40 feet.

CRIMSON KING MAPLE (*Acer platanoides Schwedleri nigrum*)—A quick-growing red-leafed variety of Norway maple, with dense foliage especially brilliant in spring and fall, with an ultimate height of 40-50 feet and a 30-foot spread.

LITTLE LEAF LINDEN (*Tilia cordata*)—A hardy, pyramidal, quick-growing tree with brown branches and dense green foliage with an ultimate height of 50 feet and a spread of 40 feet.

(3) Five Good Coniferous Shade or Specimen Trees

ATLAS CEDAR (*Cedrus Atlantica glauca*)—A rather slow-growing tree with blue needles and stiff branching, that will ultimately reach 60 feet in height and spread 30 feet.

DEODAR CEDAR (*Cedrus deodara*)—Closely related to the Cedar of Lebanon, this is a quick-growing tree with graceful, pendulous, blue-green foliage, that will reach 60 feet in height and spread out to 30 to 40 feet.

BLUE SPRUCE (*Picea pungens glauca, Kosteri or Moerheimi*)—Probably the best known and most widely grown of all conifers on account of its hardiness and unmatchable blue color. A slow grower, it will reach 40 feet in as many years, with a base of 25 feet.

NORWAY SPRUCE (*Picea excelsa*)—A symmetrical, quick-growing tree, with bright green needles, adaptable to moist conditions, and a varying height up to 100 feet, with a 30 to 40 foot spread.

AUSTRIAN PINE (*Pinus nigra austriaca*)—A stiffly branched tree with dark green, small needled foliage, that will reach 70 feet in height and 30 feet in spread.

(4) Ten Good Deciduous Flowering Trees

ORIENTAL FLOWERING CHERRY (*Prunus serrulata, var. Kwanzan*)—Double, deep pink flowers in early May, with young foliage a copper color and all foliage taking on beautiful hues in the fall. Rather upright, with a height of about 20 feet and a spread of 15 feet.

JAPANESE FLOWERING PLUM (*Prunus cerasifera atropurpureum, var. Blireiana*)—Double rosy pink bloom in April, foliage reddish purple. It grows to about 15 feet, with a 12-foot spread.

FLOWERING CRABAPPLE (*Malus purpurem, var. Eleyi*)—Wine red flowers in mid-May, bright red fruits, purplish red foliage with good fall coloration. Rather spreading in habit, with a height and spread of about 20 feet.

PACIFIC DOGWOOD (*Cornus nuttallii*)—Large white flowers, like clematis, in late April, pyramidal habit, large oval leaves that color beautifully in the fall. Will grow up to 50 feet high, with a spread of 25 feet.

ENGLISH HAWTHORNE (*Cratageus oxyacantha, var. Paul's Scarlet*) — Scarlet double flowers in May and reddish purple berries during winter. Bushy, small leaved, with a height of about 15 feet and a spread nearly the same.

SAUCER MAGNOLIA (*Magnolia soulangeana*)—White and purple, large cup shaped flowers in May before the leaves unfold. Loosely branched, pyramidal in shape, with a height of about 20 feet and a spread of 15 feet.

GOLDEN CHAIN TREE (*Laburnum alpinum, var. Vossi*)—Yellow, sweet pea shaped flowers in long pendant racemes during late May. Serrated green foliage. Grows 20 to 25 feet in height with a 15-foot spread.

EUROPEAN MOUNTAIN ASH (*Sorbus aucuparia*)—Masses of white flowers in late May, followed by large clusters of orange or red berries. Serrated foliage. It grows in a pyramidal form to 30 feet, with a 15-foot spread.

TULIP TREE (*Liriodendron tulipifera*)—Greenish-yellow, tulip-like flowers, in early summer, and fiddle-shaped leaves. A quick growing, shapely tree that reaches 20 feet in height and spreads about 15 feet.

PINK HORSE CHESNUT (*Aesculus carnea*)—Showy pink flowers in late May, dense foliage and an umbrella shape that reaches 25 feet in height, with a spread of 15 feet. Variety Brioti has brilliant red flowers.

(5) Ten Good Deciduous Flowering Shrubs

GLOSSY ABELIA (*Abelia grandiflora*)—Small, glossy green leaves, turning bronze in autumn. Small pink or white fragrant flowers from July to October. Height four to five feet.

RED JAPANESE MAPLE (*Acer palmatum atropurpureum*)—Small yellow flowers, serrated red leaves throughout the summer, turning brilliant in the fall. Grows slowly to about eight feet, with a six-foot spread.

BUTTERFLY BUSH (*Buddleia Davidii*)—Long stems with terminal spikes of lilac-like fragrant flowers (yellow, red, white or purple) that bloom in late summer. Should be cut back hard each spring. Grows about eight feet.

JAPANESE QUINCE (*Chaenomeles japonica*)—Red, orange or pink flowers on bare branches in April or earlier. Irregular branching habit, with a height of around five feet in most varieties. Dwarf varieties three feet or under.

FLOWERING CURRANT (*Ribes alpinum*)—Clusters of red flowers in late March. Tolerates shade and grows to about five feet.

GOLDENBELLS (*Forsythia*)—Masses of golden yellow bloom in March, before the leaves unfold. Needs pruning back after flowering. Many varieties are available, growing from six feet to 10 feet in height.

WINGED SPINDLE TREE (*Euonymus alatus compactus*)—Corky angles to the branches are distinctive. The tiny flowers aren't showy, but produce orange-red seeds that last throughout the winter. The fall coloration of the foliage is outstanding. A compact shrub that grows to five feet.

ROSE OF SHARON (*Hibiscus syriacus*) —Red, white or blue showy flowers in the fall. Adaptable to sun or shade and grows to about 10 feet.

MOCK ORANGE (*Philadelphus coronarius*) — Single or double white, fragrant blooms in late May. Tolerant to most soils in sun or shade. Dwarf varieties grow to four feet, others to 10 feet.

SMOKE TREE (*Rhus cotinus coggygria rubrifolius*)—Plumes of mauve or yellow flowers in midsummer, with reddish purple leaves that turn brilliant colors in fall. Grows to 12 feet, with a six-foot spread.

SNOWBALL TREE (*Viburnum Opulis sterile*)—Large, white, chrysanthemum-like flowers in June. Excellent fall coloration of foliage. Grows to eight feet. Very adaptable to soils, sun or shade.

(6) Five Good Flowering Evergreens for Border Planting

MEXICAN ORANGE (*Choisya ternata*) —Masses of scented white flowers in June. Glossy green leaves. Grows to six feet.

LAURISTINUS (*Viburnum Tinus*) — Flat clusters of pink-budded white flowers are often visible in January. Deep green foliage, black berries. Grows to eight feet.

MOUNTAIN LAUREL (*Kalmia latifolia*)—Waxy, white to pink bell-shaped flowers in June. Glossy foliage. Prefers shade and will grow up to 15 feet but usually stays less.

ESCALLONIA—Pink or white flowers, June to September. Rather irregular branching habit, glossy bright green foliage. Can be kept to six feet or less.

EVERGREEN BARBERRY (*Berberis, var. Darwini*) — Orange-yellow flowers in clusters during May, small, green holly-like leaves. Grows to six feet.

(7) Ten Good Border Perennials

DOUBLE PEONIES (*Paeonia albiflora sinensis*) — Many varieties are available, blooming during May and June. Festiva Maxima is a fine early white, Jules Elie a large flowered early pink, and Felix Crousse a brilliant free flowering red. Average height about four feet.

PERENNIAL ASTERS (*Michaelmas Daisies*)—Amellus varieties, 18-24 inches, bloom from July to September. Blue King (dark blue), Lady Hinlip (rose), and Mrs. Ralph Wood (pink), are a few of many good varieties. The Novae-Angliae and the Novi-Belgi hybrids bloom later in the season and range from two feet to five feet in height. Blandie (white), Prosperity (rosy pink), and Red Cloud (red) are good examples.

PERENNIAL SPIRAEA (*Astilbe*)—Two to six foot spikes of white, rose, pink or scarlet flowers in midsummer, foliage green or purple. Fanal (red, 2½ feet) and Serenade (pink, three feet), and Gladstone (white, three feet) are a few choice varieties.

SHASTA DAISY (*Chrysanthemum maximum*)—Originally available in white only, e.g. the famous Esther Read, these may be obtained now in yellow (Cobham Gold), pink (Clara Curtis), and red (Duchess of Edinburgh). They are hardy, bloom profusely for a long period in midsummer, with long stems for cutting. Up to three feet.

DELPHINIUMS (*Pacific Giants*)—Grow these stately plants from seed and you will get a wide range of color combinations. Some named varieties are Galahad (white), Guinevera (mauve), and Black Knight (dark violet). The pure pink, Pink Sensation, is a continual flowering, disease free addition to the family, growing about 2½ feet high compared to between four and eight feet in most other varieties.

RED HOT POKER OR TORCH LILY (*Tritoma*)—A striking subject that blooms in late summer or early fall. Brilliant orange-red, deep yellow,or all red trusses grow on stems up to three feet. Fireflame (orange-red), Royal Standard (yellow, scarlet top), and Yellow Hammer (maize yellow) are three well known varieties.

PHLOX PANICULATA — There are dozens of varieties of this favorite summer blooming perennial, with many color combinations. The latest include Blue Moon (lilac blue), Sweetheart (salmon pink), Prunella (reddish purple), Tenor (red), and Snowdrift (white). Average height 2½ feet.

GLOBE FLOWER (Trollius) — These

A GOOD EXAMPLE OF LOW BORDER PLANTING

plants with ball-shaped flowers on long stems are useful for cutting as well as garden show. The color range is somewhat limited. Lemon Queen (lemon yellow), Orange Globe (orange yellow), and Orange Princess (orange), are a few varieties, average height 2½ feet.

BLEEDING HEART (Dicentra spectabilis)—An old time favorite. Pink and white, heart-shaped flowers on long graceful stems, early in May. A hybrid named "Bountiful" has larger blooms, though the plant is only 18 inches high, compared to two feet or more with the older varieties.

BELLFLOWER (*Campanula persicifolia*)—Blue, violet or white flowers in June-July, on long stems suitable for cutting. Average height three feet.

Most of the above mentioned perennials are tall subjects, suitable for interplanting (preferably in clumps of three) with shrubs, or planted in masses as background material for foreground planting in borders or in rockeries, and we will mention some of them when discussing the latter.

(E) ROCKERIES AND PLANTERS

(1) An Approach to Rock Gardening

Most small grounds haven't suitable locations for a rock garden of any size. However, there are many properties on the Pacific coast where there are natural outcroppings of rock, with clefts and pockets suited for alpine plants, and there are many others which can be terraced with dry rock walls, where pockets may be found for many interesting subjects.

If you are fortunate enough to have natural rock, the layout of your rockery will present no problem. Plant where possible in natural pockets, and if you have to add rock to provide extra depth of soil behind it, be sure to search for rock of the same character and color as that of your rockery base.

If you have a choice of exposure, try to provide full sun. This doesn't mean that the rockery has to face south. In locations where rainfall is abundant, with less sun and heat than elsewhere, a southern or western exposure is preferable, but where there is less precipitation and considerable hot summer sun, it is better if the rockery slopes to the east or northeast.

Generally speaking, rock plants are more resistant to drought than to over abundant moisture, so soils should be of a loamy or sandy loam character. A heavy clay is just not suitable, and if you have nothing else to deal with, it would be better to forget about a rockery altogether unless you are prepared to incorporate plenty of sand, peat and compost. An acidity of about pH 6.0 is right for most rock plants and those requiring more acidity can be treated individually.

When laying out your rockery, always remember that the more natural you can make it the more pleasing it will be. Go out into the countryside and study some of the effects found in natural, unscarred rock areas. Notice how most of the rocks have been buried or covered with growth, exposing only about a third of their surface to the eye. Observe how carelessly, yet attractively, nature has scattered her plant subjects. After all, she has been rock gardening for a long time and can provide you with many valuable tips. Take your camera along and snap a few pictures of spots that appeal to you and provide a suggestion you think might blend into your home setting. Visit some well laid out rock gardens in your city and take notes of the items that interest you. When you have correlated all your notes and ideas, and boiled them down to fit your needs, start to work.

Use the largest pieces of rough, weathered rock you can handle. A dozen large rocks are better than two or three dozen small ones. When placing the rocks, don't lay them out in any particular pattern, but do try to keep the natural stratification facing the same direction in a more or less rolling contour. Whatever you do, don't dot the rockery with round clean boulders that look like blanched almonds in a cake. Bury at least half the rock in the soil, exposing the weathered surface just as you would find it in nature.

When constructing a dry wall, keep the large stones for the base, tilting them slightly downward and inward as you build. Slope back the face of the wall about three inches to the foot, to prevent possible collapse when winter rains loosen the backfill, and set the stones at right angles to this slope. Pockets should be filled with soil as you build, and may be planted at the same time if the season is right. Be sure the roots can find their way back behind the rocks, into the soil bank. Chunks of sod or sphagnum moss will help prevent new soil from washing out of rock crevices, and also provide valuable humus for the plants.

Spring is a good time to set out most alpine plants, but container grown material may be moved successfully at any period, though it is inadviseable to do it during midsummer, unless you are prepared to apply daily waterings. Spring flowering plants and bulbs should be planted as early in the fall as possible.

To assist you in selection of rockery material we will list a few subjects that have proved their usefulness over the years. A study of parks and nurseries, as we have suggested, will disclose to you many others.

(2) Five Good Conifers for Large Rockeries

TAMARIX JUNIPER (*Juniperus sabina tamariscifolia*)—Compact, deep green foliage, with a height less than one foot and a natural spread of six to eight feet in diameter.

HETZ JUNIPER (*Juniperus sinensis glauca hetzi*)—Somewhat less compact than the tamarix, steel blue foliage, with a height of two feet and a natural spread up to eight feet in diameter.

PFITZER JUNIPER (*Juniperus sinensis pfitzeriana*) — Quick growing, somewhat loose in habit until mature, green foliage, with a height up to 30 inches and a spread up to 15 feet. There are compact forms (compacta) and golden forms (aurea), with less height and spread.

OHLENDORF SPRUCE (*Picea abies ohlendorffi*) — Compact, dark green, small needles, with a height up to three feet and a spread to six feet.

DWARF JAPANESE YEW (*Taxus cuspidata nana*)—Compact, dark green leaves, with a height up to two feet and a spread up to 10 feet.

(3) Five Good Conifers
for Small Rockeries

DWARF HINOKI CYPRESS (*Chamaecyparis obtusa nana gracilis*)—Tight-growing, bright green foliage in informal whorls. Ultimate height around three feet, slightly less in diameter. The golden form (lutea) is somewhat smaller.

WAUKEGAN JUNIPER (*Juniperus horizontalis douglasi*)—Trailing habit, steel blue in summer, purplish in winter, very prostrate, can be kept within a six-foot area.

DWARF SWISS PINE (*Pinus mugho mughus*)—A slow growing globe, with fine green needles, reaching a height of two or three feet and a spread of about the same.

BERKMAN'S GOLDEN ARBORVITAE BIOTA (*Thuya orientalis biota aurea nana*)—A slow growing, gold tipped, round to oval shaped shrub, with foliage in flat parallel sprays. Reaches an ultimate height of two to three feet with a two-foot diameter.

FORSTEKENSIS (*Chamaecyparis lawsoniana forstekensis*)—A dense, hedge-hog like green cushion that will reach two feet in height and the same in spread.

(4) Five Good Broad Leafed
Evergreens for Any Rockery

JAPANESE AZALEA (*Azalea kurume*)—Compact, small-flowered varieties like Mother's Day (bright red) or Hinodegiri (crimson red), grow about 18 inches high, with a two-foot spread. The larger flowered varieties like Orange Beauty (orange) or Willy (bright pink), grow slightly taller.

EVERGREEN DWARF BARBERRY (*Berberis buxifolia nana*)—Sometimes used for hedging, this is also a useful subject for rockeries, with small yellow flowers in April-May and dark green foliage. It grows about two feet in height, with a diameter of about 18 inches.

COTONEASTER DAMMERI (*Cotoneaster humifusa*)—A very prostrate evergreen carpeter, with white flowers in summer and red berries in winter. Will wind its way informally among the rocks, or may be controlled within a three or four-foot area.

PROSTRATE BROOM (*Cytisus kewensis*)—Creamy white flowers in early spring with a height of one foot and a three or four-foot spread.

GARLAND FLOWER (*Daphne cneorum*)—A compact, small-leafed evergreen with masses of fragrant pink flowers in spring. Not over one foot in height, with a spread sometimes reaching three feet.

(5) Five Good Deciduous Shrubs
for Any Rockery

DWARF JAPANESE QUINCE (*Chaenomeles lagenaria, var. Simoni*)—Deep velvety red flowers in early spring, prostrate in habit with a spread up to four feet.

DWARF SPIRAEA (*Spiraea bumalda Newmanni*)—Red flowers in midsummer and brilliant foliage in fall. A foot in height and about the same in diameter.

DWARF POTENTILLA (*Potentilla fruticosa, var. Mandshurica*)—A low, spreading shrub bearing a succession of white flowers in summer on mats of grey foliage. A foot in height and up to three feet in spread.

JAPANESE CUT-LEAF MAPLE (*Acer palmatum dissectum*)—Very serrated leaves, green or purple, on graceful arching branches. Slow growing, with an average height of two or three feet and a spread of about the same.

AZALEA MOLLIS — There are many choice varieties of deciduous azaleas in brilliant red, orange, pink, salmon, yellow and white, that bloom during May and early June. Some are small-flowered, some, like the Knap Hill hybrids, large flowered. Many are scented. Heights vary from two to five feet.

(6) Ten Good Rockery Perennials

ASTER (*Amellus*)—Heliotrope flowers with orange hearts on eight-inch to 12-inch stems during May and June.

THE PASQUE FLOWER (*Anemone pulsatilla rubra*)—Red flowers, six inches to eight inches high, May to July.

PINKS (*Dianthus "Little Joe"*)—A new hybrid with dark red flowers on four-inch stems and with a long summer blooming period.

ROCK ROSES (*Helianthemum*) — An evergreen perennial in an assortment of colors that appear in May and, when cut back, again in September.

A LOVELY POOL WITH WATER LILIES BORDERED WITH HEATHER

DWARF PHLOX (*Phlox Subulata*)—In rose, blue, pink and white blooms, during late spring. Plants four inches to eight inches high, spreading up to two feet in diameter.

PRIMULA—Many strains like the Juliae hybrids (e.g. Wanda) available in a wide range of color combinations, with flowers around four inches high during March and April.

GENTIAN (*Gentiana acaulis*) — Large trumpet shaped blue flowers from March to May on a low, compact clump. Intense, striking color.

BELLFLOWER (*Campanula carpatica*)— A carpet of bright blue, star-shaped flowers throughout June and July, on a mound of green foliage that usually stays green all winter.

LEWISIA (*Var. Heckneri*)—Fleshy evergreen leaves, small rosy-red flowers on 12-inch stems in May.

PENSTEMON (*Var. Rupicola*) — Rose-crimson flowers on four-inch stems during June and July, a solid mat of bloom.

(7) Ten Good Heathers for Rockeries
(In order of flowering)

SPRINGWOOD WHITE (*Erica carnea*) —Strong prostrate growth, green foliage all year, spikes of white flowers from January to March.

KING GEORGE (*Erica carnea*) — An excellent prostrate, reddish purple, January to March.

VIVELII (Erica carnea)—Bronze flower buds, brilliant carmine flowers, compact, prostrate. Flowers from February to March. Bronze foliage in winter.

MRS. MAXWELL (*Erica vagans*) — A compact plant with bright green foliage all season and beautiful deep pink flowers from August to September.

C. W. NIX (*Erica calluna vulgaris*) — Dark green, compact foliage, crimson bloom from August to September.

J. W. HAMILLTON (*Erica calluna vulgaris*) — A beautiful bright salmon pink flower on a prostrate, compact plant, August to September.

TIB (*Erica calluna vulgaris*)—A double rosy pink on tight growing plant, August to September.

MAIR'S VARIETY (*Erica calluna vulgaris*)—A long spiked white flower on 12-15-inch plant, July to September.

H. E. BEALE (*Erica calluna vulgaris*)— Dull foliage in winter, dark green in summer, with striking long spikes of double-pink blooms from September to November.

DAVID EASSON (*Erica calluna vulgaris*)—A late blooming red, October to November, on semi-compact plants 12-15 inches high.

(8) A Word About Planters

In recent years there has been a great increase in the construction of the planter box as an integral part of the modern ranch-style home. Unfortunately many architects and contractors design them mainly for appearance, without regard to the demands of plant material that people might like to use in them. Many are far too narrow, some too deep, with too much wall exposure to the hot sun, some even without drainage. As a result, many gardeners who have tried to establish permanent plantings in them have been disappointed.

If you have a planter less than 18 inches wide, inside measurement, forget the idea of planting dwarf shrubs in it, for it becomes too hot and dry during the summer months. Restrict yourself to the heat loving annuals, like petunias or geraniums, or, in shady positions, begonias. If, however, the planter is two feet wide or more, with good drainage, and you are careful to maintain adequate fertilizer and moisture, there are a number of dwarf shrubs which may be used to advantage in planters, as a permanent complement to your foundation planting.

Most of the heathers and rockery perennials previously listed, are suitable, and there are a few dwarf conifers and deciduous shrubs that won't get out of hand over the years.

CRIMSON DWARF BARBERRY (*Berberis thunbergi atropurpurea nana*)—A 15-inch globular plant with bright red foliage throughout the summer.

A POTTED TUBEROUS BEGONIA READY TO SET OUTSIDE

DWARF VARIEGATED EUONYMUS (*Euonymus radicans variegata*)—Small, silvery, variegated foliage on a prostrate plant that will drop trailing branches over the planter's edge. Evergreen.

JAPANESE AZALEA (*Azalea kurume*) —The small-flowered varieties like the crimson Hinodigiri make a brilliant spring show in a planter.

VERONICA PAGEANA—Small white flowers bloom throughout late summer on a compact, silver-grey plant that always looks neat.

JAPANESE HOLLY (*Ilex crenata convexa*)—Bushy, spreading, small-leaved evergreen, with shiny, bright green foliage.

MINIATURE GOLDEN CYPRESS (*Chamaecyparis lawsoniana minima aurea*) —A dwarf, golden globe with flat, parallel sprays.

DWARF ARBORVITAE (*Thuya occidentalis pumila "Little Gem"*)—A dwarf, flattened green ball that turns a bronzy hue in winter.

DWARF MOSS CYPRESS (*Chamaecyparis pisifera aurea nana*)—A round, compact shrub with fine, gold-tinged foliage.

DWARF BROOM (*Genista sagittalis*)— A very prostrate creeper that bears bright yellow flowers during May and June.

DWARF SPRUCE (*Picea glauca albertiana conica*) — A tight-growing, conical slow growing shrub, suitable at the ends of large planters, or where an upright effect is needed.

(F) THE ROSE GARDEN

While roses may be used in border plantings like specimen shrubs, they are far more effective and easier to prune, spray and control generally if they are kept together in beds or groups.

Beds or borders three or four feet wide, in full sun, with good drainage and air circulation, are ideal. The soil is better on the clay loam side than too sandy, on the acid side (pH 5.6 to 6.0), and must be well supplied with organic material.

(1) Roses Classified

Besides climbers, which will be discussed later, roses include several types, grouped according to flowering habit, hardiness, etc. The most common and popular of the bush roses are the hybrid teas, and if you have limited room in your garden, you will probably gain greater satisfaction from a selection out of this group than any other. Hybrid tea flowers are borne one to a stem or on a cluster of three to five. There are many varieties and colors, most of which are suitable for cutting, many possessing fine fragrance. They grow between eighteen inches and four feet high, depending on the variety and pruning methods used, and should be spaced 18" to 24" apart.

Similar in appearance to the hybrid teas are the hybrid perpetuals, the June roses of grandmother's garden. They are vigorous, hardy, and make a grand display in June and July, but don't continue blooming like the hybrid teas, and their flowers lack the variety and refinement of the latter. They still have a place, however, in the shrub border, or even in some foundation plantings.

Where you have room for mass plantings and desire a gay summer show of special color effects, the polyanthas or floribundas will meet your requirements. This group bears flowers on short-stemmed clusters, single or double, and there are many choice colors. Some closely resemble small hybrid teas, and most varieties provide almost continuous bloom throughout the summer. Some of the larger flowered floribundas grow as tall as the tallest hybrid teas and should be spaced two feet apart, but the dwarf polyanthas, many of which don't exceed 18" in height, are happiest when spaced about that distance from each other.

A new class of roses called grandiflora (hybrid tea crossed with floribunda) has recently been developed and it seems destined to become very popular. Grandifloras are vigorous, easy to grow, produce more flowers than the hybrid teas on long stems suitable for cutting. They may be planted in the same beds with hybrid teas but should be spaced at least two feet apart.

For colorful and distinctive accent material beside paths or as a background in rose or perennial beds, tree roses can add dignity and elegance. Contrary to the opinion of many, these are not a distinctive class, but are simply hybrid tea, perpetual, or floribunda rose varieties grafted on specially grown "tree" stocks.

Miniature roses, with their tiny single or double blooms and delicate fragrance, are becoming more and more popular each year. Barely exceeding a foot in height, they are an ideal subject for planters or pockets in the rockery. They are quite hardy.

(2) When and How to Plant

Roses may be planted either in the fall or spring, and container grown plants may be set out even while in bloom. In the fall, sometimes the wood is slow to ripen and planting stock is unavailable until weather conditions make late planting difficult, so most roses are set out in early spring. New plants should be cut back to between six and twelve inches above the crown, the more vigorous varieties cut back the least. (See Chapter I (F). Roots should be pruned where damaged and spread outwards and downwards in an inverted cone shape from the crown, which should be set about an inch below the surface. Thorough watering at ten-day intervals will help get the young plants established, and as growth appears, spraying for diseases and insects will become necessary.

(3) Diseases and Insects That Attack Roses

Mildew and black spot are the most serious diseases that trouble roses. Powdery mildew is easily recognizable by the frost-like film which appears on leaves, stems and buds. It usually starts when the first buds are forming and continues for several weeks, subsiding during the summer and reappearing during the fall. Powdered sulphur, mildex and actidione are materials generally recommended for control.

Black spot is easily recognizable by the more or less circular spots ⅛" to ½" across, that appear on the upper side of the leaves. If left unchecked these spots merge into large patches and the leaves turn yellow and die. Overhead sprinkling and summer rains contribute to the spread of the fungus. A dormant copper spray will kill spores overwintering in infected stems and canes, and if there are still signs of black spot when the foliage appears, spray or dust with a fungicide containing captan or phaltan and repeat every two weeks until the disease has been eliminated.

Aphids and red spider mites are two of the most common insect pests found on roses and they, with chewing insects and thrips, can be controlled by sprays that include malathion, diazinon, tedion, etc., in various combinations, available at all garden centres. For best results with roses, as with everything else, a regular cultural program should be followed.

(4) Cultural Calendar

Feb. 15—Spray with dormant strength fungicide.

March 15—Prune bushes, dig in compost or rotted manure, add a handful of 6-8-6 fertilizer per bush.

April 1—Spray or dust foliage with a fungicide that contains mildex or phaltan for mildew and captan or phaltan for black spot.

April 15—Spray or dust foliage with an insecticide containing malathion or diazinon for aphids, and if it doesn't include a fungicide as well, repeat April 1 spray for diseases.

May 1—Repeat spray as before if there is any sign of disease or insect damage.

May 15—Add another handful of 6-8-6 fertilizer per bush. Irrigate well. Repeat insecticide spray or dust treatment. Mulch with peat moss.

June 1—Repeat insecticide spray or dust treatment. From now on through July make certain your insecticide contains a miticide such as tedion or malathion as red spider mites are most active during this time.

July 1—Keep dead flowers from seeding. Repeat sprays regularly every two weeks. Make certain plants are well watered.

Aug. 1—Remove dead blooms. Spray or dust for insects and possible signs of mildew. Irrigate well.

Sept. 1—Watch for return of mildew or black spot with fall rains. Continue insect control and watering program until rains arrive.

Oct. 1—Remove dead blooms and continue disease and insect controls.

Nov. 1—Cut tops off exceptionally vigorous plants to prevent wind damage, but don't attempt to prune. Make sure crowns are covered with soil to avoid any chance of frost damage. Mulch with rotted manure or compost.

(5) Rose Varieties by Color

Since there are so many good varieties of roses, with new ones being added every year, it is difficult to make a selection. However, the following are reliable varieties that have proven their performance in most sections of the Pacific northwest.

WHITE

Hybrid Teas	*Poly. & Floribundas*
White Knight	Irene of Denmark
White Swan	Ivory Fashion
Virgo	White Bouquet
McGredy's Ivory	White Pinocchio

PINK

Hybrid Teas	*Poly. & Floribundas*
Capistrano	Cecile Brunner
Helen Traubel	Fashion
The Doctor	Pink Pinocchio
Symphonie	Lilibet

RED

Hybrid Teas	*Poly. & Floribundas*
Ena Harkness	Frensham
Charles Mallerin	Alain
Chrysler Imperial	Floradora
New Yorker	Red Ripples

YELLOW

Hybrid Teas	Poly. & Floribundas
Peace	Yellow Pinocchio
Isobel Harkness	Goldilocks
Golden Sceptre	Gold Cup
McGredy's Yellow	Golden Fleece

ORANGE

Hybrid Teas	Poly. & Floribundas
Fred Edmunds	Jiminy Cricket
Mojave	Fusilier

BI-COLOR

Hybrid Teas	Poly. & Floribundas
Saturnia	Masquerade
Fortyniner	Circus
Shot Silk	The Optimist
Signora	Oberon

New Grandifloras

Queen Elisabeth—	pink
Carrousel—	red
Buccaneer—	yellow
Montezuma—	orange

(G) CLIMBERS AND CREEPERS

(1) Climbing Roses

Since we have been discussing roses, it might be as well at this point to assess the place of the climbing rose in the garden. Nearly every home has a spot for one or two, and sometimes there are locations where nothing is quite as effective.

They make an excellent screen to hide a bare wall or add an accent of color to foundation planting. They provide a brilliant show when trained along a fence and may be used as a substitute for a fence or hedge, if given adequate support. The pillar type roses, trained on posts or upright trellises are especially useful to relieve formality around a car port.

Climbing roses fall into three distinct sub groups: climbers, ramblers, and pillars. The term "climber," which in a sense describes them all, is applied particularly to a stiff-caned variety that blooms on shoots from one or two-year-old wood. Care must be taken when pruning, therefore, not to remove growth that will flower the following year. A thinning of old canes and a shortening of long laterals is all that is necessary.

A rambler has long, thin, pliable canes which will lie on the ground if unsupported, and it flowers on the previous season's wood. All older wood should be removed immediately after flowering to throw the strength of the plant into new cane growth.

A pillar rose, or climbing hybrid tea, is actually an extension of the bush rose, with rigid growth like that of the teas, requiring the same type of spring pruning, but not cut back as far.

Here are a few easy to grow varieties in each sub group.

Climbers—

Blaze—Bright red, medium size double blooms, a long bloomer.

Golden Showers — Brilliant canary yellow, medium size double blooms.

New Dawn — Flesh pink, medium size blooms like tea roses.

Ramblers—

Chevy Chase — Small scarlet blooms. Very floriferous.

Carpet of Gold — Masses of yellow bloom.

Dorothy Perkins — Popular small flowered pink.

Pillars and Climbing H.T.s—

Paul's Lemon — Almost white, exceptionally large blooms.

Cl. New Yorker — L a r g e, fragrant, scarlet flowers.

Cl. Shot Silk — Salmon pink, large blooms.

(2) Eight Popular Climbing Plants

THE CLEMATIS is a climber which stands shoulder to shoulder with the climbing rose in popularity, and in value as an accent plant. A little more delicate than the rose, and somewhat more selective in soil requirements, it is nevertheless not difficult to grow if certain conditions are met. It likes its feet kept cool and shaded and its head in the sun. It prefers a sandy, well drained soil with plenty of humus and a pH around 7.0. A trellis or other support must be provided for the vine tendrils to cling to. There are many spectacular varieties but a few of the most reliable include Jackmanni (single, large-flowered deep purple), Duchess of Edinburgh (white, double, large-flowered), Ville de Lyon (single, large-flowered wine red), and Montana Rubens (small-flowered, very floriferous pink, early bloomer).

CHINESE WISTERIA (*Wisteria sinensis*) is a quick growing climber that produces panicles of mauve flowers that hang down like bunches of grapes. Usually it is trained as a vine on an arbor or trellis, but may be trained to a tree form by tying a newly planted shoot to a strong stake and keeping the side shoots rubbed off to let the top develop. After a couple of years of judicious pruning to shape and shorten the branches, you can develop an attractive standard. Wisteria likes a rich, fairly deep soil, full sunlight, and the withered blooms should be removed right after flowering to keep it attractive.

DUTCHMAN'S PIPE (*Aristolochia sipho*) is a hardy climbing plant with large tropical-like leaves and purplish flowers shaped like a pipe. The flowers bloom in the spring, but there is another variety (sempervirens) with small evergreen leaves and yellowish pipes that bloom in late summer.

HONEYSUCKLE (*Lonicera*) is popular chiefly on account of the outstanding fragrance of several of its varieties. It is adaptable to shade or sun, but prefers the latter, and likes well drained soil with plenty of humus. It requires a trellis or arbor to climb upon. There are both evergreen and deciduous varieties. Of the latter, Caprifolium (yellow), and Heckrotti (apricot), are two of the best for both color and fragrance, and Halliani is an evergreen Japanese variety with creamy-white perfumed flowers.

IVY (*Hedera*) has been always widely used in gardens, both as a climber and a creeper, and is perhaps the hardiest and most adaptable in the group. It will grow in dense shade, full sun, and in almost any type of soil.

ENGLISH IVY (*Hedera helix*), either with plain green or silver and gold variegated leaves, may be used to cover walls, hide unsightly stumps, etc.

IRISH IVY (*Hedera helix hibernica*), with its sharply pointed leaves, is equally hardy and adaptable.

VIRGINIA CREEPER (*Parthenocissus quinquefolia*) is a deciduous vine, also used extensively for covering walls and fences, and is noted particularly for its brilliant fall coloring. It requires a support for its tendrils to cling to, but there is a close relative (*parthenocissus tricuspidata*), known as BOSTON IVY, which clings tenaciously with sucker-like tips to hard surfaces without support and is often used on brick or stone buildings, outside chimneys, etc. Its dense summer green foliage also turns beautiful colors in the fall. Both are adaptable to most well drained soils.

HYDRANGEA PETIOLARIS is another hardy self-clinging climber that will grow in sun or shade, is tolerant of most soil conditions, and throws masses of small white flowers in early summer.

THE SILVER FLEECE VINE (*Polygonum aubertii*) also produces small white flowers, and is a very vigorous grower, requiring support and room to spread. It is particularly suitable for large arbors.

(3) Groundcovers for Dry Areas

In spots too dry or too shady for a lawn to grow, where grass is difficult to mow, and where rain erodes sloping ground, the groundcovers come into their own. Many of them require less care than a lawn and provide very charming effects.

CREEPING THYME (*Thymus serpyllum*) is an evergreen, aromatic creeper that makes a prostrate mat. Tiny purplish flowers bloom in midsummer. It will grow in rather poor, rocky soils. There are variations with gold or silver-gray foliage.

ARROW BROOM (*Genista sagittalis*) is a very prostrate, small leafed evergreen that takes considerable heat and drought. Small pea-like yellow flowers bloom in late May and June.

PHLOX SUBULATA is an alpine favorite, in a wide range of colors, that will soften a rocky bank with masses of bright flowers in early summer. It is not over six inches high and is adaptable to a wide range of soils.

ST. JOHNSWORT (*Hypericum calycinum*) is excellent for sandy or gravelly soils. It is a semi-evergreen with 4" leaves and yellow bloom that continues throughout most of the summer. It grows about ten inches high.

(4) Groundcovers for Shady Areas

JAPANESE SPURGE (*Pachysandra terminalis*) is one of the best in dense shade,

NATURALIZING WITH AZALEAS, RHODODENDRONS, WITH A BACKGROUND OF NATIVE TREES

under heavily foliaged trees, or on banks where grass won't grow. The foliage is lustrous, evergreen, and doesn't exceed eight inches in height. The small white flowers are inconspicuous in contrast to the leaves. It likes humus, but will do well in almost any soil.

PERIWINKLE (*Vinca minor*) is a trailing groundcover that thrives in all but the deepest shade. Its glossy evergreen leaves and blue or white flowers produced throughout spring and summer, make it an exceptionally attractive plant. It will do well in fairly poor soil, provided there is ample moisture.

ENGLISH IVY (*Hedera Helix*) has been described already under climbers, but it also makes an excellent evergreen ground cover for shaded locations and is particularly suited to formal borders. It is difficult sometimes to keep it confined.

CARPET BUGLE (*Ajuga reptans*) forms a neat carpet of long narrow leaves, with blue, white, or purple flowers on upright spikes during May. Semi-evergreen, it spreads quickly and is tolerant to most soils.

ALPINE EPIMEDIUM (*Epimedium alpinum*) is a fine plant for partial shade. The heart-heaped leaves, more or less evergreen, turn brown and yellow in the winter and the yellowish flowers in June add to its attractiveness. It grows about a foot high and does well in average soil.

VIOLETS (*Viola*) are the favorite of those who love scent and color combined. The long blooming English violet (V. odorata sempervirens) is hard to equal in a semi-shaded area. The stemless bird's foot violet (Viola pedata) is better for sandy soil, but not as easy to naturalize as the other.

(H)   BULBS AND ANNUALS

The uses of bulbs and annuals in the landscape picture can be as varied as the personalities of the gardeners employing them. To those fond of spectacular color effects, and who don't mind the chore of planting, digging and replanting, the garden can become a gallery of changing tapestries from spring to fall. For those less ambitious, bulbs and annuals can serve to fill in bare spots along borders, between shrubs and perennials or under deciduous trees. They can add accents of color beside driveways, in planter boxes, or along foundations.

Generally speaking, neither bulbs nor annuals should be planted in single, or even in double, rows. In small gardens they should be grown in clumps, in larger gardens in masses. Care should be taken to see that they bloom in color harmony with other shrubs, perennials or trees flowering at the same time, and that their soil requirements approximate those of established subjects.

(1) Bulbs Classified

Bulbs may be classified as hardy bulbs, like daffodils, crocus, and lilies, which can be left in the ground from year to year, or tender bulbs, like gladiolus and begonias, which must be lifted after flowering, and stored.

. The spring flowering bulbs, which include aconite, snowdrops, crocus, hyacinths, tulips, Dutch iris and early lilies, must be planted in autumn, the earlier the better. Summer flowering bulbs, like begonias and gladiolus, are planted in the spring, and the autumn flowering bulbs, like autumn crocus and colchicums, should be planted in midsummer.

All bulbs like a friable, well drained soil which contains a generous supply of organic material. While some bulbs, like daffodils, will flower satisfactorily in partial shade or filtered sunlight, for the most part bulbs like full sun. Begonias are the outstanding exception.

There has been so much hybridizing done with bulbs, particularly with daffodils, tulips, lilies and gladiolus, that there are now literally thousands of varieties, with new ones appearing every year. Those wishing to specialize, or keep up with the latest developments, should study texts or magazines devoted to their particular pet subject. To those who merely want general information on the most common bulbs and varieties used in the Pacific northwest area, the following chart may be of service.

NOTE: There are so many new varieties of roses, bulbs and perennials brought out annually that it is impossible for the average home gardener to keep up unless he wishes to specialize. In this case it would be wise to join a group interested mainly in the plant specialty. E.g. Gladiolus Society, Chrysanthemum Society, Rose Society, etc. For those just seeking general information, membership in a local Horticultural Society can be very helpful and enjoyable.

NAME	Planting Time	Depth & spacing	Flowering height	Flowering period	Some Varieties
Glory of the Snow (Chionodoxa)	Sept.-Oct.	2"	5"	Jan.-Feb.	Lucillae—lilac blue Rosea—rose
Snowdrop (Galanthus)	Sept.-Oct.	3"	4"	Jan.-Feb.	Elwesi—single white Nivalis—double white
Winter Aconite (Eranthis hyemalis)	Sept.-Oct.	3"	3"	Feb.-Mar.	Yellow
Crocus (Crocus vernus)	Sept.-Oct.	3"	3"	Feb.-Mar.	Golden Yellow—yellow Purpurea—purple Snowstorm—white
Hyacinths	Sept.-Oct.	6"	8"	Mar.-Apr.	L'Innocence—white Jan Bos—scarlet Bismark—sky blue
Grape Hyacinths (Muscari)	Sept.-Oct.	4"	6"	Mar.-Apr.	Alba—white Armeniacum—blue
Squills (Scilla campanulata)	Sept.-Oct.	4"	8"	Mar.-Apr.	Blue Coeurlea—blue Alba—white Rosea—**pink**
Daffodils	Sept.-Oct.	8"	15"	Mar.-Apr.	Golden Harvest—yellow Mary Copland—cream Troubadour—pink
Narcissi	Sept.-Oct.	8"	15"	April	Mount Hood—white Carlton—soft yellow Red Marley—yel. orange
Narcissi species and Paperwhites	Sept.-Oct.	8"	15"	April	Angel's Tears—white Trevithian—yellow
TULIPS Single and double early	Sept.-Oct.	6"	12"	April-May	Olympiad—single yellow Pink Beauty—single rose Pr. of Austria—orange
Darwin Tulips	Sept.-Oct.	6"	24"	May	Sunkist—yellow Pr. Elisabeth—pink Wm. Pitt—scarlet
Parrot Tulips	Sept.-Oct.	6"	18"	May	Texas Gold—yellow Fantasy—rose Parrot Wonder—red
Species Tulips (For rockeries)	Sept.-Oct.	6"	6-12"	Early April	Kaufmanniana Hybrids in pink, white and carmine Red Emperor—red
Anemone	Sept. to Feb.	3"	8"	May	St. Brigid double mixed
Ranunculus	Sept. to Feb.	3"	6"	May	Mixed colors
Begonias	Start in Feb. inside	½" deep 12" apart	8-12"	June to Oct.	Mixed colors, single, double, camellia type or ruffled
Dutch Iris	Sept.-Oct.	5"	10"	May	Yellow Queen—yellow Wedgewood—blue Imperator—dark blue
LILIES The Gold Band Lily (Lilium auratum)	Sept.-Oct.	6"	3-4 ft.	Aug.-Sept.	Auratum Platyphllum —white and gold
The Regal Lily (Lilium regale)	Sept.-Oct.	6"	3-5 ft.	June-July	Regale—white Royal Gold—hybrid yellow
Aurelian Trumpet Lily	Sept.-Oct.	6"	5-7 ft.	July	Golden Clarion—yellow Olympic Hybrids—cream, pink
The Tiger Lily (Lilium tigridum)	Sept.-Oct.	6"	3 ft.	June-July	Red with purple spots
The Croft Lily (Easter Lily)	Sept.-Oct.	6"	10"	June (Unless forced)	White
Gladiolus (M) Medium early (75-100 days) (E) Early (60-75 days)	Apr.-June	6"	3 ft.	July to Oct.	Fl. Nightingale (M) white Snowdrift (E)—cream Dr. Fleming (M)—rose Friendship (E)—pink Polynesia (E)—salmon Spotlight (M)—yellow Dieppe (M)—scarlet Jo Wagenaar (M) dark red King David (M)—purple
Autumn Crocus	July	2"	4"	Oct.-Nov.	C. Asturicus — violet C. Sativus — lilac C. Speciosus Albus—white
Colchicums (Colchicum autumnale)	July	4"	8"	Oct.-Nov.	White, lilac, violet
Montbretia	Sept. to Mar.	3"	24"	Aug.-Sept.	A. E. Amos—yellow Lord Lamberne—red

(3) Annuals Classified

Annuals can be very useful as a follow up in bulb plantings. They help hide the untidy bulb foliage while it is ripening, and provide continuous color. Seeds of many may be sown among the bulbs while they are flowering, or before, or young plants may be set out between them. They may be used in the same way to take over after the flowering of perennials.

Annuals may be divided into three groups, according to their temperature reaction. While there is no definite line of demarkation, and a certain amount of overlapping, they may be grouped fairly well as hardy, half hardy or tender. In the first group, for example, sweet peas or larkspur may be sown in late fall or very early spring and will winter without difficulty. The half hardy annuals like alyssum should not be sown until the chances of hard frosts are slim and the ground temperatures have reached 50 deg. F. The tender annuals like petunias must wait until all danger of frost has passed and ground temperatures approximate 60 deg. F.

Most annuals are adaptable to a wide range of soil and climatic conditions, but generally speaking they favor full sun, a pH around 6.0, and respond to a well drained soil with a reasonably generous supply of organic matter. Some will thrive even on poor soils, but a sprinkling of fertilizer is usually necessary for best results.

While seed may be sown outdoors when temperatures are right, and the plants subsequently thinned out, many gardeners prefer to start the plants indoors or in cold frames, or buy them already established for bedding out. By doing this, blooming can be speeded up, particularly with slow germinating plants like snapdragons and slow maturing plants like petunias. Also ground temperatures are more likely to be stable around the first of May than a month earlier, and the plants have a better chance for the steady growth so essential for top performance. While any seed catalogue will give you a list of annuals, with varietal and other information, the following chart, briefly classifying some of the most useful, may be of assistance when making a choice.

ANNUAL INFORMATION CHART (Forty Common Annuals)

HARDY ANNUALS

NAME	Outdoor Planting Time (Indoors 4 wks earlier)	Spacing	Flower Height	Approx. Flowering Time	Some Varieties
Calliopsis	Mar. 15	6″	24″	Late June	Golden Crown—yellow
Calendula	″	6″	8″	″	Campfire—orange
Carnation	″	10″	18″	July	Chabaud's Mixed
Cornflower	″	6″	30″	″	Cyanus double mixed
Dianthus (pinks)	″	10″	12″	″	Chinese double mixed
Gaillardia	″	8″	24″	″	Picta Lorenziana
Larkspur	″	6″	48″	″	Cockade mixed
Mathiola (stocks)	″	8″	18″	″	Mathiola Bicornis
Morning Glory	″	10″	10′ vine	″	Heavenly Blue
Pansies	″	6″	8″	July-Aug.	Swiss Giants mixed
Shirley Poppy	″	6″	18″	″	Shirley mixed
Stocks (10 weeks)	″	8″	12″	June	Double dwarf mixed
Sweet Peas	Mar. 1st	6″	8′ vine	July	Cuthbertson mixed
Viola	″	6″	6″	″	Bambini mixed

HALF HARDY ANNUALS

NAME	Indoor Planting Time	Spacing	Flower Height	Approx. Flowering Time	Some Varieties
Antirrhinum (Snaps)	Feb. 15	8″	Dwf 6″, tall 3′	July-Aug.	{ F1. Hybrids mixed / Maiestic mixed
Ageratum	″	6″	6″	June-July	Blue Cap—blue
Alyssum	″	8″	4-6″	″	{ Pink Heather—pink / Carpet of Snow—white
Asters	″	10″	24″	Aug.-Sept.	Crego mixed
Balsam	″	8″	18″	July	Camellia flower mixed
Candytuft	″	10″	12″	June	Umbellata mixed
Celosia	″	10″	36″	July	Golden Fleece—yellow
Chrysanthemum	″	10″	30″	July-Aug.	Rainbow mixture
Cosmos	″	10″	48″	″	Sensation mixture
Daisy	″	10″	36″	″	Super Enorma mixed
Escholtzia	″	8″	12″	″	Southern Jewels mixed
Four O'clock	″	10″	36″	″	Mixed
Godetia	″	8″	12″	June-July	Duke of York—rose
Gypsophila	″	8″	24″	″	Elegans Carminea—red
Lobelia	Feb. 1	8″	6″	″	{ Crystal Palace—blue / Sapphire Trailing—blue
Mignonette	Outdoors April 1	6″	12″	July-Aug.	Sweet Scented
Phlox Drummondi	Feb. 15	8″	18″	June-July	Grandiflora mixed
Portulaca	″	6″	6″	″	Double mixed
Rudbeckia	″	10″	36″	″	Gold Flame—yellow
Scabiosa	″	10″	30″	July-Aug.	Imperial Giants mixed
Viscaria	″	6″	12″	″	Mixed

TENDER ANNUALS

NAME	Indoor Planting Time (Outdoors Apr. 15)	Spacing	Flower Height	Approx. Flowering Time	Some Varieties
Helianthus	April 1	10″	6-8′	July-Aug.	Russian Giants
Marigold	″	8″	Dwf. 8″, tall 3′	″	{ Dwarf Double French / Tall African
Nasturtium	Outdoors April 15	10″	24″	″	Gleam Hybrids
Nemesia	April 1	8″	12″	″	Carnival mixed
Nicotiana	″	8″	30″	″	Sensation mixed
Petunias	Mar. 15-Apr. 1	10″	18″	″	F1. Hybrids
Salpiglossis	April 1	8″	30″	″	Emperor Hybrids
Salvia	Mar. 15-Apr. 1	10″	12″	Aug.-Oct.	Blaze of Fire
Zinnia	″	10″	Dwf. 18″, tall 3′	″	{ Dahlia Fl. mixed / Lilliput mixed

PACIFIC NORTHWEST GARDENING CALENDAR

JANUARY

	PLANT	PRUNE	SPRAY	FERTILIZE	Miscellaneous
ANNUALS, PERENNIALS and BULBS	Plant peonies, delphiniums, bleeding hearts, etc. if weather permits.	Cut back dead foliage of mums, daisies, fuchsia, montbretia, etc. Shear flags to six inches.		Top dress rock plants with compost.	Order seeds. Check stored bulbs and tubers Prepare soil for flats.
TREES and SHRUBS	Plant fruit trees, ornamentals deciduous shrubs and roses, if ground is frost free and not soggy.	Prune fruit trees, fl. trees, and shrubs like buddleia and hydrangea, if not done in fall.	Spray fruit trees, roses and ornamentals with fungicide. Spray peaches for leaf curl as early as possible.	Lime orchard if necessary. Apply boron if need is indicated. Top dress evergreens with peat moss or compost.	Turn compost heap. Clean up prunings. Check trees for disease.
SMALL FRUITS and VEGETABLES	Plant currants, raspberries, etc. Start lettuce, cabbage and caul. in cold frame toward end of month.	Prune grapes. Cut out old raspberry and boysen canes, and prune currants if not done before.	Spray currants and gooseberries with fungicide.	Lime garden if necessary.	Plan spring planting. Check stored vegetables. Dig garden if soil permits. Clean tools. Force rhubarb.
LAWNS					Sharpen mower Keep lawn free of leaves.

FEBRUARY

	PLANT	PRUNE	SPRAY	FERTILIZE	Miscellaneous
ANNUALS, PERENNIALS and BULBS	Start tuberous begonias indoors. Start hardy annuals (see table). Plant daylilies. Sow sweetpeas outside.		Water seed flats with fungicide to prevent damping off.	Give perennials a dressing of complete fertilizer	Pot up geraniums. Take carnation cuttings.
TREES and SHRUBS	Plant fruit trees, flowering trees, shrubs, roses, conifers.	Finish pruning fruit trees and ornamentals. Prune blueberries. Cut back rasps to five feet if not done before.	Spray trees and roses if not done in January.	Punch holes around fruit and ornamental trees and fertilize. One pound per inch diam. of trunk.	Treat pruning wounds with asphalt emulsion.
SMALL FRUITS and VEGETABLES	Plant bush and cane fruits. Rhubarb, shallots, broad beans, peas, leeks, radish, parsley. (See table.)	Prune blueberries and currants if not done previously.	Spray for slugs. Set out bait at 10-day intervals.	Dress rows of strawberries, raspberries and currants with complete fertilizer.	Finish digging. Prick off seedlings. Sprout early potatoes in sun.
LAWNS				Alum. sulphate, 1 lb. per 100 sq. ft. will control moss.	Aerate lawn with fork or aerator.

MARCH

	PLANT	PRUNE	SPRAY	FERTILIZE	MISCELLANEOUS
ANNUALS, PERENNIALS and BULBS	Prick off annuals started Feb. Sow tender annuals (Table) Plant out hardy annuals at end of month.		Stir 5% granular diazinon into soil before planting. Spray or dust for slugs.	Scatter complete 6-8-6 fertilizer in soil where annuals will be planted.	Harden off flats of hardy annuals. Prepare ground
TREES and SHRUBS	Complete tree and rose plantings. Plant deciduous and evergreen shrubs.	Finish tree pruning. Prune roses after 15th Trim old hedges.	Last chance to spray trees and roses with dormant-strength fungicide.	Dress roses with nitrogen fertilizer. Dress evergreens with peat, compost and organics.	Layer rhododendrons. Graft fruit trees. Transplant rooted cuttings.
SMALL FRUITS and VEG.	Sow tomatoes under glass. Plant strawberries, onions, spinach, parsnips, chard, early potatoes. Set out lettuce & cabbage plants.		Stir 5% granular diazinon in soil before planting annuals.	Rake in a complete fertilizer before planting veg. seeds or plants. Feed rhubarb with ammonium sulphate or liquid fish.	Tie up logan and boysenberry canes.
LAWNS	Sow grass seed after 15th.		Repeat above soil treatment before planting new lawn.	Apply complete 8-6-4 fertilizer, or ureaform.	Keep new lawn moist.

APRIL

	PLANT	PRUNE	SPRAY	FERTILIZE	MISCELLANEOUS
ANNUALS, PERENNIALS and BULBS	Set out hardy annuals, primulas, dahlias and glads. Start cucumbers under glass. Also marigolds and zinnias.		Spray early for insect pests.	Feed all spring flowering bulbs and perennials with 6-8-6 commercial fert. or liquid fish.	Cultivate lightly and keep plants watered.
TREES and SHRUBS	Plant conifers, camellias, rhododendrons, etc.	Shear winter heathers and broom lightly after flowering	Spray apple and pear trees in pink bud stage. Spray holly, azaleas and roses and conifers with malathion.	Mulch evergreens.	Water newly planted nursery stock.
SMALL FRUITS and VEG.	Sow main crop peas, lettuce, carrots, beets, runner beans.	Pinch out tops of broad beans.	Spray gooseberries and currants with methoxychlor after flowering. Dust veg. with rotenone.	Side dress slow growing leaf veg. with nitroprills.	Tie-up rasp. canes if not done. Prepare cucumber bed.
LAWNS	Don't delay lawn planting.		Spray for weeds on warm day. 70 deg. F.	If grass pale in color dress with high nitrogen fertilizer.	Water during morning hours. Wash in fertilizer.

MAY

	PLANT	PRUNE	SPRAY	FERTILIZE	MISCELLANEOUS
ANNUALS PERENNIALS and BULBS	Set out begonias and geraniums after 15th, and plant salvia, zinnias, etc. Plant succession of gladiolus.	Shear lightly perennials like aubretia, alyssum after flowering. Break off tulip heads.	Keep young plants sprayed or dusted with insecticide.		Divide and replant perennials that have bloomed. Pull up wall flowers and forget-me-nots.
TREES and SHRUBS	Plant evergreens without delay.	Thumb nail prune soft new growths of young trees and shrubs to shape them. Cut flowering wood off forsythia, fl. currant, etc.	Use multispray on fruit trees to catch codling moth. Spray roses, azaleas and rhododendrons	Water camellias, rhodos and azaleas with fish fertilizer. Mulch with peat moss.	Spray foliage of newly planted evergreens with water on sunny, windy days.
SMALL FRUITS and VEG.	Sow a succession of carrots, beets. Plant tomatoes after 15th, and cucumbers, squash, at end of month. Sow bush beans.	Cut off strawberry runners.	Spray carrots with diazinon as soon as they show forked leaves.		Net strawberries, cultivate veg. plants. Stake tall peas. Thin beets and carrots.
LAWNS	Last chance for lawn planting before hot weather.		Control broadleaf weeds with 2-4-D on warm day.		Cut grass weekly. Set mower 1" high.

JUNE

	PLANT	PRUNE	SPRAY	FERTILIZE	MISCELLANEOUS
ANNUALS, PERENNIALS and BULBS	Plant geraniums and begonias if not done in May.	Cut off dead foliage on spring flowering bulbs.	Spread earwig bait and spray ground with diazinon for ants, etc.	Give liquid fish fertilizer to sweet peas and begonias.	Repot mums. Divide iris. Stake tall perennials. Lift early bulbs.
TREES and SHRUBS	Plant container grown evergreens without delay.	Thin fruit on trees and grapes. Cut seed pods off lilacs, rhodos and azaleas.	Dust or spray roses with all-purpose material. Watch fruit trees for aphids. Spray cherries for fly.	If growth is poor or leaves yellow-ish, water with liquid fish fertilizer.	Water heavily, but not too often.
SMALL FRUITS and VEG.	Sow turnip and N.Z. spinach.	Prune side growths out of staked tomatoes.	Spray boysens and logans with malathion, and dust vegetables with rotenone.		Hill potatoes. Turn compost pile. Thin carrots.
LAWNS			Spray with diazinon to control insects.	Feed lawns with liquid fish or a urea compound if a poor color.	Water deeply but not too often.

JULY

	PLANT	PRUNE	SPRAY	FERTILIZE	MISCELLANEOUS
ANNUALS, PERENNIALS and BULBS	Sow seed of biennials like wallflowers, forget-me-nots, and pansies. Plant fall crocus and colchicums.	Shear lavender lightly. Also heathers after flowering.	Spray gladiolus for thrips.	Feed chrysanthemums.	Take softwood cuttings. Dig tulips. Divide spring perennials. Layer carnations.
TREES and SHRUBS		Cut out flowering wood of rambler roses. Prune back wisteria. Trim hedges. Thin fruit on trees if not done.	Spray roses with pesticide. Spray fruit trees for codling moth and aphids. Spray conifers, hollies, with malathion.		Bud roses. Water garden thoroughly. Cultivate lightly afterwards.
SMALL FRUITS and VEG.	Set out plants of celery, fall cabbage and broccoli.	Cut out all fruited canes on rasps, logans, etc. Summer prune espalier trees.	Dust vegetables with rotenone and potatoes with copper spray for blight.		Dig shallots. Pull soil away from globe onions.
LAWNS		Treat for weeds if necessary.			Make sure mower is sharp. Set at 1½".

AUGUST

	PLANT	PRUNE	SPRAY	FERTILIZE	MISCELLANEOUS
ANNUALS, PERENNIALS and VEG.	Transplant biennials or perennials seeded earlier. Plant spring bulbs.	Cut old flower heads off dahlias glads and roses.		Feed glads, zinnias and asters with liquid fish. Use bone meal with bulb plantings.	Transplant rooted carnation layers. Dig spring bulbs.
TREES and SHRUBS		Finish pruning old wood from cane fruits. Thin currant wood. Summer prune espalier trees.	Keep spraying roses. Spray fruit trees for codling moth and scab.	Keep trees and shrubs mulched, especially evergreens.	Make sure watering is thorough.
SMALL FRUITS and VEG.	Sow lettuce or spinach for fall use. Plant leeks.	Top tomato plants at 4th truss.	Dust vegetables with rotenone.	Give strawberries a feed of ammon. phosphate. Give celery, melons, liquid fish.	Harvest early potatoes. Bend onions for ripening.
LAWNS				Treat grass with liquid nitrogen, ureaform, or 8-6-4 mix.	Make sure water is penetrating.

SEPTEMBER

	PLANT	PRUNE	SPRAY	FERTILIZE	MISCELLANEOUS
ANNUALS PERENNIALS and BULBS	Plant wallflowers, violas, pansies, primulas, spring flowering bulbs, peonies, tritoma, etc.		Stir 5% granular diazinon in soil before planting bulbs.	Feed mums for last time before bloom.	Divide summer perennials. Cultivate for fall weeds.
TREES and SHRUBS	Plant container grown evergreens, heathers, etc.	Trim hedges.	Spray cherries, pears and hawthornes for black slugs. Spray roses for mildew.	Mulch evergreens.	Take cuttings of evergreens. Harvest fruit. Keep plants watered till rains come.
SMALL FRUITS and VEG.	Sow onion seed for spring. Peg boysen or black-berry tips in ground to start new plants.			Manure space for next years veg. garden. Feed everbearing strawberries.	Harvest carrots, beets and onions. Earth up leeks. Turn compost. Dig vacant spaces.
LAWNS	Plant new lawns or renovate old ones.		Give final spray for weeds if necessary.	Aerify lawn if compacted and fertilize with organic nitrogen.	Keep watering, especially newly seeded areas.

OCTOBER

	PLANT	PRUNE	SPRAY	FERTILIZE	MISCELLANEOUS
ANNUALS, PERENNIALS and BULBS	Plant spring flowering bulbs and perennials. Pot bulbs for forcing.	Take geranium cuttings.	Stir 5% granular diazinon in soil before planting bulbs.	Feed mums in pots with liquid fertilizer.	Dig dahlias, glads. Divide peonies. Clean up borders. Lift begonias. Weed rockery.
TREES and SHRUBS	Plant evergreens and deciduous trees and shrubs toward end of month.	Cut out old flowering wood from shrubs.	Spray fruit trees with copper spray for anthracnose.	Mulch trees and shrubs with manure or compost if available.	Water newly planted shrubs and trees well. Harvest late pears and apples.
SMALL FRUITS and VEG.	Plant bush fruits, rhubarb, etc.		Stir 5% granular diazinon in soil before planting bush fruits.	Mulch bush fruits with manure or compost, if available.	Gather grapes. Dig vacant spaces. Dig late potatoes.
LAWNS	Plant grass seed until 10th of month.		Above treatment in new lawn planting.		Keep lawn free of leaves. Keep cutting it as long as it grows.

NOVEMBER AND DECEMBER

These are mainly planting and clean-up months. There is little to do in the way of pruning, spraying or fertilizing. November is probably the best month of the year for planting fruit trees and other deciduous material. It is not too late to plant spring flowering bulbs although they are better planted earlier. If you want to take a chance on a sowing of early peas and broad beans for spring, now is the time. It is also the time for planting fall rye as a green crop to be turned under in spring.

As you get into December it would be wise to spray your peach trees for leaf curl, cut back the tops of tall varieties of roses, and tie up loosely branched conifers for possible snow damage. Keep the leaves raked up so they won't smother your lawn, and keep them off the rockery, too.

December is a good month to complete your records, check stored bulbs and vegetables, clean and oil tools, etc., and leave everything ship-shape for a good start the following year.

Summary

The previously outlined calendar is by no means complete. It merely suggests some of the most important things to look for each month. Every gardener has his own special interests and should, therefore, prepare his own special calendar. A closely kept diary is invaluable for the preparation of such a calendar, and we suggest that the reader maintain one for at least one full year, to guide his future gardening activities.

PLANTS FOR SPECIAL PROBLEMS

(A) For Sunny Dry Areas

Evergreen Trees—
Pines (*Mugho, White Pine, Scotch Pine*)
Arizona Cypress (*Cupressus Arizonica*)
Madrona (*Arbutus Menziesii*)

Deciduous Trees—
Red Oak (*Quercus coccinea*)
Chesnut (*Castanea*)
Flowering Peach (*Prunus mume*)
Silver Maple (*Acer negundo variegatum*)
Catalpa
Hawthorne (*Cratageus*)
Mountain Ash (*Sorbus aucuparia*)
Siberian Elm (*Ulmus pumila*)
Larch (*Larix*)
Lime (*Tilia*)

Evergreen Shrubs—
Evergreen Barberry (*Berberis Wilsonae, Darwini, Julianae*)
Heaths (*Calluna vulgaris*)
Ceanothus
Cotoneasters (*Franchetti, microphylla, dammeri*)
Broom (*Cytisus*)
Euonymus Radicans
Mexican Orange (*Choisya ternata*)
Holly Mahonia (*Mahonia aquifolium*)

Spanish Broom (*Spartium junceum*)
St. John's Wort (*Hypericum*)
Veronica (*Buxifolia, traversi, pageana*)

Deciduous Shrubs—
Japanese Barberry (*Berberis thunbergi*)
Smoke Tree (*Rhus cotinus*)
Lavender (*Lavandula*)
Tamarix (*Tamarisk*)

Perennials—
Sun Rose (*Helianthemum*)
Anemone Japonica
Catmint (*Nepeta mussini*)
Yucca

(B) Moist Areas, Full Sun

Evergreen Trees—
Spruce (*Picea*)
Fir (*Abies*)
Cedar (*Cedrus*)
Japanese Cedar (*Cryptomeria*)
Thuya (*Arborvitae*)

Deciduous Trees—
Magnolia
Poplars (*Populus*)
Willows (*Salix*)
Alder (*Alnus*)
Beech (*Fagus*)

Laburnum
Flowering Crabapples (*Malus*)
Flowering Plums (*Prunus*)
Flowering Cherries (*Prunus*)

Evergreen Shrubs—
Abelia
Arbutus Unedo
Azalea Kurume
Cotoneaster Henryana
Erica Carnea
Pernettya
Pyracantha
Escallonia

Deciduous Shrubs—
Hibiscus (*Althea*)
Butterfly Bush (*Buddleia*)
Quince (*Chaenomeles*)
Potentilla
Golden Bells (*Forsythia*)
Beauty Bush (*Kolkwitzia*)
Lilac (*Syringa*)
Mock Orange (*Philadelphus*)
Snowball (*Viburnum opulus sterile*)
Spirea Bumalda varieties

Perennials—
Astilbe
Aster
Gentian
Iris
Phlox
Lily (*Hemerocallis*)
Bluebells (*Campanula carpatica*)
Pinks (*Dianthus*)
Candytuft (*Iberis sempervirens*)
Pyrethrum
Rudbeckia
Scabiosa
Red Hot Poker or Torchlily (*Tritoma*)

(C) Moist Areas, Partial Shade

Evergreen Trees—
Western Hemlock (*Tsuga heterophylla*)
Cypress (*Chamaecyparis*)
Holly (*Ilex*)

Deciduous Trees—
Native Dogwood (*Cornus nutallii*)
Judas Tree (*Cercis*)
Poplar (*Populus*)
Norway Maple (*Acer planatoides*)
Japanese Maple (*Acer palmatum*)

Evergreen Shrubs—
Pieris Japonica (*Andromeda*)

Holly Mahonia (*Mahonia aquifolium*)
Evergreen Barberry (*Berberis Darwini*)
Boxwood (*Buxus*)
Camellia Japonica
Daphne Odora
Rhododendron Hybrids
Portugal Laurel (*Prunus laurocerasus*)
Skimmia
Periwinkle (*Vinca minor*)
Mexican Orange (*Choisya ternata*)
St. John's Wort (*Hypericum*)
Spurge (*Pachysandra terminalis*)
Junipers (*Tamarix, sabina, pfitzeriana, etc.*)
Euonymus Radicans
Ivy (*Hedera*)

Deciduous Shrubs—
Azalea Mollis
Clematis Species
Cotoneaster Horizontalis
Daphne Mezereum
Enkianthus
Hydrangea
Kerria Japonica
Flowering Currant (*Ribes alpinum*)
Elder (*Sambucus*)
Flowering Quince (*Chaenomeles*)
Dogwood (*Cornus Alba*)
Japanese Honeysuckle
    (*Lonicera japonica*)

Perennials—
Narcissus
Day Lily (*Hemerocallis*)
Columbine (*Aquilegia*)
Foxglove (*Digitalis*)
Periwinkle (*Vinca minor*)
Shasta Daisy (*Chrysanthemum maximum*)
Violet (*Viola*)

(D) Moist Areas, Deep Shade

Evergreen Shrubs—
Variegated Laurel (*Aucuba japonica*)
Holly (*Ilex latifolia*)
Skimmia Japonica
Rhododendron Hybrids
Camellia Japonica
English Yew (*Taxus baccata*)
Boxwood (*Buxus*)
Irish Juniper (*Communis hibernica*)

Deciduous Shrubs—
Daphne Mezereum

Hydrangea Hortensis
Red Twigged Dogwood (*Cornus alba sibirica*)

Perennials—
Lily of the Valley
Violet (*Viola*)
Bleeding Heart (*Dicentra*)
Christmas Rose (*Helleborus niger*)

(E) For Seaside Planting

Evergreen Trees—
Arbutus Menziesi
Fir (*Abies*)
Pine (*Pinus mugho, nigra, etc.*)
English Holly (*Ilex aquifolium*)

Evergreen Shrubs—
Evergreen Barberry (*Berberis Wilsonae*)
Mexican Orange (*Choisya ternata*)
Broom (*Cytisus*)
Euonymus Radicans
Cotoneaster Franchetti
Juniperus Chinensis
Veronica
Escallonia
Olearia Haastii

Deciduous Trees—
Red Oak (*Quercus rubra*)
Red Maple (*Acer rubra*)
Sweet Gum (*Liquidambar*)
Willow (*Salix*)
Poplar (*Populus*)
Mountain Ash (*Sorbus aucuparia*)
Laburnum
Hawthorne (*Cratageus*)

Deciduous Shrubs—
Buddleia Davidi
Ceanothus
Euonymus Europea
Cotoneaster Horizontalis
Fuchsia Ricartoni
Lilac (*Syringa*)
Tamarix (*Tamarisk*)
Hydrangea
Roses (*Rosa*)

Perennials—
Most varieties of perennials.

(F) Lime Lovers (pH 6.5-7.5)

Evergreen Trees—
Yew (*Taxus*)

Deciduous Trees—
Flowering Plums and Cherries (*Prunus*)

Mountain Ash (*Sorbus aucuparia*)
Beech (*Fagus*)
Laburnum
Filbert (*Corylus*)
Maple (*Acer*), except Japanese varieties
Hawthorne (*Cratageus*)
Sumac (*Rhus*)

Evergreen Shrubs—
Evergreen Barberry (*Berberis Darwini, etc.*)
Boxwood (*Buxus*)
Irish Juniper (*Communis hibernica*)
Savin Juniper (*J. Sabina and tamariscifolia*)
Yew (*Taxus repandens and fastigiata*)
Firethorn (*Pyracantha*)

Deciduous Shrubs—
Clematis
Cotoneaster Horizontalis
Euonymus Europeus
Privet (*Ligustrum vulgare*)
Mock Orange (*Philadelphus*)
Smoke Tree (*Rhus cotinus*)
Lilac (*Syringa*)
Snowball (*Viburnum opulus sterile*)
Althea (*Hibiscus*)
Flowering Currant (*Ribes alpinum*)
Spirea (*Thunbergi, Van Houttei, etc.*)

Perennials—
Pinks (*Dianthus*)
Aster (*Michaelmas daisy*)
Carnation
Perennial Sunflower (*Helianthus*)
Lewisia
Catmint (*Nepeta*)
Peony
Perennial Salvia
Sedums
Perennial Poppy (*Papaver*)

(G) Acid Lovers (pH 4.5-6.0)

Evergreen Trees—
Holly (*Ilex*)
Madrone (*Arbutus menziesii*)
Fir (*Abies*)
Pine (*Pinus*)
Spruce (*Picea*)
Hemlock (*Tsuga*)

Deciduous Trees—
Japanese Maples (*Acer palmatum*)
Birch (*Betula*)
Magnolia Soulangeana

Oak (*Quercus*)
Willow (*Salix*)
Flowering Crabapples (*Malus*)

Evergreen Shrubs—
Andromeda (*Pieris japonica*)
Japanese Azaleas (*Azalea kurume*)
Camellia Japonica
Broom (*Cytisus*)
Heathers (*Erica and calluna*)
Pernettya
Rhododendrons
Juniperus Horizontalis
Daphne Odora
Mountain Laurel (*Kalmia latifolia*)

Deciduous Shrubs—
Fuchsia Riccartonii
Witch Hazel (*Hamamelis*)
Azalea Mollis

Enkianthus
Hydrangea
Roses
Blueberry (*Vaccinium corymbosum*)
Cranberry (*Vaccinium macrocarpon*)

Perennials—
Alyssum
Calla Lilies
Delphinium
Crocus
Phlox
Ivy (*Hedera*)
Ferns
Strawberry

Most plants not mentioned above will tolerate a range from slightly acid (pH 6.0) to neutral (pH 7.0).

PLANTS WITH DISTINCTIVE FOLIAGE

(A) GREY and GREY-GREEN FOLIAGE
Cotoneaster Franchetti
Fletcher Cypress (*C. lawsoniana fletcheri*)
Moss Cypress (*C. pisifera plumosa squarrosa*)
Broom (*Cytisus*)
Andorra Juniper (*J. horizontalis plumosa*)
Irish Juniper (*J. communis hibernica*)
Hetz Juniper (*J. sinensis glauca Hetzi*)
Himalayan Weeping Cedar (*Cedrus Deodara*)
Tamarix
Veronica Pageana
Lavender (*Lavandula*)
Pinks (*Dianthus*)
Arabis
Artemesia

(B) BLUE and BLUE-GREEN FOLIAGE
Atlas Cedar (*Cedrus Atlantica glauca*)
Blue Columnar Cypress (*C. lawsoniana columnaris glauca*)
Triumph of Boskoop Cypress (*C. lawsoniana Triumph of Boskoop*)
Waukegan Juniper (*J. horizontalis Douglasi*)
Blue Columnar Juniper (*J. chinensis columnaris glauca*)
Spiny Greek Juniper (*J. chinensis stricta*)
Himalayan Blue Juniper (*J. squamata meyeri*)
Dwarf Scotch Pine (*Pinus sylvestris nana*)
Blue Spruce (*Picea pungens glauca Kosteri or Moorheimi*)

(C) GOLDEN FOLIAGE
Golden Cypress (*C. lawsoniana Stewarti or Lanei*)
Golden Plume Cypress (*C. pisifera plumosa aurea*)
Golden Thread Cypress (*C. pisifera filifera aurea*)
Dwarf Golden Cypress (*C. lawsoniana minima aurea*)
Golden Biota (*Thuya biota orientalis aurea*)

Golden Spreading Juniper (*J. communis depressa aurea*)
Golden Plume Juniper (*J. sinensis plumosa aurea*)
Golden Pfitzer Juniper (*J. sinensis pfitzeriana aurea*)
Golden Irish Yew (*Taxus fastigiata aureo-marginata*)
Golden Dwarf Arborvitae (*Thuya occidentalis Rheingold*)
Golden Leafed Elder (*Sambucus Canadensis aurea*)
Golden Catalpa (*Catalpa bignoniodes aurea*)
Golden Heather (*Calluna vulgaris serlei aurea*)
Golden Leafed Mock Orange (*Philadelphus coronarius aureus*)
Golden Leafed Poplar (*Populus Canadensis aurea*)

(D) RED and PURPLE FOLIAGE
Bloodleaf Japanese Maple (*Acer palmatum atropurpurea*)
Crimson King Maple (*Acer schwedleri nigra*)
Purple Leafed Filbert (*Corylus avellana atropurpurea*)
Purple Leafed Flowering Plum (*Prunus pissardi nigra*)
Copper Beech (*Fagus sylvatica atropurpurea*)
Scarlet Oak (*Quercus coccinea splendens*)
Redleaf Barberry (*Berberis thunbergi atropurpurea*)
Purple Leafed Smoke Tree (*Rhus cotinus atropurpurea*)
Purple Leafed Weigela (*Weigela rosea purpurea*)
Purple Leafed Dahlia

(E) VARIEGATED FOLIAGE
Variegated Laurel (*Aucuba japonica variegata*)
Euonymus Fortunei Silver Gem or Variegata
Variegated Holly (*Ilex aquifolium variegata*)
Golden-variegated Privet (*Ligustrum ovalifolium aureo marginatum*)
Pieris Japonica Variegata
Silver Leafed Variegated Maple (*Acer negundo arg. variegatum*)
Variegated Weigela (*Weigela rosea nana variegata*)
Variegated Boxwood (*Buxus sempervirens variegata*)
Variegated Plume Cypress (*Pisifera plumosa nana aureo-variegata*)
Variegated Dogwood (*Cornus Nuttalii Eddei*)
Variegated Juniper (*J. sinensis albo-variegata*)
Golden-variegated Cedar (*Thuya lobbi semperaurea*)
Variegated Ivy (*Hedera canariensis variegata*)
Silver-variegated Geranium

(F) OUTSTANDING AUTUMN FOLIAGE
Maples, particularly the Canadian Red Maple (*Acer pseudoplatanus rubrum*)
Amelanchier
Azalea Mollis (*Some varieties*)
Japanese Barberry (*Berberis thunbergi*)
Enkianthus
Euonymus Alatus
Ginkgo Biloba
Japanese Flowering Cherries (*Prunus kwanzan*)
Sumac (*Rhus*)
Pin Oak (*Quercus palustris*)
Scarlet Oak (*Quercus rubra*)
Sweet Gum (*Liquidambar*)
Witch Hazel (*Hamamelis*)
Snowball (*Viburnum opulus sterile*)
Bridal Wreath Spirea (*Spirea prunifolia flore plena*)

A SELECTED LIST OF PLANTS FOR SUCCESSION OF BLOOM

JANUARY-FEBRUARY
BULBS—Snowdrops, crocus, aconite.
PERENNIALS—Christmas Rose (*Helleborus niger*).
SHRUBS—Witch Hazel (*Hamamelis mollis*)
    Winter Flowering Jasmine (*Jasminum nudiflorum*)
    Winter Flowering Heathers (*Erica carnea* "Darleyensis," "King George,"
        "Springwood White")
    Viburnum Fragrans
    Daphne Mezereum
    Camellia Japonica (In warmer areas)
    Rhododendron Hybrids (Some varieties, like "Christmas Cheer")

MARCH
BULBS—Daffodils, narcissus, hyacinths (in warmer areas)
PERENNIALS—Aubretia, primulas (some varieties), saxifrage.
SHRUBS—Camellia Japonica
    Lily-of-the-Valley Shrub (*Pieris Japonica*)
    Goldenbells (*Forsythia*)
    Garland Spirea (*Spirea Arguta*)
    Lauristinus (*Viburnum Tinus*)
    Star Magnolia (*Magnolia stellata*)
    Spring Flowering Heathers (*Erica carnea* "Springwood Pink," "Vivelli,"
        "Ruby Glow")
TREES—Japanese Flowering Plums (*Prunus pissardi, blireiana, moseri*)
    Japanese Flowering Peach (*Prunus mume*)

APRIL
BULBS—Daffodils, narcissi, muscari, hyacinths, scilla, tulip species, aenome.
PERENNIALS—Aubretia, allyssum saxtile, primulas, saxifrage.
SHRUBS—Flowering Quince (*Chaenomeles lagenaria*)
    Flowering Currant (*Ribes alpinum*)
    Pearl Bush (*Exochorda racemosa*)
    Spindle Tree (*Euonymus alatus*)
    Viburnum Carlesi and Burkwoodi
    Broom (*Cytisus praecox, kewensis*)
    Bridal Wreath Spiraea (*Spiraea pruniflora flora plena*)
    Daphne Burkwoodi and cneorum
    Japanese Azaleas (*Kurume*)
    Rhododendron Hybrids (*Early varieties*)
    Flowering Almond (*Prunus triloba*)
TREES—Flowering Almond (*Prunus Pollardi*)
    Flowering Crabapples (Early varieties like floribunda and profusion)

MAY
BULBS—Tulips, ranunculus, aenome, Dutch iris.
PERENNIALS—Peony, gentian aucaulis, bleeding heart (*dicentra*), candytuft,
    phlox amoena, polyanthus, helianthemum.
SHRUBS—Spiraea Van Houtte
    Azalea Mollis
    Rhododendron Hybrids
    Lilac (*Syringa vulgaris*)
    Beauty Bush (*Kolkwitzia amabilis*)
    Weigela
    Mock Orange (*Philadelphus*)
    Viburnum opulus and tomentosum
    Cotoneaster horizontalis, microphylla, dammeri, etc.

Broom (Cytisus scoparius hybrids like Red Wings, Burkwoodi, etc.)
Evergreen Barberry (*Berberis darwini, julianae, etc.*)
Mountain Laurel (*Kalmia latifolia*)
TREES—Flowering Crabapples (Later varieties like Eleyi)
Hawthorne (*Cratageus*)
Laburnum
Japanese Flowering Cherries (*Prunus kwanzan, shidare sakura, etc.*)
Magnolia (*Soulangeana*)
Dogwood (*Cornus nutallii*)
Horse Chesnut (*Aesculus*)

JUNE
BULBS—Lilies (Regale, croft, tiger lily).
PERENNIALS—Pinks (*dianthus*), columbine (*aquiligia*), astilbe, honeysuckle, alpine aster (*alpinus*), bluebells (*campanula*), Shasta daisies, delphinium, German iris, salvia (sage), peonies.
SHRUBS—Hybrid Tea roses, climbing roses, polyanthus roses.
Hydrangea arborescens
Deutzia gracilis (white)
Lavender (*lavandula*)
Potentilla fruticosa
Heather (*Erica cineria coccinea*)
St. John's Wort (*Hypericum*)
Pernettya
Smoke Tree (*Rhus cotinus*)
TREES—Tulip Tree (*Liriodendron*)

JULY
BULBS—Gladiolus, begonia, Aurelian trumpet lily, the tiger lily, tritoma.
PERENNIALS—Geum, Aster (Michaelmas Daisy), phlox paniculata, clematis hybrids, campanula lactiflora, perennial poppy (papaver), coneflower, globe flower, (trollius), veronica speedwell, fuchsia, yucca.
SHRUBS—Spirea Froebelli and Anthony Waterer
Abelia
Butterfly Bush (*Buddleia*)
Fuchsia Riccartonii
Hydrangea Hortensis
Rose of Sharon (*Hibiscus syriacus*)
Spanish Broom (*Spartium junceum*)
Escallonia
Ceanothus
Heathers (*Calluna vulgaris* "C. W. Nix," Alporti)
Tamarisk

AUGUST
BULBS—Gladiolus, begonia, montbretia, dahlia (tuberous)
PERENNIALS—Aster (Michaelmas daisy), geum, sunflower (*helianthus*), torchlily (*tritoma*), black-eyed susan (*rudbeckia*), goldenrod.
SHRUBS—Butterfly Bush (*Buddleia*)
Heather (*Erica vagans* "Mrs. Maxwell," "Lyonesse')
(*Calluna vulgaris* "Alba Plena," "J. H. Hamilton," "Tib")
Rose of Sharon (*Hibiscus syriacus*)
Hydrangea *paniculata grandiflora*
Tamarisk

SEPTEMBER
BULBS—Gladiolus, begonia, montbretia, dahlia (tuberous)
PERENNIALS—Aster (Michaelmas daisy), chrysanthemum, torchlily (*tritoma*).

PLANTS FOR PATIO PLANTERS (Cement, plastic, or wooden containers)

BROADLEAFED EVERGREENS (Sunny exposure)

DWARF RHODODENDRONS—Such as Blue Diamond (early April, 3 ft.), Gypsy Queen (rose pink, early May, 3 ft.), Elizabeth (early April, deep red, 3 ft.), and Fabia (late May, orange-salmon, 3 ft.).

KURUME AZALEAS (*Azalea japonica*)—Such as Vuyk's Scarlet, Hino-Crimson. Elizabeth Gable (rose pink), Adonis (white), and Purple Splendor. Height varies from 18" to 2 ft.

EVERGREEN BERBERIS—Such as Irwini (pendulous habit, small holly-like leaves, golden yellow flowers in May, 3 ft.), and Orange King (upright, bright orange flowers in May, 4 ft.)

PERNETTYA MUCRONATA—Variety Bell's Seedling (small pointed leaves, white flowers in June, large red berries in fall and winter, 3 ft.)

MAHONIA AQUIFOLIUM—Variety Bealei (erect habit, large glossy leaves, fragrant yellow flowers in April, followed by dark purple fruits, 2 to 3 ft.)

BROADLEAFED EVERGREENS (Shade, partial or full)

SEMI-DWARF RHODODENDRONS—Such as Blue Peter (lavender, early May, 4 ft.), Unique (peach, late April, 3 ft.), King Tut (deep pink, early May 3 ft.), and Kluis Sensation (scarlet, early May, 4 ft.).

PIERIS (Lily-of-the-valley shrub)—Variety Formosa Forresti (white flowers March-April, 4 ft.), and Pieris japonica variegata (silver-edged foliage, white flowers, March-April, 2 ft.).

LEUCOTHOE CATESBAEI—Somewhat similar to Pieris, but with large, glossy green leaves and white flowers in May, 3 ft.

JAPANESE HOLLY (*Ilex crenata rotundifolia*)—Erect, dense habit, with small glossy leaves, white flowers in May and black fruits, 3 ft.

VIBURNUM DAVIDII—Spreading habit, large oval leaves, clusters of small white flowers in May, followed by blue fruits, 3 ft.

CONIFEROUS EVERGREENS (Sun or shade)

DWARF SPRUCE (*Picea Albertiana conica*)—Compact, small needles, conical, rarely exceeds 3 ft. when grown in containers.

DWARF CYPRESS—Such as Obtusa nana gracilis (dark green, whorled foliage, can be kept to 3 ft.)

DWARF PINE—Such as Sylvestris nana, globular form of Scotch pine, with blue needles, 4 ft.

DWARF JUNIPER—Such as Communis hibernica compressa, with silvery green foliage, tight vertical habit, 3-4 ft.

DWARF ARBORVITAE—Such as Thuya orientalis aurea nana (dense, ovoid, golden foliage, 3 ft. Commonly called Biota.).

DECIDUOUS TREES AND/OR SHRUBS (Sun and shade)

JAPANESE DWARF MAPLE—Such as Acer palmatum dissectum, with green or purplish thread-like leaflets and spreading habit to 4 ft. wide and 4 ft. high.

HIGHBUSH BLUEBERRY—An attractive shrub with clusters of white flowers in May, followed by edible blue fruits and brilliant autumn leaf coloration, 4 ft.

FUCHSIA RICCARTONII—A hardy variety with red and blue flowers in late summer. Can be controlled to 4 ft.

HYDRANGEA PANICULATA GRANDIFLORA (*Peegee hydrangea*) —Grown as a standard, i.e. grafted on a 3 or 4 foot stem, it makes an attractive shrub with its clusters of tapered white flowers in August.

TREE PEONY—Single or double, large white, pink, yellow or purple blooms in May and June. Attractive foliage, 3 to 4 ft.

STANDARD ROSES—Hybrid Teas or Floribundas grafted on 3 or 4 ft. rugosa stems.

DWARF PEACH—Variety Bonanza, a small shrubby tree (5 ft.) that produces an abundance of excellent fruit.

SHRUBS—Heathers (*Calluna vulgaris* H. E. Beale, Searlei aurea, Goldsworth Crimson)
    Hydrangea *paniculata grandiflora*
    Roses
    Veronica Autumn Glory

OCTOBER

BULBS—Gladiolus, begonia, autumn crocus, dahlia (tuberous)
PERENNIALS—Aster (Michaelmas daisy), chrysanthemum, tritoma, pampas grass.
SHRUBS—Heathers (*Calluna vulgaris* David Easson, H. E. Beale, Goldsworth Crimson)
TREES—Dogwood (*Cornus nutallii*—sometimes blooms in fall as well as spring)
    Autumn Flowering Cherry (*Prunus subhirtella autumnalis rosea*—shows some bloom in the fall and again in spring)

There is very little significant bloom during November and December.

PLANTS WITH OUTSTANDING FRAGRANCE

EVERGREEN TREES
Magnolia Grandiflora
Arbutus Menziesii
Balsam Fir (*Balsamea*)

DECIDUOUS TREES
European Linden (*Tilia europaea*)
Laburnum
Horse Chesnut (*Aesculus*)
Flowering Almond (*Prunus Pollardii*)
Flowering Cherry (*Prunus Shirotae*)

EVERGREEN SHRUBS
Mexican Orange (*Choisya ternata*)
Lily-of-the-Valley Shrub (*Pieris floribunda*)
Holly-Leaf Barberry (*Mahonia aquifolium*)
Buddleia Globosa
Rhododendrons Loderi and Fortunei
Rosemary (*Rosmarius*)
Spanish Broom (*Spartium junceum*)
Broom (*Cytisus* and *Genista*)

ANNUALS
Sweet Alyssum
Candytuft
Wallflowers
Pinks
Carnations
Sweet Peas
Lupines
Stocks
Nicotiana
Mignonette

Scabiosa
Verbena

BULBS
Lily-of-the-Valley
Crocus vernus
Hyacinth
Lilium auratum
Lilium regale
Narcissi

DECIDUOUS SHRUBS and VINES
Daphne Mezereum
Honeysuckle (*Lonicera japonica*)
Mock Orange (*Philadelphus coronarius*)
Viburnum Hybrids—Carlesi, Burkwoodi
Wisteria chinensis
Witch Hazel (*Hamamelis*)
Summer-Flowering Jasmine (*J. offininale*)
Privet (*Ligustrum*)
Lilac (*Syringa*)
Thyme (*Thymus*)
Rose (*Rosa*)

PERENNIALS
Sage (*Salvia officinalis*)
Mint
Peony
Auricula, Primrose, Polyanthus
Violet (*Viola odorata*)
Candytuft (*Iberis*)
Lavender (*Lavandula*)
Phlox paniculata
Verbena

SOME PACIFIC NORTHWEST NATIVE PLANTS ADAPTABLE TO HOME GARDENS

EVERGREEN TREES

SITKA SPRUCE (*Picea sitchensis*)—A tall (150') conifer with bristling needles and drooping branchlets. Suitable specimen for large estates.

WESTERN HEMLOCK (*Tsuga heterophylla*)—A large tree (up to 150') with dark green needles. Thrives in shade and moist areas. Excellent for tall hedges or windbreaks.

BALSAM FIR (*Abies amabilis*)—A symmetrical, flat-needled conifer that grows up to 100 feet in moist shady locations. A nice specimen in a large lawn area.

WESTERN RED CEDAR (*Thuya plicata*)—A tall (150') tree with flat, yellowish green foliage, drooping branches and stringy, reddish bark. Too large as a specimen for most home gardens, but may be planted small and kept clipped to form an attractive hedge.

WESTERN YEW (*Taxus brevifolia*)—A bushy, irregular small (25') tree, with flat pointed needles. Its main attribute is its ability to thrive in deep shade.

ARBUTUS (*Arbutus menziesii*)—The only native Canadian broad leafed evergreen tree. A tree of twisted, irregular reddish trunk and limbs. It grows up to 50 feet high in rocky, well drained, sunny locations. Creamy bell-shaped flowers in May are followed by masses of orange-red berries.

DECIDUOUS TREES

PACIFIC DOGWOOD (*Cornus nuttallii*)—The unofficial floral emblem of B.C. A bushy, irregular tree up to 80 feet high, with large white blooms in early spring and often again in September. Foliage colors beautifully in the fall.

GARRY OAK (*Quercus garryana*)—The only oak native to B.C. An irregular tree that grows up to 50 feet, with huge gnarled limbs and grey, ridged bark. Likes good drainage.

BROADLEAF MAPLE (*Acer macrophyllum*)—A massive tree, up to 80 feet, with leaves nearly a foot across. Pale yellow flowers hang in long clusters in early April. A good shade tree in a large estate, or acreage.

VINE MAPLE (*Acer circinatum*)—A bushy tree, up to 20 feet, but usually only half that size. It is valued mainly for its outstanding fall coloring.

EVERGREEN SHRUBS

HOLLY MAHONIA (*Mahonia aquifolium*)—An irregular, often sprawling shrub, up to five feet high, with glossy dark evergreen leaves, bright yellow flowers in May, followed by dark blue edible berries. Suitable for large rockeries or border plantings. Brilliant fall leaf coloring. A smaller variety (M. nervosa), commonly called Oregon Grape, does best in partial shade.

WHITE RHODODENDRON (*Rhododendron albiflorum*) — A thickly branched shrub up to six feet, with oval hairy leaves and bell-like white clustered flowers in May. A good shrub for naturalizing, or in a wide border.

DWARF JUNIPER (*Juniperus communis*)—A sprawling shrub with narrow, pointed leaves, reddish bark, and dark blue berries. A hardy plant for rockeries and dry locations.

EVERGREEN HUCKLEBERRY (*Vaccinium ovatum*)—A bushy shrub up to six feet high, with waxy green-toothed leaves, clusters of pink flowers in May, and shiny black edible berries in October.

DECIDUOUS SHRUBS

RED FLOWERING CURRANT (*Ribes sanguineum*)—A loose bush averaging five feet in height, with drooping clusters of small red flowers in early April, followed by blue-black berries.

WAXBERRY or SNOWBERRY (*Symphoricarpus albus*)—A thin-stemmed shrub about three feet high, with pinkish bell-like flowers in May, followed by clumps of waxy white berries during fall and winter. Suitable for a low hedge.

RED HUCKLEBERRY (*Vaccinium parvifolium*)—A lacy, bright green, compact bush up to six feet high, with small oval leaves, pink blooms in May and tart red edible berries in September. Grows well in shade.

ORANGE HONEYSUCKLE (*Lonicera celiosa*)—A climbing vine with large oval whitish leaves, clusters of tube-like fragrant orange flowers, followed by coral red berries in fall. Useful along a back fence or arbor.

PERENNIAL FLOWERS and FERNS

CAMAS (*Camassia quamash*)—A bulb that produces grassy foliage and one-inch bluish purple flowers on stems up to two feet high, in early April. Fine for naturalizing with narcissi.

WESTERN TRILLIUM (*Trillium ovatum*)—Three large net-veined leaves cradle a short stemmed white flower in mid April. A good rockery subject.

EASTER LILY (*Erythronium oregonum*)—A deep growing bulb that produces mottled glossy leaves and takes five years or more to develop its first flower, a dainty white bloom with golden anthers. There is also a pink variety.

WILD TIGER LILY (*Lilium parviflorum*)—Similar to the cultivated variety except that the bloom is smaller and more delicate. Height 15 inches to thirty inches. Blooms in early June. Suitable for moist soils.

YELLOW COLUMBINE (*Aquilegia flavescens*)—A lovely yellow bloom with orange spurs, on stems up to three feet high, mid-May to June. Fine for partial shade.

RUSTY SAXIFRAGE (*Saxifraga rufidula*)—Thick leathery leaves, red underneath, surround the short (six-inch) purple flower stems that carry white blooms with orange stamens in May and June. An interesting rockery plant.

VERONICA (*Veronica alpine*)—A dwarf plant with oval leaves and small blue and cream flowers that appear in June and July. Useful for midsummer bloom in a border or rockery.

BUNCHBERRY (*Cornus canadensis*)—A miniature dogwood, up to eight inches high, with white flower bracts an inch across in May and sometimes again in late summer. A showy carpeter for under trees.

THRIFT (*Statice armeria*)—Similar to cultivated Thrift, with a clump of needle-like leaves and pink tufts of bloom in late spring. A good seaside plant.

BLEEDING HEART (*Dicentra formosa*)—A more delicately formed plant than some cultivated varieties, but with smaller flowers. Blooms in May, is fragrant, and prefers some shade.

STAR FLOWER (*Trientalis latifolia*)—A delicate eight-inch plant with large, glossy, oval leaves and small starlike white flowers in May. Likes moisture and shade.

STONECROP (*Sedum*)—Clusters of yellow blooms rise six inches above rosettes of fleshy leaves in May and June. A rockery plant that stands dry conditions.

GOLDENROD (*Solidago elongata*)—This variety is only a foot high and makes a showy summer groundcover on moist but well drained soil.

BLUE-EYED MARY (*Collinsia parviflora*)—A dwarf, delicate-looking plant with tiny blue flowers in April and May. Likes sunny dry locations.

GENTIANS (*Gentiana propinqua*)—Less than a foot high, with blue notched flowers in early summer. It likes moisture and some shade.

HARVEST BRODIAEA (*Brodiaea coronaria*)—Commonly called wild hyacinth, it grows about a foot high, with narrow leaves and beautiful blue or purple trumpet-shaped flowers. A good seashore and rockery plant.

LITTLE FLOWER PENSTEMON (*Penstemon procerus*)—A 12-inch plant with dark blue trumpet-shaped flowers in midsummer. Likes sandy soil and sun.

PARSLEY FERN (*Cryptogramma acrostichoides*)—A dwarf (8-inch) tufted fern suitable for rockeries.

LADY FERN (*Athyrium filix-femina*)—A graceful four-foot fern with arching tapered fronds, happiest in moist shady areas.

MAIDENHAIR FERN (*Adiantum pedatum aleuticum*)—A delicate fern with fringed leaf fronds and black stems. Grows about two feet and likes damp shaded areas.

SWORD FERN (*Polystichum munitum*)—As the name suggests, the leaves are sharply pointed. Grows about three feet and will stand sun better than most varieties.

ALPHABETICAL GUIDE TO 250 IMPORTANT PLANTS

Introduction

Names, botanical and/or common, will appear in alphabetical order, with cross references whenever required. The description of the plant will follow either the botanical name or the common name, whichever occurs first, and the cross reference will refer back. For example, the botanical name for a fir tree is "abies." Since "a" comes before "f," the plant description will follow "abies." But if you don't know the botanical name and look under "fir," you will be referred back to "abies" for the description. In a case where both botanical and common names are the same, like "camellia," of course there will be no cross reference.

The first abbreviation will always refer to the plant's hardiness, as follows:

H.A.—Hardy annual	H.P.—Hardy perennial
H.H.A.—Half hardy annual	H.H.P.—Half hardy perennial
T.A.—Tender annual	T.P.—Tender perennial
H.B.—Hardy bulb	H.S.—Hardy shrub
H.H.B.—Half hardy bulb	H.H.S.—Half hardy shrub
T.B.—Tender bulb	H.T.—Hardy tree

Next will come reference to the plant's soil requirements and its approximate position on the pH scale to indicate its acid tolerance. (See Fig. 2.)

Following this will be a brief description of the plant, it's height, width, habit of growth, time and color of bloom.

Where it's important, special pruning requirements will be mentioned, and the easiest method of propagation.

Finally, brief mention will be made of anything special or unusual about the plant.

ABELIA GRANDIFLORA—H.S. Average loam, pH 6.0. About four feet high, bushy, arching habit, pink, bell-like flowers June to Oct. Glossy, almost evergreen leaves. There is a low growing variety (prostrata) with white flowers. Prune lightly after flowering. Propagate from hardwood cuttings. Tolerates shade.

ABIES (Fir)—H.T. Sandy loam, pH 5.5. Up to 200 feet high, symmetrical, with upright cones. Propagated from spring sown seed, dwarf forms from grafting. Likes sun.

SOME HOME GARDEN VARIETIES: (Note: Planting restricted due to woolly aphid.)

A. *Concolor* (Silver or White Fir)—Up to 30 feet, silver-blue foliage, horizontal branching, quick grower, stands clipping, resists drought.

A. *Nordmanniana* (Nordmann Fir)—Up to 30 feet, glossy green foliage, silver beneath, horizontal branching, graceful habit.

A. *Koreana* (Korean Fir)—Up to 15 feet, pyramidal, deep green foliage and two-inch purple cones. The Nikko Fir (*A. homolepsis*) is similar, but grows up to 70 feet.

A. *balsamea nana* (Dwarf Balsam Fir)—Up to 15 feet, globular, deep green, fragrant. The regular balsam (*A. balsamea*) grows to 50 feet.

A. *arizonica compacta* (Dwarf Arizona Fir)—Up to eight feet, pyramidal, blue, small-needled foliage, stands drought. The only dwarf blue fir.

ACER (Maple)—H.T. Good moist loam, pH 6.5 (except Japanese varieties, pH 5.5). Height from four feet to 100 feet. Ornamental foliage widely varied in serration and color. Early spring flowering. Propagated from spring sown seed, layerage or graftage.

SOME HOME GARDEN VARIETIES:

A. *pseudoplatanus rubrum* (Canadian Red Maple)—Up to 30 feet high, 20 feet spread, with red flowers in spring and brilliant fall coloration.

A. *platanoides schwedleri* (Norway Maple)—Average height 30 feet with a 20-foot spread, symmetrical pyramid, red leaves in spring and fall. A fine shade tree.

Variety *nigrum* (Crimson King Maple), has the same habit, but the leaves are reddish-purple all season.

A. *negundo variegatum* (Variegated Maple)—About 20 feet high, 15-foot spread, with large leaves pencilled with silver or gold. A good shade tree for small gardens. Fairly drought resistant.

A. *palmatum atropurpureum* (Japanese Blood Leaf Maple)—Up to 10 feet with brilliant red, serrated leaves. Subject to leaf scorch in full sun or wind exposure. Variety *dissectum* grows up to six feet with green or purplish thread-like leaflets. A spreading habit, suitable for rockeries or beside pools.

ACONITE (*Eranthis hyemalis*)—H.B. Friable loam, pH 6.0. Yellow blooms, three inches high, in Feb.-March. One of the earliest of all spring flowers.

ACONITUM (Monkshood)—H.P. Average well-drained soil, pH 6.0. Pale or dark blue flowers three to five feet high during midsummer. Propagated by seed or root division. Won't stand drought. Roots are poisonous.

AESCULUS (Horse Chesnut)—H.T. Well drained loam, pH 5.0-6.0. Up to 20 feet high, symmetrical, compact, with white, pink or red flowers in spring. Propagated by planting nuts in fall, or grafting. Good boulevard or lawn specimen.

AGERATUM—H.H.A. Average soil, pH 6.0. Clusters of blue flowers, three to six inches, in June-July. Best started in heat.

AILANTHUS (Tree of Heaven)—H.T. Average to poor soil, pH 5.0-6.0. Height 50 to 100 feet. Large pinnate leaves. Best propagated from female tree root cuttings. The common *Ailanthus altissima* is a hardy disease-free shade tree, but too large for the average garden.

AJUGA Reptans (Carpet Bugle)—Hardy perennial creeper. Average soil, pH 5.0-6.0. Flat, almost evergreen four-inch leaves and blue, white or purple flowers in mid-summer. Forms a dense groundcover in sun or shade. Best propagated from layers or root divisions.

ALDER (Alnus)—H.T. Adapted to wet heavy soil, pH 5.0-6.0 Up to 75 feet, quick growing, a good shade tree. The Red Alder (A. *rubra*) is native to B.C. The Black Alder (A. *glutinosa*) is a shapely tree with several foliage variations. A. *incana aurea* has golden yellow leaves, while the leaves on A. *laciniata* are finely serrated. Propagated from seeds or layers.

ALMOND, FLOWERING (*Prunus Amygdalus, var. flora roseo-plena*)—H.T. Average well drained soil, pH 6.0-6.5. A 20-foot symmetrical tree with semi-double silvery pink flowers in early spring, and self-pollinated hardshelled nuts in fall. Best propagated by graftage on seedling peach stock.

SOME DWARF VARIETIES:

Prunus triloba—A shrub sometimes reaching 10 feet with a profusion of double pink rosette blooms in early spring.

Prunus tenella, or Dwarf Russian Almond, only grows four feet with white, pink or rose-red blooms.

Prunus glandulosa, a native of China and Japan, grows to five feet with white or pink blooms.

ALPINE CURRANT (*Ribes alpinum*)—H.S. Average soil, pH 5.0-6.0, up to eight feet with long racemes of gold, pink or red flowers before the leaves appear in early spring. Adapted to shade. Used effectively for low hedges. Propagated from cuttings. R. *sanguineum* is a pink flowered native of the Pacific northwest. A hybridized variety, King Edward VII has an intense crimson color.

ALTHAEA (For perennial, see Hollyhock.)

ALTHAEA (Hibiscus)—H.S. Average moist loam, pH 6.0-6.5. Grows up to 10 feet with large flowers in many colors during midsummer. Best propagated from cuttings, softwood or hardwood. *Hibiscus syriacus* has many named varieties such as Woodbridge (ruby red), Hambo (blush crimson), and Jeanne D'Arc (white).

ALYSSUM—H.H.A. Average soil, pH 5.0-6.0. White, pink or purple blooms on a compact plant three inches to four inches high. Start indoors from seed for early bloom.

ALYSSUM (Saxatile)—H.P. Light soil, pH 5.0-6.0. Makes a solid golden mat in early spring. Must be cut back hard after flowering. A good rockery plant. May be propagated from seed or cuttings.

AMELANCHIER (Juneberry)—H.T. Average soil, pH 6.0. A compact tree, up to 20 feet high, with racemes of white blooms in spring before the leaves show. Silvery foliage, very colorful in fall. Best variety is A. *canadensis.* Propagated from seed or cuttings.

AMPELOPSIS (See *Parthenocissus*)

ANDROMEDA POLIFOLIA (Bog Rosemary)—H.S. Peaty loam, pH 4.5 to 5.0. A 12-inch evergreen shrub with drooping pink flowers in April. Propagated from seed or cuttings. Favors moist, partially shaded areas.

ANEMONE (Windflower)—H.P. Light, well-drained limey soil, ph 6.5 to 7.0 From six inches high to three feet, according to variety. Wide color range. Propagated from seed, cuttings and tubers. Fine plants for herbaceous border and rock garden.

ANTIRRHINUM (Snapdragon)—H. A. Moist loam, pH 6.0. From six inches to 36 inches high in a wide color range. Seeds sown indoors February 1st will bloom in midsummer. They like full sun. Tall varieties like the Rocket Hybrids are excellent for cut flowers.

APPLE (*Malus*)—H.T. Any good well-drained loam, pH 5.5-6.5. From eight feet high in dwarfs to 25 feet in standards. May be pruned in various ways (see Fig. 9). See page 27 for variety table. Propagated by graftage (March) or budding (August). The most popular and adaptable fruit for home gardens.

APRICOT (*Prunus*)—H.T. Well drained light loam, pH 6.5. From eight feet high in dwarfs to 20 feet in standards. Summer prune to keep growth from getting too dense. Likes heat. See Part I (C) for variety table. Propagated by graftage (March) or budding (August). An early bloomer, hence subject to trouble in frost zones.

APRICOT, JAPANESE (*Prunus mume*)—H.T. Well drained light loam, pH 6.5. Reaches 20 feet in height, and blooms very early in spring, either in double white (*albo-plena*) or double pink (*roseo-plena*). Subject to late frosts. A beautiful ornamental for more sheltered areas.

AQUILEGIA (Columbine)—H.P. Moist loam, pH 6.0 From six inches to 24 inches high, late spring to midsummer. Grown mainly from seed. Prefers partial shade, though some rock garden varieties like A. *glandulosa,* will stand sun fairly well.

ARABIS (Rock Cress)—H.P. Average to poor soil, pH 5.0-6.0. Six-inch white flowers February-April, above tufted grey foliage. Good rockery plant. Propagated from seeds or root divisions. Sometimes difficult to contain. Cut back hard after blooming.

ARAUCARIA (Monkey Puzzle Tree or Chile Pine)—H.T. Moist loam, pH 5.5 to 6.0 Grows to about 15 feet in the Pacific northwest. Dark green, leathery, spiny leaves and large seed cones. A garden novelty. Propagated from seed.

ARBORVITAE (*Thuya*)—H.T. Does well in a wide range of soils, but favors the moist clay loams, pH 5.0 There are many variations in height and form from three feet to 60 feet. Propagated from seed or cuttings.

SOME HOME GARDEN VARIETIES:

T. *occidentalis* (American Arborvitate)—A large (50 foot) tree, useful for high hedges or screening.

T. *occidentalis pyramidalis compacta*—Very columnar, to 20 feet high, bright green foliage, an excellent hedge plant.

T.*occidentalis globosa*—A dwarf (eight feet) round form, suitable for foundation work.

T. *occidentalis pumila* (Little Gem)—A two-foot flattened ball, useful in planters and rockeries.

T. *orientalis* (Oriental Arborvitae or Biota)—Very variable in character but may be recognized by its flattened, parallel branching habit.

T.*orientalis aurea nana* (Berkman's Golden Arborvitae)—A dwarf (two feet) globe, light green with gold tips. Stands dry locations. A good foundation or rockery plant.

T. orientalis Rosedalis—A dwarf (four feet) form, with soft grey juvenile foliage, tipped yellow in spring.

ARUNDINARIA (Bamboo)—H.P. Moist clay loam, pH 6.0. Height varies from three feet to 15 feet or more. Dwarf varieties best suited for home landscaping. Will grow in sun or shade but should be planted where roots can be controlled. Propagated from root divisions.

ASH (Fraxinus)—H.T. Average moist loam, pH 6.0 Height varies from 20 feet to 120 feet. The smaller trees make good lawn specimens, and some, like the Manna Ash (*F. ornus*) has very attractive white bloom in May. The Weeping Ash (*F. excelsior pendula*) makes an excellent garden arbor and the Golden Ash (*F. excelsior aurea*) has distinctive yellow bark. Easily propagated from seed or grafting. This genus is not to be confused with the European Mountain Ash or Rowan tree. (See *sorbus.*)

ASTER (Michaelmas Daisy)—H.P. Light rich loam, pH 6.0-6.5. Height varies from six inches to 48 inches. Suitable for rock gardens, sunny herbaceous borders or open woodlands.
Alpinus—White, pink or blue, May-June. Two feet. Good rockery plant.
Amellus—Pink, violet, rose, blue, July-Sept. 1½ feet to two feet.
Novae-Angliae—Blue, pink, red, Sept.-Oct. Four feet to five feet.
Novi-Belgi Hybrids—White, pink, red, blue, Sept.-Oct. Two to three feet.
Subdivide roots after flowering to keep up bloom. Propagated by root divisions.

ASTILBE (Perennial Spiraea)—H.P. Average loam, pH 6.0. Moisture lovers. Height from one foot to six feet in white, pink, rose, purple and red. The plume-like flowers are very showy from June to August. May be propagated from seed or root divisions. Especially attractive near garden pools or ponds.

AUBRETIA (Purple Rock Cress)—H.P. Light soil, pH 6.0. Mauve to wine-colored mats of bloom in April, on grey-green foliage. Propagate from seed or root division. Shear back hard after flowering. Ideal for sunny rock walls.

AUCUBA JAPONICA VARIEGATA (Gold Dust Tree)—H.S. Average soil, pH 5.0-6.0. height, six feet. Large laurel-like foliage, male plants green, female plants flecked or striped with gold. Does best in full shade. Propagated easily from cuttings.

AVENS (Geum)—H.P. Light loam, pH 6.0. Flowers 12 inches to 24 inches high in scarlet, orange and yellow, July-Aug. Propagated from seed or root divisions. A good border perennial.

AZALEA—Hardy and half hardy shrubs for lime-free loamy soils. Many sub-species and varieties, from a few inches in height to 20 feet.
A. mollis—Up to 10 feet high, with brilliant bloom in early spring before the leaves appear. Colors in white, pink, orange, salmon and yellow. Exbury and Knap Hill strains are exceptionally large flowered, some with fragrance. Will grow in sun or partial shade. Propagated from seed or cuttings.
A. kurume—Dwarf, Japanese evergreen, up to three feet. Requires an acid soil, pH 5.0. Many choice varieties in a wide color range. Best propagated from cuttings. Fine rockery or planter subject.

BABY'S BREATH (Gypsophila)—H.A. and H.P. Average soil, pH 6.0-6.5. Height from six inches in dwarf varieties (repens), to three feet. White, yellow, pink or red flowers in late summer. Propagate the annual from seed and the perennial from root divisions.

BACHELOR'S BUTTONS (*Centaurea*)—H.A. (Cornflower). Average to poor soil, pH 6.0. Height of bloom from 10 inches to 2½ feet, in blue, pink or white. Sow seed in autumn for early spring flowering, or spring for summer bloom.
H.P. (Knapweeds). Average soil, pH 6.0. Height of bloom 18 inches to three feet. Foliage silvery, flowers in spiked petals, crown-shaped, white or blue, during July-August. Propagated by root division.

BALSAM (*Impatiens*)—H.H.A. Friable, well-drained soil, pH 6.0. Height of bloom 18 inches in mixed colors, July-August. Sow in heat during February. A good border annual.

BALSAM FIR (See *Abies*)

BAMBOO (See *Arundinaria*)

BARBERRY (*Berberis*)—Hardy and half hardy deciduous or evergreen shrub. Wide range of soils, pH 5.5-6.0. Height varies from 1 ft. to 8 ft. Many varieties, most of which bloom during May and June. Propagated from seed or hardwood cuttings.

SOME HOME GARDEN VARIETIES:

B. *buxifolia nana*—Dwarf (2 ft.) evergreen for low hedge or rockery.

B. *verruculosa*—Dwarf (2 ft.) evergreen, yellow bloom, April-May.

B. *Darwinii*—Erect, 6 ft. evergreen, fragrant orange bloom.

B. *Julianae*—A 6 ft. evergreen with yellow bloom and blue fruits.

B. *Thunbergii*—(Chinese barberry). Height 3-5 ft. thickly branched, deciduous, yellow blooms followed by red berries and brilliant fall coloration of foliage.

B. *Thunbergii atropurpurea*—Same as above, with reddish-purple leaves all summer. A dwarf variation (*minor*) grows only 15" high and is a fine shrub for rockeries, planters or low hedges.

B. *Thunbergii erecta*—Narrow, upright to 8 ft., fine for hedging.

BARRENWORT (*Epimedium*)—Hardy groundcover. Sandy loam, pH 5.5-6.0. About 12" high, with white, pink, yellow, or violet bloom in April-May. Propagated by root divisions. Does best in partial shade.

BEAUTY BUSH (*Kolkwitzia amabilis*)—H.S. Average loamy soil, pH 6.0. Grows 8 ft. high and produces bell shaped pink and yellow flowers in May and June. Grey green foliage. Propagated from seed or cuttings. Should be pruned back hard after flowering. Likes sun.

BEECH (*Fagus*)—H.T. Average soil, pH 6.0-6.5. The American Beech, *F. grandifolia* grows up to 100 ft. but the one best suited for home gardens, the European Beech, *F. sylvatica*, rarely reaches half that height. The copper leafed form, *F. sylvatica atropurpurea*, is the most popular, and may be grown from select seedlings or may be a grafted variety (Riversi). Hedges of beech form an excellent screen or windbreak.

BEGONIA—A tender tuber or fibrous-rooted plant with spectacular flowers and/or leaves, favoring friable soil with plenty of humus, pH 5.5-6.0. Height varies from 9" to 18" and colors range from white, pink, salmon, orange and yellow, into reds and bicolors, in double camellia-like flowers, ruffled carnation types, or small single multifloras. May be grown from seed, or tubers. Tubers started indoors in early Feb. will bloom in July. Partial or full shade essential for good blooms.

BELLFLOWER (*Campanula*)—Hardy annual, biennial and perennial plants, with wide variation in height and habit. Prefer light, well drained soil, pH 6.0. Propagate from seed, perennials from root divisions.

SOME ROCK GARDEN PERENNIAL VARIETIES:

C. *carpatica* (Carpathian Bellflower)—Saucer shaped blue or white flowers in a carpet of bright green foliage. Height 6".

C. *caespitosa*—A dwarf spreading plant 4-5" high, with blue flowers in June. Fine for dry walls or between flagstones.

SAME BORDER PERENNIAL VARIETIES:

C. *glomerata* (Clustered Bellflower)—Large clusters of violet purple blooms on 18" stems in June.

C. *persicifolia* (Peach-leaved Bellflower)—Blue or white cup shaped flowers on leafy stems, 2-3 ft., in June-July.

C. *pyramidalis* (Chimney Bellflower)—A vigorous plant, 4-5 ft. with blue or white flowers in July-Aug.

BERBERIS (See Barberry).

BETULA (Birch)—H.T. Average garden soil, pH 5.5-6.5. Height up to 100 ft. Propagated from seed. Dwarf and weeping varieties grafted. A fine shade and ornamental tree.

B. pendula alba is a handsome tree, with white bark and graceful habit. Average height around 40 ft.

B. pendula laciniata is a cut leaf semi-weeping tree, that grows slightly smaller.

B. pendula Youngii is a low growing (20 ft.) dome-shaped tree with slender pendulous branches.

BLACKBERRY—H.C. Rich, well-drained loam, pH 5.5-6.0. Blooms in June, fruits in July. After fruiting, old canes should be cut out. Propagate by tip layering. See Chapter I (C) for planting details. The Pacific blackberry is a fine hybrid trailing variety with excellent flavor and a heavy yield. The Marion blackberry is somewhat larger than the Pacific, hardy and productive.

BLEEDING HEART (*Dicentra*)—H.P. Loamy, fibrous soil, pH 6.0. Pinnate, light green leaves with heart shaped, drooping pink and white flowers in April-May. *D. spectablis* is the most common variety, and it prefers partial shade. Propagated from seed or root divisions.

BLUEBERRY, HIGHBUSH (*Vaccinium corymbosum*)—H.S. Moist peaty loam with high acidity (pH 4.0-5.2). Height up to 6 ft. Clusters of white flowers in May-June are followed by blue fruits in July-Aug. Propagated from seed or hardwood cuttings. Lovely fall leaf colorations. Some recent large fruited varieties include Bluecrop, Earliblue, Ivanhoe, Coville and Berkeley. Older varieties such as Rubel, Rancocas, Pioneer and Concord are still grown but are much inferior.

BOSTON IVY (See *Parthenocissus*).

BOYSENBERRY—H.C. Well drained rich loam, pH 5.5-6.0. Canes grow 8-10 ft. long and require support. Blooms in May-June and fruits in July. Cut out old canes after fruiting, leave new canes on ground until following spring. Propagate by tip layering. See Chapter I (C) for planting details.

BOXWOOD (*Buxus*)—H.S. Average well drained soil, pH 6.0-6.5. Height varies from 1 ft. to 6 ft. according to variety. An excellent evergreen hedge plant. Propagated from cuttings or root divisions.

B. sempervirens, the common Box, is used extensively for topiary work and hedging. Will reach 6 ft. but is better at about 4 ft.

B. sempervirens elegantissima has narrow leaves, edged with white, and makes a nice specimen in sun or shade.

B. sempervirens suffruticosa, the edging Box, is naturally dwarf and can be kept as low as 8" by constant clipping.

B. microphylla koreana, the Korean Box, is lighter in color than B. sempervirens, but very hardy.

BROOM (*Cytisus* and *Genista*)—H.S. Light, well drained soil, pH 5.5-6.0. Height varies from a few inches in prostrate varieties to 10 ft. White, cream, yellow or red flowers in spring and summer. Best propagated from cuttings. Good rockery plants that stand drought and seaside conditions well. Tall varieties should be pruned back after bloom.

Cytisus praecox—Creamy white, fragrant flowers, 4 ft. early spring.

Cytisus kewensis—White fragrant flowers, early spring, prostrate.

Cytisus scoparius and hybrids—Various colors, late spring, to 5 ft.

Genista saggitalis, or Winged Broom, is a prostrate evergreen plant with bright yellow flowers in May-June.

Genista tinctoria—Yellow flowers, June-July, up to 2 ft. high.

BROOM, SPANISH (*Spartium junceum*)—Light sandy soil, pH 5.5-6.0. Will grow to 10 ft. but best kept pruned to 5 ft. Large pea-like golden flowers from June to September, very fragrant. Best grown from seed. Stands sun and seaside conditions well.

BUDDLEIA (Butterfly Bush)—H.S. Loamy, well drained soil, pH 6.0-6.5. Varieties of Buddleia Davidii (*variabilis*), will grow up to 10 ft. with large spikes of white, red, lilac, blue or purple, in July-Aug. These should be cut back hard each spring. Varieties of Buddleia *globosa,* the evergreen Orange Ball Tree, should not be pruned until after flowering in May-June. Buddleias may be grown from seed but named varieties should be propagated from cuttings.

BULBS (See Chapter II (H).

BUTTERCUP (*Ranunculus*)—H.P. Loamy soil, pH 6.0. The common double yellow Buttercup, *R. acris flore-pleno*, grows up to 2 ft. and blooms in May-June. Easily increased by root division. There are many other border and alpine varieties. The Turban and Persian Ranunculi, *R. asiaticus*, are grown from tubers set out from Sept. to Feb. Plant 2" deep in light fertile soil, in full sun. There are many bright colors. They grow about a foot high.

BUTTERNUT (*Juglans cinerea*)—H.T. Well drained loam, pH 6.0-6.5. Up to 100 ft. high. Light smooth bark, compound pinnated leaves. Propagated from seed or graftage. A good large shade tree with self pollinated sweet oily nuts in October.

BUXUS (See Boxwood).

CALENDULA (Pot Marigolds)—H.A. Average soil, pH 5.5-6.0. Height 6"-18". Yellow, lemon or orange flowers, May to Dec. Freely self seeding.

CALIFORNIA POPPY (*Eschscholtzia*) — H.A. Light, dry soil, pH 6.0. Yellow, orange, red and white flowers, one foot high. Sow outdoors in March for summer flowering and in Aug. or Sept. for early spring.

CALLA AETHEOPICA (The Arum Lily)—H.B. Moist friable loam, pH 5.5-6.0. Height 2 ft. White flowers in summer. Propagate from seeds or offsets.

CALLIOPSIS (*Coreopsis*)—H.A. Average soil, pH 6.0-6.5. Height 18" to 3 ft. Yellow and crimson flowers in June-July. Sow outdoors in March.

CALLUNA and ERICA (Heather and Heath)—Note: There is so much similarity between these two types of evergreen shrubs that for all gardening purposes they can be grouped together.

Calluna, commonly known as Scotch Heather, has only one species, *C. vulgaris*, but many varieties. It likes peaty, lime free soil, pH 4.5-5.5, good drainage and full sun. Best propagated from cuttings. Useful for ground cover, planters and rockeries. A summer bloomer.

C. vulgaris Camla, double pink, 9" high, July.
C. vulgaris Mair's White, white, 2½ ft., July-Aug.
C. vulgaris Hammondi, white, 2½ ft., July-Aug.
C. vulgaris Alporti, crimson, 2 ft., July-Aug.
C. vulgaris Serlei aurea, white, golden foliage, 2 ft., Aug.-Sept.
C. vulgaris alba plena, white, 18", Sept.-Oct.
C. vulgaris H. E. Beale, double pink, 2 ft., Sept.-Nov.
C. vulgaris David Easson, red, 12", Oct.-Nov.

Erica, or Heath, for the most part likes the same peaty, acid soil as Heather, but a few species like *E. mediterranea*, *E. carnea*, and *E. darleyensis* will tolerate a little lime, pH 5.5-6.0. The Tree Heaths, such as *E. arborea* and *E. mediterranea* grow up to 12 ft. with white or rose-purple flowers in early spring. There are many varieties of the commonly planted Heath, *E. carnea*, most of which are under 2 ft. in height.

E. carnea King George, reddish purple, 6", Jan.-Mar.
E. carnea Springwood White, white, 10", Jan.-Mar.
E. carnea Springwood Pink, pink, 10", Jan.-Mar.
E. carnea Vivelii, carmine, 6", bronzy foliage, Feb.-Mar.
E. carnea Ruby Glow, deep pink, 8", Mar.-April.

The Cornish Heath, *Erica vagans*, is a spreading plant up to 2 ft. high, blooming in late summer and autumn.

E. vagans Lyonesse, white, 18", Aug.-Sept.
E. vagans Mrs. Maxwell, bright pink, 18", Aug.-Sept.
E. darleyensis, with purple or white flowers, Nov.-May, is a very hardy hybrid of spreading growth, 12"-18" high.

CAMELLIA (Tea Plant)—H.H.S. Friable, peaty loam, pH 5.0. Height up to 20 ft. but average six to eight feet. White, pink, red and variegated colors from Feb. to April. Propagated from seed or semi-hardwood cuttings. Best in partial shade, sheltered from wind. Most garden varieties belong to three species, *C. Sasanqua*, *C. reticulata*, and *C. japonica*, with the latter by far the most popular.

Some *C. japonica* varieties suitable for Northwest gardens:
Alba Plena and Purity are good double whites.
Debutante and Perfection are reliable double pinks.
Cheerful, Mme. Sarmont, and Glen 40 are hardy double light reds.
Julia Drayton and Col. Fiery are excellent scarlet reds.

CAMPANULA (See Bellflower).

CANDYTUFT, ANNUAL—H.A. Average soil, pH 6.0. Height from 6" to 1 ft. Mixed pastel colors in June-July, if sown outdoors in April. A good edging plant.

CANDYTUFT, EVERGREEN (*Iberis sempervirens*)—Average well drained soil, pH 6.0. Low spreading habit, with white or lilac pink blooms in April-May. Easily grown from seed or cuttings. A good edging or wall garden plant in sun or partial shade.

CARAGANA (Pea Tree)—H.S. Well drained sandy soil, pH 6.0-6.5. Makes a hardy hedge plant, with pinnate leaves and yellow blooms in May. Best grown from seed.

CARNATION (*Dianthus Caryophyllus*)—H.P. Light, limed soil, pH 6.5-7.0. Outdoor Border Carnations usually grow 18" to 24" high. Double, scented flowers in white, pink, rose, yellow, scarlet and orange, on long stems and spiky grey foliage. Need tying up. Seed sown in Feb. will bloom in Aug.-Sept. Cuttings or layers taken in March will bloom July-Aug. A fine cut flower for both show and perfume.

CARPET BUGLE (See *Ajuga reptans*)

CARYOPTERIS (Bluebeard)—H.S. Well drained sandy loam, pH 6.0. Height about 4 ft. Masses of powdery blue, fringed flowers, bloom in late summer. Prune back after flowering. Propagated from cuttings.

CASTANEA (Sweet Chesnut)—H.T. Well drained moist loam, pH 6.0. Height of Chinese seedlings and hybrids is about 25 ft. Serrated round leaves and sweet soft shelled nuts. Two required for pollination. *C. Mollissima* varieties are blight resistant. Propagate from seed or by grafting. Likes a warm location.

CATALPA, WESTERN (*C. speciosa*)—H.T. Deep, loamy, well drained soil, pH 6.0-6.5. A handsome pyramid 40-80 ft. with large ovate leaves and panicles of white frilled flowers, spotted with yellow and purple, in June-July. A good shade tree.

CEANOTHUS—H.S. Prefers light, well drained loam, pH 6.0. The summer flowering hybrids grow 8-10 ft. and produce a wealth of blue, rose or pink flowers, July-Oct. Need hard pruning to keep shaped. Propagated from cuttings. Gloire de Versailles (deep blue), and Marie Simon (pink), are good varieties.

CEDAR (Cedrus)—H.T. Rich, well drained loam, pH 5.5-6.0. Height 60-100 ft. Propagated from seed or graftage. Not to be confused with the native Western Red Cedar (*Thuya plicata*), Yellow Cedar (*Chamaecyparis nootkatensis*), or Japanese Cedars (*Cryptomeria*). The true cedars have dense clusters of spurlike leaf growths encircling terminal shoots at irregular intervals.
C. libani, the Lebanon Cedar, is a pyramidal tree, up to 100 ft. high with a 60 ft. spread, with dark green foliage.
C. Atlantica, the Atlas Cedar, grows about the same height, and the variety *glauca* is a beautiful bluish specimen for large lawns.
C. Deodara, the Himalayan Cedar, is a graceful, pyramidal tree with blue-green foliage, pendulous branching, and a height between 60-100 ft. in mature trees. The golden form, *C. Deodara aurea* grows somewhat smaller.

CELOSIA (Cockscomb)—H.H.A. Average soil, pH 6.0. Height 12" to 36".
C. cristata bears flattish, dense heads of crimson, yellow orange or pink flowers. A good pot plant.
C. plumosa has plumelike inflorescences in scarlet, crimson and gold. Seed sown indoors in Feb. will bloom outdoors in July. A showy border plant.

CENTAUREA (See Bachelor's Buttons).

CERCIS (Judas Tree or Redbud)—H.T. Rich light loam, pH 6.0. Varies in height from a large, 15 ft., bush to a broad round-headed tree up to 40 ft. *C. canadensis*

(American Redbud) produces short clusters or rosy-pink flowers in May. Propagated from seed or graftage.

CHAENOMELES LAGENARIA or CYDONIA JAPONICA (Japanese Flowering Quince)—H.S. Average soil, up to 10 ft. high, with red, pink, salmon or white blooms in early spring, before the foliage appears. Propagated from seed, layers or cuttings. A good wall plant or border specimen. Dwarf varieties like *C. japonica Simoni,* a brilliant red, are excellent rock garden plants.

CHAMAECYPARIS (False Cypress)—H.T. Well drained moist loam, pH 5.5-6.0. Varieties vary in height from 2 ft. to 100 ft. or more. Propagated from seed, cuttings or graftage. Probably more variations in form, color and size than in any other class of evergreens. Somewhat subject to root diseases, especially in heavy wet soils.

THE LAWSON GROUP (*C. Lawsoniana*)

C. Lawsoniana—a silvery green, quick growing tree, up to 100 ft. or more. Useful for screens and tall hedges.

C. Lawsoniana Allumii and *columnaris glauca*—blue-green specimens, compact, pyramidal, up to 15 ft.

C. Lawsoniana Triomphe de Boskoop and *Fraseri*—similar to above in size, with blue-gray foliage.

C. Lawsoniana erecta viridis—upright branching, bright green.

C. Lawsoniana Fletcheri—gray, feathery, good hedge plant.

C. Lawsoniana Elwoodii—conical, compact, blue-green, to 15 ft.

C. Lawsoniana Stewartii—pyramidal, golden foliage, 10 ft.

C. Lawsoniana Wiselii—narrow column, tufted glaucous foliage.

C. Lawsoniana minima glauca, and *aurea*—dwarf, round, green and gold forms suitable for the rock garden.

THE HINOKI GROUP (*C. obtusa*)

C. obtusa—the Hinoki Cypress of Japan, where it grows to 100 ft. or more. A decorative specimen for a large estate. Bright green foliage.

C. obtusa Crippsi—an open-branched, gold-tipped form, averaging 8 ft.

C. obtusa nana gracilis—brilliant green foliage in tight whorls, 5 ft. The golden form, *nana aurea,* rarely exceeds 2 ft.

C. obtusa pygmaea—informal arched green branches, bronze in winter, 4 ft.

C. obtusa caespitosa—a 4" dwarf for the rock garden.

THE SARAWA (PLUME CYPRESS) GROUP (*C. pisifera*)

C. pisifera—the Sarawa Cypress of Japan, where it grows 90 ft. high.

C. pisifera plumosa and *plumosa aurea* are green and gold-tipped forms with juvenile soft foliage, that grow up to 8 ft. in conical habit. Useful for hedging or wide borders. *C. pisifera nana* is a green, 2 ft. flattened globe, and *C. pisifera nana aureo-variegata* is flecked with gold.

C. pisifera squarrosa—sometimes called Moss Cypress, on account of its soft gray-green foliage, is a pyramidal tree averaging 10 ft.

C. pisifera squarrosa intermedia—a globular form of the above, reaching 4 ft. with a subvariety *nana* only half that size.

C. pisifera filifera—sometimes called Thread Cypress, on account of whiplike pendent branches, grows to 6 ft. with a dwarf subvariety *nana* reaching only 2 ft. There is also a golden form.

CHEIRANTHUS (Wallflower)—H.H.P. Usually treated as biennials. Firm clay loam, pH 6.0-6.5. Height varies from 6" to 36". Seeds sown in June-July and transplanted in October, will bloom the following April and May. Wide range of named varieties in many colors, primrose, dark red, yellow, orange and purple. Very popular as a spring bedding plant.

CHERRY, FRUIT (*Prunus avium* (Mazzard) or *prunus Malaheb* rootstocks)—H.T. Light rich loam, pH 6.0-6.5. Height of sweet cherries is around 20 ft. and sour cherries around 15 ft. Sweet varieties need compatible pollenizers (See Part I (C) for variety table). Propagated by grafting or budding named varieties on seedling rootstocks. Good drainage and light pruning are essential for best results.

CHERRY, FLOWERING (*Prunus*)—H.T. Light rich calcareous loam, pH 6.0-6.5. Height from 10 ft. to 40 ft. according to variety. White or pink, single or double flowers in May, except *P. subhirtella autumnalis* which flowers intermittently from Oct. to Mar. Propagated by grafting or budding on seedling stocks. The Japanese flowering cherries are exceptionally beautiful and useful plants for home gardens, and there are many fine varieties.
P. serrulata Kwanzan—Height 20-25 ft., upright habit. Double rose-pink flowers in early May, coppery foliage in spring and fall. A fine boulevard or border tree.
P. serrulata Kiku Shidare—Height 15 ft., long pendent branches wreathed in clusters of double rose-pink blossoms. A fine weeping specimen near a pool or rock.
P. serrulata grandiflora (Ukon) — Height 20 ft., semidouble yellowish white flowers, in May, coppery foliage in spring and fall.
P. serrulata Shimidsu Sakura (Oku Miyako)—Height 15-20 ft., large double fringed flowers open pale pink and change to white, in late May.
P. subhirtella or Rosebud Cherry—Height 10 ft., with an abundance of pale pink flowers in early spring. Subvariety *autumnalis* and *autumnalis rosea* have white and light pink blooms from fall till spring.
CHESNUT (See *Aesculus* and *Castanea*).
CHIONODOXA (Glory of the Snow)—H.B. Light rich soil, pH 6.0. Blue, white or pink flowers about 6" high on slender stems in Feb.-Mar. Propagation by seed or offsets. Fine for rock gardens.
CHOISYA TERNATA (Mexican Orange Flower)—H.H.S. Light rich soil, pH 6.5. Height 6-8 ft. Glossy-green evergreen leaves, fragrant white flowers resembling orange blossoms in midsummer. Best propagated from cuttings. Good for seaside planting. Prune back in spring.
CHRISTMAS ROSE (*Helleborus*)—H.P. Moist but well drained rich soil, pH 6.5. Large leaves and purple, pink or green flowers, as well as white, on erect stems 12-18" high, from Feb.-April. Best propagated from root divisions after flowering. Prefers some shade. *Helleborus niger* (white) and *Helleborus orientalis* (pink or green), are two well known varieties.
CHRYSANTHEMUM (*C. maximum or Shasta Daisy*)—H.P. Average soil, pH 6.0. Forms evergreen tufts close to thte ground with large single or double flowers on stems 2-3 ft. in midsummer. Propagated from root divisions. Excellent for cut flowers. Well known variety Esther Read has large white double blooms, Cobham Gold is cream with a yellow centre. Another hardy herbaceous chrysanthemum of similar habit is *C. rubellum*, with 3 ft. rose-pink single flowers in Sept.-Oct.
CHRYSANTHEMUM (Border Type)—H.P. Average light soil, pH 6.0-6.5. This group includes dozens of varieties, from the 6" cushion mums to the 3-4 ft. cutting varieties. There is a wide range of colors, and blooms extend from midsummer into late fall. May be grown from seed but are usually propagated from cuttings or root division. Special study and culture are prerequisites to success, especially with the less hardy Japanese greenhouse types. They are one of the showiest of border perennials and finest of cut flowers. There is also a hardy annual chrysanthemum with single and double blooms in yellow, white and crimson, (Marguerites).
CINQUEFOIL (Potentilla)—H.P. and H.S. Well drained loam, pH 6.0. The herbaceous perennials vary in height from 4" to 2 ft. and bloom during June-July, in red yellow or orange combinations. May be grown from seed or propagated from root divisions. *P. nitida* is a fine 6" plant, with gray leaves and pink flowers, suitable for rock gardens. Miss Willmott, a pink variety of *P. nepalensis*, grows about 12" high and is suitable for either a border or rockery. Most of the shrubby Potentillas suitable for gardens are varieties of *P. fruticosa*, which grows 2-3 ft. and bears large yellow or cream colored flowers during May-June. Best propagated from cuttings. All Potentillas like full sun.
CISTUS (Rock Rose)—H.H.S. Well drained sandy loam, pH 6.0. An evergreen shrub

that grows 4-6 ft. high, with single roselike flowers, white or crimson blotched, in June-July. Grown from seed or cuttings. It stands drought well and is fine for a sunny bank or border. Not to be confused with Helianthemum, also sometimes called Rock Rose.

CLEMATIS—Hardy and half-hardy climber. Manured, sandy loam, pH 6.5-7.0. The brittle, clinging vines require support. Propagated from softwood cuttings or layers. Flowers in a wide range of colors, May-Sept., according to variety. Best in partial shade. Pruning practice varies with type.

C. montana and *montana rubens* will grow up to 50 ft. Cut back or shorten old shoots after flowering in May. White or pink small blooms.

C. Armandii is a hardy evergreen that grows 15-20 ft. with clusters of cream-white flowers April-May.

Large flowered varieties of the Patens Type bloom in May-June on old wood. Pruning on varieties like Nelly Moser and The President should be done after flowering. Old wood without new shoots should be removed.

Double flowered varieties of the Florida Type, bloom on old wood from May to Aug. Duchess of Edinburgh, a favorite white scented variety is one example. Remove weak shoots right after flowering.

The Lanuginosa Type, which includes such varieties as Crimson King, and Henryi, a cream-white, bloom in late summer and fall on short side growths of old wood, and should be pruned in spring.

The Viticella Type, with medium sized blooms, July-Oct., includes the red Ernest Markham, purple Lady Balfour and wine-colored Ville de Lyon. They flower on the current season's growth and should be pruned hard in Feb.

The large-flowered Jackmanni Type also bloom on fresh growths of the current year, and should be cut back almost to the ground every spring.

COLCHICUM (Autumn Crocus) — H.B. Good moist loam, pH 6.0. Pale purple flowers on eight inch stems appear before foliage in Aug.-Sept. Propagated from seeds grown into corms. Should be planted as corms in July-Aug. The yellow-flowered *C. luteum* blooms in spring.

COLUMBINE (See *Aquilegia*) .

CONEFLOWER (*Rudbeckia*)—H.A. Average soil, pH 6.0. Mixed yellow, brown or purple flowers, 3 ft. in July-Aug. Sow seeds outdoors in April.
—H.P. The perennial grows up to 6 ft., blooming in late summer. Varieties include Autumn Sun (yellow), Purpurea (purple) and The King (crimson). Best propagated from root divisions.

CONVOLVULUS (Morning Glory)—H.A. climber. Average soil, pH 6. Throws 10 ft. shoots with trumpet-shaped blue or mixed flowers in midsummer, if seed is sown in April. Likes sun. There is a dwarf variety, Royal Marine, only a foot high. Most perennial varieties are so hard to control they are considered weeds.

COREOPSIS—H.P. Average soil, pH 6.0. Golden flowers on 2 ft. stems in July. Propagate from root divisions. Likes sun.

CORNFLOWER (See *Centaurea*).

CORNUS (Dogwood)—Hardy shrub and hardy tree. Both like moist loam with lots of humus, pH 5.5-6.0. Propagated from seed or cuttings. Useful for shrubbery borders and woodland planting.

SOME HOME GARDEN VARIETIES:

C. alba (Red Twig Dogwood)—A shrub that grows 8-10 ft. with small white flowers in May-June, and striking red bark. Useful for winter color.

C. florida (Eastern Flowering Dogwood)—A small tree, 15-30 ft. covered in spring with small flower clusters surrounded by white or pink bracts. Striking foliage in autumn.

C. Nuttallii (Pacific or Western Dogwood)—A tree native to the Pacific coast that grows up to 80 ft. and produces large cream-white bracts in April-May and often again in the fall. Good autumn leaf coloring. Best propagated from seeds and container grown until transplanted. Likes its roots shaded.

C. Kousa (Japanese Flowering Dogwood)—A spreading tree, up to 20 ft. high, with large creamy white floral bracts in May-June. Excellent fall coloration.

CORTADERIA (Pampas Grass)—H.P. Rich light soil, pH 6.5. Yellowish, white, or purple plumes, up to 6 ft. in autumn. Best propagated from root divisions in spring. Should be divided every two or three years. Cut back after flowering.

CORYLUS AVELLANA (Filbert)—H.T. Average friable well drained loam, pH 6.5. Height 12-15 ft. Catkins and flowers are self sterile, requiring two compatible varieties for pollination. Blooms Jan.-Mar. Some combinations are Du Chilly-Nooksack and Barcelona-Daviana. Propagated from seed nuts, cuttings or layers, usually the latter. Excellent edible nuts.

C. Avellana contorta is an ornamental filbert with curiously twisted branches.

C. maxima purpurea is a decorative shrub with purple leaves throughout the summer.

COSMOS (Mexican Aster)—H.H.A. Light soil, pH 6.5. Single, double and semi-double flowers in soft pink, red and orange shades. Height from 2 ft. to 5 ft. Sow in heat during Feb. to bloom July-Aug. Likes sun.

COTONEASTER—H.S. Average soil, pH 5.5-6.0. There are many forms, deciduous and evergreen, prostrate and upright. Most are easily propagated from seed, layers or cuttings. Fine for borders and rockeries.

SOME GOOD HOME GARDEN VARIETIES:

C. horizontalis (Rockspray)—Small rounded leaves on branches with fishbone pattern. Height up to 3 ft. Deciduous, but covered with red berries in winter. Good for foundations, banks, etc.

C. microphylla, thymifolia and *conspicua decora* are dwarf spreading evergreens, with large red or purplish red berries, suitable for the rock garden or border plantings.

C. Dammeri is a prostrate shrub with long trailing branches, medium sized leaves and large red berries in winter. A fine carpeter and rockery plant.

C. Simonsi is an upright shrub, to 8 ft. deciduous, with large orange-red berries in winter. A good hedge plant.

C. Franchetii is upright to 8 ft. with graceful arching branches, silvery evergreen and red berries.

COTTONWOOD (*Populus*)—H.T. Most any type of moist soil, even boggy places, pH 6.0. Many species and varieties, all hardy and fast growing. Mainly propagated from cuttings. Most varieties are too large for small gardens. Widespread root systems. Best suited for shelter belts, screening or high hedges. Good seaside trees.

P. alba pyramidalis (Bolleana) is a pyramidal, white-barked tree, up to 80 ft. with silvery foliage.

P. nigra italica (Lombardy) has stiff erect branches and a narrow habit of growth, to 80 ft., that makes it suitable for high screening or hedging. A subvariety, The Birch-leaved Poplar (*betulifolia*) has smaller leaves, hairy shoots and a burred trunk.

P. canadensis aurea, the Golden-leaved Poplar, is a quick growing variety with yellow leaves.

CRABAPPLE (Malus)—See Part I (C) for fruiting varieties. The flowering varieties like well drained average loam, pH 6.0. They vary in height from 12 ft. to 35 ft. and bloom from late April to May, in white, pink or red. Named varieties propagated by grafting or budding on seedling stocks. Fine ornamental trees.

SOME HOME GARDEN VARIETIES:

M. floribunda is a 15 ft. tree, very floriferous, with deep pink buds opening to pale pink, fading to white. An early bloomer.   Var. Hillieri is a semi-weeper.

M. sylvestris aldenhamensis has purplish leaves, deep red flowers in April-May, and large dark red fruits, suitable for jelly.

M. sylvestris Eleyi also has dark red flowers and large red fruits.

M. sylvestris Lemoinei is a 20 ft. tree with bronzy foliage and purple-red flowers.

M. sylvestris Almey, the Rosybloom Crab, is a 25 ft. tree with flame red flowers and long maroon-colored fruits.

M. sylvestris Profusion is a 20 ft. tree with masses of bright red bloom in early May.

M. sylvestris Dolgo is a vigorous 30 ft. tree with white flowers and bright red fruits, excellent for jelly. A good dual purpose tree.

CRANBERRY (*Vaccinium macrocarpon*)—H.S. Moist, peaty soil, pH 5.0. Highbush varieties grow up to 8 ft. Propagated from cuttings or root divisions. Very specialized growing requirements. Check with agricultural agency before any extensive planting.

CRATAEGUS (Hawthorne)—H.T. Average soil, pH 6.0-7.0. Height varies from 12 ft. to 30 ft. Propagated from seed or graftage. White, pink or scarlet blooms in April-May. Hardy and widely grown for boulevard trees or home garden specimens.
SOME HOME GARDEN VARIETIES:
C. *Oxyacantha* (English Hawthorne)—Best varieties include *flore-plena* (double white), Pauli (Paul's double scarlet), and *flore-plena rosea,* double pink.
C. *Lavallei* (carrieri)—Semi-evergreen, about 25 ft. high, with white flowers in late May, followed by large orange berries.
C. *Toba*—A hardy small hybrid with fragrant light pink flowers and red berries.

CROCUS VERNUS (Crocus)—Hardy corm (bulb). Average well drained soil, pH 6.0. Yellow, white or purple flowers, 4" high, in very early spring. Propagated from offsets. Fine for edging or rockery.

CRYPTOMERIA (Japanese Cedar)—H.T. Moist loam pH 5.5-6.0. An evergreen tree varying from 3 ft. in dwarf varieties to 100 ft. or more in the original C. *japonica*. Seeds of this are easily grown, but variations must be propagated from cuttings.
C. *japonica elegans* is an upright, graceful tree, to 20 feet. with feathery green foliage, bronze in winter. A good lawn tree.
C. *japonica Jindai-Sugi* is a conical, compact tree, up to 30 ft. with green foliage.
C. *japonica Vilmoriniana* is the tiniest globular form, not over 3 ft. Bright green in summer, bronzy in winter, a fine planter box or rockery subject.

CUPRESSUS (Cypress)—H.H.T. Light, well drained soil, pH 6.0 Height varies but doesn't often exceed 30 ft. Many kinds previously named Cupressus are now called Chamaecyparis.
C. *arizonica* is a grey foliaged evergreen that will reach 25 ft. and is often used for hedging. A good seaside plant.
C. *macrocarpa,* the Monterey Cypress, has been widely planted on the Pacific coast as a hedge plant, but hasn't proved hardy in severe winters.
C. *sempervirens,* the Italian Cypress, is a bright green very erect tree, also subject to damage during low temperatures.

CURRANTS, RED AND BLACK—Moist rich loam, pH 6.0-6.5. Propagation is best from hardwood cuttings in fall. Red currants should be pruned to six or seven main branches, with laterals shortened to 2 or 3 inches. Red Lake and Perfection are two good varieties. Fruiting wood on black currants should be cut back after harvesting to new side growths, in order to maintain plenty of new wood. Boskoop Giant and Baldwin are excellent varieties.

CURRANT, FLOWERING (See Alpine Currant).

CYDONIA (Quince)—See *Chaenomeles.*

CYTISUS (See Broom).

DAFFODILS (Narcissi)—H.B. Well drained light loam, pH 6.0. Numerous varieties and colors, from rockery miniatures only a few inches high to the long stemmed King Alfred. May be propagated from seed, but more commonly from offsets. Do well in partial shade. Narcissi include the cluster-flowered jonquils and multi-flowered paperwhites extensively used for forcing. See Part II (H) for planting and variety table.

DAHLIA—H.H.P. Well drained soil with plenty of humus, pH 6.5. Height varies from 4" in miniatures to 5 ft. in border varieties. Many classifications, based on size or formation, including the large flowered Decoratives, Cactus Dahlias, Ball Dahlias, and the small Pompon and Miniature types. Colors in white, yellow, sowing seeds, from cuttings, or most commonly, by root divisions. One of the chrysanthemums, has resulted in hundreds of named varieties. Propagated by sowing seeds, from cuttings, or most commonly, by root divisions. One of the showiest of all border perennials.

DAISY, MICHAELMAS (See Aster).

DAISY, SHASTA (See Chrysanthemum).

DAISY, ENGLISH (*Bellis perennis*)—H.P. Average soil, pH 6.0. Scarlet, pink, or white flowers, 4" high, in early spring, above rosettes of pale green leaves. Propagated from seed or root division. Must be divided often. A showy edging plant.

DAPHNE—Friable, well drained loam, pH 5.5-6.0. From 1 ft. to 5 ft. high, in deciduous and evergreen varieties. Propagated from seed, layers of cuttings. Most varieties prefer shade. Some are exceptionally fragrant.

SOME GOOD HOME GARDEN VARIETIES:

D. Cneorum, the Garland Flower, is a 9-12" evergreen with flat heads of scented pink flowers in May. Likes peaty soil. Fine for planter boxes or rockeries.

D. Mezereum is a shapely deciduous shrub, to 4 ft., with fragrant reddish-purple flowers in Feb. before the leaves appear, followed by bright red poisonous berries.

D. Burkwoodi Somerset is an upright deciduous shrub, to 5 ft., with masses of pale pink fragrant flowers in April-May.

D. Laureola is a large leafed evergreen, around 3 ft. with scented pink flowers in April-May. Prefers some shade.

DAY LILY (*Hemerocallis*)—H.P. Average well-drained soil, pH 6.0 with plenty of humus. Flowers on stems 8" to 3 ft. in June-July. Colors are mostly yellow and red. Foliage resembles grass. Suitable around a pool. Propagated from root divisions.

DELPHINIUM—H.P. Deep, manured well-drained loam, pH 5.5-6.0. Vary in height from 4-6 ft. with long spikes of white, blue, mauve, lavender, indigo and pink. Seed sown in March will produce plants that will flower the following year. Also propagated from root divisions. Plants cut back right after spring flowering often bloom again in late fall. Staking and thinning out of weak shoots are essential for best results. A good mildew resistant strain for the Pacific northwest is the Pacific Giant Hybrids.

DEUTZIA—H.S. Average soil, pH 5.5-6.5. Height varies between 2 ft. and 4 ft. with double white or pink flowers in late May or early June. Propagated from hardwood cuttings. Thin out and prune back old wood after flowering, to avoid legginess and ripen new wood. Prefers sun.

D. gracilis and *D. candelabrum* are two good white flowering kinds, about 4 ft. high, and *D. rosea* and *D. rosea floribunda* are about the same height, with pink flowers.

DIANTHUS (Pinks. Also see Carnations)—H.A. (Japanese Pinks). Light sandy soil, pH 6.5-7.0. Pink, rose, crimson and white, single or double flowers that bloom in July-Aug. from seed sown in March. H.P. (Alpine or Rock Pinks). Light limey soil. Flowers vary from 6" to 12" high in June-July. Propagated from seed, cuttings or root divisions. Fine rock garden or border plants.

D. deltoides, the Maiden Pink, is a low trailing plant with fragrant single rose, red or white flowers.

D. caesius, the Cheddar Pink, is a 6" tufted plant, with rose bloom.

D. alpinus, the Alpine Pink, is a compact plant with large rose colored bloom. All pinks like sun.

DICENTRA (See Bleeding Heart).

DOGWOOD (See Cornus).

DOUGLAS FIR (*Pseudotsuga taxifolia*)—H.T. Light, well-drained moist soil, pH 5.0-6.0. Height 30 to 150 ft. A rapid grower with bluish-green foliage and branches set in regular horizontal whorls. Propagated from seed. A native coastal tree so common and so large that it is not used extensively in home gardens.

127

DUTCHMAN'S PIPE (*Aristolchia Sipho*)—H.C. Average soil, pH 6.0. A hardy climbing plant with large heart shaped leaves and purple, pipe-shaped flowers in summer. Propagated from layers or cuttings.

ECHINOPS (*Globe Thistle*) — H.P. Average light soil, pH 6.0. Grayish serrated leaves and round heads of thistle-like pale blue flowers on 3-4 ft. stems in summer and fall. Best propagated by root division or root cuttings. *E. Ritro* is one of the best varieties. A suitable plant for the herbaceous border.

ELAEAGNUS (Oleaster)—Hardy and half hardy small trees or shrubs, deciduous and evergreen. Average garden loam, pH 6.0. White or cream fragrant flowers in midsummer. Propagated by seed or cuttings.
E. angustifolia (Russian Olive) is a feathery shrub, up to 20 ft. with silvery tapered leaves, small white flowers and yellow fruits.
E. pungens aureo-maculata is an interesting evergreen variety that grows up to 10 ft. with yellow-blotched leaves. Not hardy in colder coastal areas.

ELM (*Ulmus*)—H.T. Average soil, pH 5.5-6.5. Height varies from 25 ft. to 140 ft. Propagated from seed, layers or grafting. On account of the Dutch Elm Disease, planting of European and American varieties is risky. Chinese and Siberian Elms are resistant and one of the best for home gardens is the Siberian Elm, *E. pumila*, which is a graceful tree of around 40 ft. with small pale green leaves. It stands dry conditions well.

ENKIANTHUS CAMPANULATUS — H.S. Average friable lime-free soil, pH 5.5-6.0. Up to 12 ft., erect, with reddish-orange, bell-like flowers in May and brilliant fall coloration of foliage. Propagated from seed or cuttings. Treat like azaleas and rhododendrons.

EPIMEDIUM (See Barrenworts).

ERANTHUS (See Aconite).

ERICA (See Calluna). (

ERIGERON (Fleabane)—H.P. Light rich soil, pH 6.0. Blooms vary from 6" high to 2 ft. according to strain. White, pink, rose, red and violet daisy-like flowers appear in midsummer.
E. speciosus is a favorite for the border, with 2 ft. flowers.
E. aurantiacus and *E. alpinus* are good 9" rockery plants.

ERYTHRONIUM (Dog's-Tooth Violet)—H.B. Sandy loam, with leaf mold or peat, pH 5.5-6.5. *E. oregonum*, or Easter lily, is native to the Pacific coast, and produces a dainty white bloom with yellow anthers during April. Its mottled glossy leaves add to its attractiveness. May be propagated from seed or offsets. A fine rock garden plant.

ESCALLONIA—H.S. Well drained average soil, pH 5.5-6.5. Height 3 ft. to 8 ft., evergreen foliage, with pink, red or white tubular-shaped flowers, June-Aug. Propagated from cuttings or layers. May be used for hedging or wall shrubs. A good shrub for the sea shore. Some good hybrids are E. Apple Blossom, soft pink, C. F. Ball, 10 ft., rosy carmine, Donard Seedling, pink, 6 ft. and Donard Brilliant, 5 ft., red.

ESCHSCHOLZIA (See California Poppy).

EUONYMUS (Spindle Tree)—H.S. Average well drained loam pH 6.0. From 6" to 8 ft. or more, with pink, white or purplish flowers in summer. Its main attractions are not the bloom but the variegated foliage, red fruits and brilliant fall coloring. Propagated from cuttings or layers.
E. europaeus, commonly called the Spindle Tree, is a deciduous shrub of about 15 ft. with red seeds and good fall coloration.
E. alatus, or Winged Burning Bush, is probably the most brilliantly colored of any variety in autumn.
E. Fortunei coloratus, or Purple-leaf Wintercreeper, is an evergreen groundcover, useful beneath trees or where grass won't grow.
E. Fortunei gracilis is a small-leafed variety with variegated evergreen foliage, and climbs by rootlets that attach themselves to walls or supports.

E. Fortunei radicans is similar but creeps along the ground and is useful in rockeries or planters.

EXOCHORDA (Pearl Bush)—H.S. Average loamy soil, pH 6.0-6.5. Height up to 10 ft. Large five-petalled white flowers, April-June. Easily propagated from cuttings. Prefers full sun. A good border shrub.

FAGUS (See Beech).

FERNS—H.P. Moist, but well drained soil, with lots of humus, pH 5.0-5.5. There are many varieties, most of which are greenhouse or indoor types, not hardy for garden planting. There are, however, several ferns native to the Pacific northwest. (See chapter on native plants). Ferns may be propagated from root divisions or spores. Nearly all prefer shade and moist conditions.

FIG (*Ficus carica*)—Tender tree. Light soil, not too rich, pH 6.0-6.5. Needs shelter from the wind even where it is winter hardy. Steady moisture supply essential. Propagated from cuttings or layers. They produce two crops a year but only one ripens. Brown Turkey and Mission are the hardiest for the Pacific northwest.

FILBERT (See *Corylus*).

FIR (See *Abies* and Douglas Fir).

FIRETHORN (*Pyracantha*) — H.H.S. Well drained loamy soil, pH 6.0-6.5. Will reach a height of 10-12 ft. but is usually kept pruned lower. Leaves are evergreen, and masses of tiny white flowers appear in June-July, followed by red, yellow, or orange berries. Propagated from cuttings or layers. Best used against a wall, with a southern exposure.
P. coccinea Lalandii is a hardy variety, with orange-red berries.
P. crenulata Rogersiana is a small-leaved species of good habit, with red berries, and subvarieties with bright yellow berries (*flava*), or rich orange-yellow berries (*aurantiaca*).

FLEABANE (See *Erigeron*).

FLEECE VINE (*Polygonum Aubertii*)—Hardy climber. Average soil, pH 6.0. A twining, fast growing climber with masses of fleecy white flowers in summer. Propagated from layers or cuttings. Suitable for trellises or fences.

FORGET-ME-NOT (*Myosotis*)—H.P. Average soil, pH 6.0-6.5. Height 6" to 18", in blue, white or rose flowers in midsummer. Propagated from seed or root divisions. Blue Ball, Victoria Alba and Carmine King are some good varieties.

FORSYTHIA (Golden Bells)—H.S. Average soil, well drained, pH 6.0. Height 4 feet to 10 feet. Golden yellow flowers appear in March before the leaves are fully out. Best propagated from cuttings. Stands partial shade. Should be pruned back right after flowering.
Forsythia intermedia Lynwood Gold is a broad leaved, large flowered shrub of about 5 feet with deep yellow blooms.
Forsythia intermedia spectabilis is a sturdy well branched shrub, 6-9 feet with rich golden blooms.
Forsythia suspensa is a Chinese variety with arching branches.
Forsythia ovata or Korean Golden Bell, is a compact, dwarf hardy variety with very early primrose yellow flowers.

FUCHSIA—H.H.S. Well drained composted soil, pH 6.0-6.5. There are many choice varieties suitable for greenhouse culture, but for the home garden very few are hardy.
F. magellanica Riccartonii forms a large bush 6-10 feet with red and blue flowers in late summer and fall. Makes an effective hedge. It should be cut back almost to the ground each fall. Easily propagated from cuttings.
F. magellanica pumila (Tom Thumb) is a small leaved dwarf suitable for planter boxes or rockeries.

GAILLARDIA—H.A. Average light loam, pH 6.0. Height 1 ft. to 3 ft. Colors mostly yellow and crimson. Sow outside in April for late summer bloom.
H.P. The perennial is similar to the annual, blooming through midsummer into fall. Propagated from seed or rooted offsets.

GALANTHUS (Snowdrop)—Flowers are single or double, white, or white with a green tinge. Blooming period January-March. Propagated from offsets. Thrives in sun or shade.

GARLAND FLOWER (See Daphne)

GENISTA (See Broom)

GENTIAN (*Gentiana*)—H.P. Light, moist, well drained loam, pH 6.5. Height from 3 in. to 3 ft. Blue, white, yellow and purple flowers, in early summer. Propagated by seed or root divisions.
Variety *G. acaulis* is one of the most intense blues in the floral world. Suitable for edging or a sunny spot in the rockery. Varieties of *G. sino-ornata* prefer a peaty, more acid soil, with ample moisture. The tallest kind, *G. Lutea*, has 3 ft. spikes of yellow star-shaped flowers. A good border plant.

GERANIUM (Crane's-bill)—H.P. Average light soil, pH 6.0. Height varies from 4 in. in rock garden varieties to 2½ ft. for border planting. Easily increased by root division.
G. argenteum a 6 in. rose-pink, with silvery foliage, and *G. sanguineum prostratum*, a 4 in. rose-crimson, are two good plants for the rock garden.
G. pratense, a 2 ft. light blue, is suitable for borders.

GERANIUM (*Pelargonium*)—T.P. Sandy loam, pH 6.0, not too rich or too moist. From dwarfs 8-9 in. high to regular varieties 3-4 ft. There are single, semi-double and double-flowered varieties in white, salmon, pink, crimson, red and purple. For summer bedding, cuttings are taken from old plants in the fall and rooted in damp sand, potted in spring, and set out in May-June. They may be grown from seed as well.
Distinct from the common Zonal Pelargoniums, are the Ivy-leaved types, particularly useful for hanging baskets, and the Regal Pelargoniums (Martha Washington), with large pansy-like blooms in various color combinations.

GEUM (See Avens)

GINKGO BILOBA (Maidenhair Tree)—H.T. Well drained loamy soil, pH 6.0. Average height is around 25 ft. though it will grow taller. Unusual bright green fan-shaped leaves that turn gold in autumn. A good park or garden specimen, not always thrifty in some coastal areas.

GLADIOLUS—H.H.B. Well drained soil, pH 6.0, with lots of humus. Height varies from 6 in. in the miniatures to 4 ft. in standard varieties. Color range is very wide. Blooming period depends on when the corms are set out, though there are early-flowering varieties such as the dwarf *nanus* types, and *Tubergenii* types, and summer-flowering varieties that include all the popular hybrids. (See Part II (H), Bulb Planting Chart).
May be propagated from seed, but most often from corms or bulblets. One of the finest of all flowers for cutting. Need spraying or dusting for thrip, and careful harvesting.

GLEDITSIA (Honey Locust)—H.T. Deep, well drained but moist loam. Some varieties like the Black Locust reach a height of 125 ft. but home garden varieties, like the Moraine Locust (*G. triacanthos*), don't reach half that height. The Sunburst Locust, is a smaller tree again, with bright yellow foliage, and is probably the best variety for home gardens. It is thornless and its serrated yellow leaves make an interesting contrast against a background of evergreens. Keeps its color best in full sun.

GLOBE FLOWER (Trollius)—H.P. Moist, heavy loam, pH 6.0 Eighteen inches to 3 ft. Yellow, orange or lilac flowers bloom in May-June. Propagated from seed or root divisions.

GLOBE THISTLE (See Echinops).

GLORY OF THE SNOW (See Chinodoxa).

GODETIA—H.A. Average soil, pH 6.0-6.5. Height 9 in. to 2 ft. in white, rose, orange, salmon and blue. Sow outdoors in March for summer bloom, or August-September for early spring bloom. Not easily transplanted. Very showy for mass plantings.

GOLDEN BELL (See Forsythia).

GOLDEN CHAIN (Laburnum)—H.T. Average soil, pH 6.0-6.5. Height around 25 ft. Long racemes of yellow flowers appear in May and June, with light green, serrated foliage.

L. alpinum, the Scotch Laburnum, is a shrubby, hardy small tree with yellow blooms in June.

L. Vossi is a hybrid with enormous racemes in late May. Propagation of the commoner kinds is by seeds, but above named varieties are increased by grafting or budding. Seeds and shoots are poisonous.

GOLDENROD (Solidago)—H.P. Average soil, pH 6.0. Height from 10 in. to 2 ft. Golden yellow flowers in masses on long stems in midsummer. Propagated from root divisions.

GOOSEBERRIES—H.S. Rich moist loam, pH 6.0-6.5. Height up to 4 ft. There are two types, the English Gooseberry, *Ribes Grossularia,* with green, white, yellow and red fruits, and the American Gooseberry, *R. hirtellum,* in green, pinkish, and red. Of the English type, the varieties Whitesmith (yellow) and Hansa (green), are two of the most trouble-free for coastal planting, while Oregon Champion (green) and Pixwell (pink) are vigorous, productive American types.

Gooseberries may be propagated from cuttings or layering, with a preference for the latter.

GRAPES—*(Vitis vinifera and vitis Labrusca).* Hardy and half hardy vines that prefer deep fertile sandy loam, with good drainage, pH 6.5. Should be on elevated sites where there is good air circulation.

American Grapes of the Labrusca varieties are easily propagated from hardwood cuttings. See Part I (C) for suitable varieties, and Part I (F) for special pruning requirements.

The European Grapes require long, hot, dry summers, and are not suitable for planting in the Pacific northwest.

GRAPE HYACINTH (Muscari)—H.B. Average soil, pH 6.0. Height 6-8 in., in bright blue or white flowers in early spring. Propagated from offsets. A good subject for edging or naturalizing.

GYPSOPHILA (Baby's Breath)—H.A. Average soil, pH 6.0. Height around 2 ft. White, rose and red flowers in June-July if seed is started indoors in February. H.P. The perennial grows from 6 in. to 3 ft. with single or double blooms in late summer. Propagated from root divisions. Bristol Fairy (white, 3 ft.), Flamingo (lilac pink, 2 ft.) and Rosy Veil (rose pink, 12 in.), are good subjects for the herbaceous border. For the rock garden there are several creeping kinds, such as *G. repens* (white), and *G. repens rosea* (pink).

HAMAMELIS (Witch Hazel)—H.S. Moisty sandy loam, pH 5.5-6.0. Height up to 10 ft. but usually stays smaller. Fragrant golden flowers, December-February. Propagated from layers or cuttings.

H. mollis brevipetala is a Chinese variety with orange-yellow bloom and very large leaves.

H. japonica arborea is a wide-spreading Japanese variety with either yellow or reddish flowers. A good woodland shrub.

HAWTHORNE (See Crataegus).

HAZEL (See Corylus).

HEATH (See Calluna).

HEDERA (Ivy)—H.C. Average soil, pH 5.5-6.0, sun or shade. provided there is ample moisture. Easily propagated by cuttings or layers. Widely used as an evergreen wall cover or groundcover.

Hedera Helix, English Ivy, may have either large or small leaves, with subvarieties having gold or silver variegations.

Hedera Helix hibernica, Irish Ivy, has large pointed leaves.

Hedera Helix baltica has green and white foliage.

Hedera colchica dentata has large green and yellow leaves, and is somewhat tender.

HELIANTHEMUM (Sun Rose)—H.P. Sandy loam, pH 6.0. Height 9 in. to 3 ft. Yellow, pink, red, salmon or white flowers, May-July. If cut back after flowering it will often flower again later in the fall. Propagated from seed or cuttings. A good rockery or border plant that stands drought well. Some good named varieties of *Helianthemum nummularium* are The Bride (white), Fireball (red), Butter and Eggs (orange), and Wisley Primrose.

HELIANTHUS (Sunflower)H.A. Good rich loam, pH 6.0-6.5. Height 4 ft. to 8 ft. Golden yellow or reddish blooms in midsummer if planted outdoors early April. H.P. The perennial makes a fine yellow cut flower. Propagated from seed or root divisions.

HELICHRYSUM (Everlasting Flower)—H.A. Average light, well-drained soil, pH 6.5. Height 1 ft. to 3 ft. in a wide range of colors. Seed sown outdoors in late March will bloom in midsummer, when the flower heads are often cut and dried for inside decoration.
There is also a hardy perennial *H. arenarium,* 10 in. high, with bright yellow flowers.

HELLEBORUS (See Christmas Rose).

HEMEROCALLIS (See Day Lily).

HEMLOCK, WESTERN—(*Tsuga heterophylla*)—H.T. Average moist soil, pH 5.5-6.0. A quick growing native conifer, up to 150 ft., that tolerates shade well, and stands clipping when used for large hedges. Propagated from seeds.

HEPATICA (Liverwort)—H.P. Rich peaty soil, pH 5.5-6.0. Height of bloom from 6 in. to 12 in. Red, blue or white, single or double flowers resembling the Buttercup, appear in early spring. Propagated from seeds or root divisions. A good subject for shady nooks in the rock garden.

HIBISCUS (See Althaea).

HOLLYHOCK—H.P. Average soil, pH 6.0. Height 4 ft. to 10 ft. Wide range of colors, flowering in late summer. Chaters Double Mixed grows to about 5 ft. Propagated from seed or root divisions. Good background plant in perennial borders.

HOLLY (*Ilex*)—H.T. Light moist loam, with plenty of humus, pH 5.5-6.0. Height varies from 4 ft. in dwarf Japanese varieties to 30 ft. or more in English and American varieties. Mainly propagated from cuttings. Can be grown from seed, but it takes a long time to germinate and there is a high percentage of male trees (without berries). Many named varieties are available.
Ilex Aquifolium, the English Holly, averages around 25 ft. It has dark green prickly leaves, with bright red berries. The traditional Christmas holly. Also used for hedging. There are several excellent varieties of English Holly with gold or silver variegations in the foliage. A hybrid, J. C. Tol, is self-pollinating.
Ilex opaca, the American Holly, is not as attractive as the English holly, but is hardier.
Ilex crenata, the Japanese Holly, is a compact shrub with smooth leaves and black berries, that stands shearing well and is suitable for rock gardens and foundation planting.

HONESTY (Money Plant)—H.B. Average light soil, pH 6.0. Height 2-3 ft. Seed sown in April or May and transplanted in August will bloom the following year. Blooms are pink, white or purple, followed by seed pods the size of half dollars.

HONEYSUCKLE (Lonicera)—Hardy shrub and hardy climber. Average soil, pH 6.0. The bush honeysuckles vary in height from 4 ft. to 10 ft. Blooms are cream or creamy-yellow in May-June. There are a few varieties with white or pink flowers.
L. fragrantissima is a Chinese shrub 6-8 ft. with fragrant cream-colored flowers on leafless branches in early spring.
L. tatarica is slightly larger, with pink bloom in May.
L. nitida is a compact evergreen bush, 4-5 ft. that makes an excellent low hedge.
The climbing honeysuckle, like the shrub, will grow in most any soil and is easily propagated from cuttings or layers.
L. Caprifolium has creamy, very fragrant flowers in May.
L. Heckrottii Goldflame is an everblooming pink with large blooms.
L. japonica Halliana is an evergreen with yellowish fragrant flowers in May. A good ground cover.

HORSE CHESNUT (See Aesculus).

HYACINTHUS (Hyacinth)—H.B. Well-drained loamy soil, pH 6.0-6.5. Propagated from offsets. Likes the sun. For varieties and planting see Part II (H)—Bulb Planting Chart.

HYDRANGEA—Hardy and half hardy shrubs and climbers. Rich, moist, well-drained loam, pH 5.5-6.5. Height varies from 3 ft. to 12 ft. according to variety, and color varies according to soil acidity as well as variety. Propagated from cuttings.

H. hortensis varieties are the most commonly known hydrangeas, with large blue, pink or white flower heads in June-July. Acid soils keep the blooms blue, while limed soils favor pink and red colors. Prune out old flowering shoots right after blooming.

H. arborescens grandiflora (Hills of Snow) is a 4-5 ft. shrub with large creamy-white blooms July-September.

H. paniculata grandiflora (Peegee Hydrangea) is a 6-10 ft. shrub with clusters of tapered white flowers in August, which turn pinkish as they age.

H. petiolaris (scandens) is a leaf-losing climber from Japan, very useful for covering walls, particularly in the shade.

HYPERICUM (St. John's-wort)—H.S. Average to poor light soil, pH 6.5. Height varies from 1 ft. to 4 ft. Flowers mostly yellow, blooming in midsummer. Propagated from layers or cuttings. Stands drought conditions and seaside planting.

H. calycinum (Aaron's-Beard) is a good low groundcover for banks in sun or semi-shade. Should be sheared back each spring.

H. patulum Henryi is a 3 ft. shrub with bright yellow bloom.

IBERIS (Candytuft)—H.A. Light loam, pH 6.0-6.5. Up to 1 ft. in mixed colors. Sow in March outdoors to bloom in June-July. Good border plant and cut flower.

H.P. The perennial likes the same type of soil and is an excellent edging or rockery plant. Propagated from seed or cuttings.

I. sempervirens is a low small-leaved evergreen with white or lilac bloom in early spring.

ILEX (See Holly).

IRIS—H.P. Average soil, pH 6.0-6.5. Preferably on the light side for bulbous varieties and heavier loams for rhizome rooted types. Height varies from 6 in. to 4 ft. Propagated from seed, offsets or rhizomes.

Iris Germanica or Bearded Iris is rhizome rooted, and comes in a wide range of colors, with dwarf types (*I. pumila,* 10 in.) flowering around the first of April, and taller types, 18 in. - 4 ft., blooming a month later. There is a wide range of colors in both with many named varieties.

Iris Kaempferi or Japanese Iris is fibrous rooted, with grasslike foliage, and likes moisture. White, blue or red flowers appear in June.

English, Spanish and Dutch Irises are bulbous kinds very popular for greenhouse forcing, but equally valuable for planting in borders or rockeries for show or cutting. There are many choice named varieties.

IVY (See Hedera).

JASMINE (Jasminum)—H.S. Average soil, pH 6.0. From a 3 ft. shrub to a 10 ft. vine-like climber. Yellow, pink or white flowers in winter or summer, according to variety. Propagated from cuttings or layers. Likes full sun.

Jasminum nudiflorum, or Winter Jasmine, is a Chinese variety with small yellow blooms, November through February, and is usually trained against a wall or trellis. Cut back flowering shoots right after blooming.

J. officinale is a vigorous climbing plant with fragrant white blooms in June-July.

JUDAS TREE (See *Cercis*).

JUGLANS (Walnut)—H.T. Deep well-drained loam, pH 6.5. Height up to 80 ft. Most varieties are self-pollinating. Propagated from seeds or graftage. All pruning should be done between June and Christmas to avoid bleeding.

Juglans regia (Persian or English Walnut) is commonly grown for commercial walnuts. Varieties Broadview, Franquette and Mayette are hardy in the Pacific northwest.

Juglans nigra (Eastern Black Walnut) is a highly prized timber tree, but also produces fine-flavored nuts. Huber, Ohio and Thomas are good named varieties. *Juglans cinera* (Butternut) produces oily, richly-flavored nuts as well as satin-like wood, highly prized for cabinets.

J. Sieboldiana cordiformis (Japanese Walnut or Heartnut) is a beautiful fast-growing shade tree, up to 50 ft., with clusters of tasty, heart-shaped nuts.

JUNIPERUS (Juniper)—H.S. Average soil, pH 5.5-6.5. Over fifty variations in size, form and color, make the junipers one of the most valuable classes of ornamental evergreens. Propagated from seed, layers or cuttings.

UPRIGHT VARIETIES

J. Virginiana Burki, Canaertii, and *Hillii* are dense pyramidal forms, with green or glaucous foliage that becomes plum-colored in winter. Will reach 20 ft. if not pruned.

J. communis hibernica (Irish Juniper) and *J. communis suecica* (Swedish Juniper), have a stiff columnar habit, and are fairly slow growing, up to 10 ft. Good foundation plants.

J. communis compressa is a tight-growing, very columnar shrub up to 5 ft. A good rockery or planter box subject.

J. sinensis stricta (Spiny Greek Juniper) is cone-shaped, bluish-green, with sharp leaf points. Slow growing, to 10 ft.

SEMI-PROSTRATE VARIETIES

J. squamata Meyeri is a blue-foliaged, informal shrub, up to 6 ft. with graceful arching branches.

J. Sabina (Savin juniper) is a hardy, vigorous shrub with ascending green branches (4 ft.) and a pungent odor. Spreads 8-10 ft.

J. sinensis Blaaw's Variety is a bushy plant up to 5 ft. with soft bluish-colored sprays of foliage.

PROSTRATE VARIETIES

J. sinensis Pfitzeriana forms an attractive, spreading, medium-green, shrub, very useful for banks and large rockeries. Not over 3 ft. high, but with a diameter of 10 ft. or more. The golden form, *Pfitzeriana aurea* grows slightly smaller. There is also a dwarf variation, *compacta,* for smaller rockeries or planters.

J. Sabina tamariscifolia (Tamarix Savin) is a spreading, deep green, feathery shrub, compact, not over 24 in. above the ground.

J. horizontalis (Creeping Juniper) is an excellent ground cover, and has many variations, including *J. horizontalis Douglasii* (Waukegan Juniper) with beautiful steel-blue foliage, and *J. horizontalis glauca,* (Bar Harbour) with blue-grey foliage in summer and plum-colored foliage in winter.

KALMIA (Mountain Laurel)—H.S. Moist peaty soil, pH 5.0-5.5. Grows 2 ft. to 15 ft. according to variety. Pink, rosy-red or white flowers appear in early summer. The evergreen leaves resemble those of rhododendrons. Propagated from seed, layers or cuttings.

K. latifolia has shiny evergreen leaves with racemes of pink, bell-shaped flowers in late May and early June. Average height 8-10 ft.

K. angustifolia, the Sheep Laurel, is a 2 ft. to 4 ft. evergreen rose-red flowers in June. *K. polifolia* is a dwarf small-leaved shrub with purplish-pink flowers in May. Best suited for bog gardens.

KERRIA JAPONICA—H.S. Loamy, fairly rich soil, pH 6.0. Button-like yellow flowers bloom along the light green stems in May. The double-flowered variety, *flore pleno,* reaches 8-10 ft. in height. Variety *variegata* has silver-variegated leaves. Propagated easily from layers or root divisions. Old flowering wood should be pruned out right after blooming.

KNIPHOFIA (Tritoma, Torch Lily or Poker Plant)—H.P. Well-drained, manured soil, pH 6.0. Brilliant orange, red and yellow flower spikes on 2-5 ft. stems, June-Sept. Best propagated from root divisions in spring. A showy addition to a border or rockery.

KOLKWITZIA (See Beauty Bush).

LABURNUM (See Golden Chain).

LARKSPUR—H.A. Average soil, pH 6.0. Height around 4 ft. Blue, white, rose and violet flowers appear on long stems in midsummer from seed sown outdoors in early March. Seed sown in Sept. will flower the next May.

LAUREL (*Prunus laurocerasus*)—H.S. Average moist soil, pH 5.5-6.0. Broad, shiny evergreen leaves, white flowers in summer and black or purple berries in winter. Commonly used for hedges up to 10 ft. Propagated from cuttings.
P. Reynvani has deep green leaves, is hardy, and makes an excellent specimen shrub of 6-8 ft.
P. Zabeliana is a low spreading plant with long narrow leaves and arching branches. Good for foundation planting, even as a groundcover.

LAUREL, PORTUGUESE (*Prunus lusitanica*)—A strong growing shrub, up to 10 ft., with medium-sized evergreen leaves on reddish stems, racemes of white flowers in midsummer, and purple berries in winter. May be used for hedging or as a large specimen evergreen.

LAURISTINUS (*Viburnum Tinus*)—H.S. Average light soil, pH 5.5-6.0. Up to 10 ft. high. Evergreen oblong leaves and flat clusters of pink-budded flowers that open white Jan.-March. May be used as a hedge or an ornamental bush. Propagated from layers or cutting. A good foundation shrub.

LAVANDULA (Lavender)—H.S. Light, well-drained rich loam, pH 6.5. From 9 in. to 4 ft. high. Easily propagated from root divisions in fall.
L. officinalis, the English Lavender, grows up to 4 ft. and needs hard pruning after flowering to keep from getting woody. There is a white bloom as well as the ordinary mauve color.
L. officinalis nana, sometimes called Dwarf French Lavender only grows a foot high, and the Munstead Dwarf about 18 in., with early dark lavender-blue flowers.
Besides being useful for border plants or low hedges, the dried flowers are widely used for perfume sachets.

LEUCOTHOE CATESBAEI—H.S. Well-drained peaty soil, pH 5.0-5.5. A 3 ft. arching shrub with lily-of-the-valley type of white flowers in May. Glossy evergreen leaves take on fine autumn coloration. Propagated from cuttings. Likes shade. Very similar to some types of Andromeda.

LEWISIA—H.P. Well-drained sandy soil, pH 6.0-6.5. Height 6 in. to 12 in. according to variety. Fleshy evergreen leaves form a rosette from which starry pink, cream or apricot flowers appear in May-June. Excellent alpine plant for the rock garden. Propagated from seed or root divisions.
Lewisia Heckneri has dark pink flowers on 12 in. stems in May.
Lewisia Howellii is a fine plant with waved leaves and apricot-pink blooms on 9 in. stems.
Lewisia Tweedyi has broad leaves with large (2 in.) waxlike apricot-colored blooms on 6 in. stems in May-June.

LIGUSTRUM (Privet)—H.S. Moist but well-drained soil, pH 6.5. Height varies from 4 ft. to 10 ft. according to variety. Used extensively for hedging. Some varieties are evergreen. Propagated from seed or root divisions, but more commonly from cuttings.
L. vulgare atrovirens, the Common or English Privet, grows up to 10 ft. and usually stays evergreen in the Pacific northwest. Purple berries in winter.
L. vulgare lodense is a glossy-leaved evergreen suitable for hedges up to 4 ft.
L. ovalifolium, the California Privet, makes a 12 ft. bush if left unclipped, but is usually found as a hedge. It bears white slightly malodorous flowers in midsummer and in normal winters holds its leaves. The variety *aureo-marginatum,* Golden Privet, makes a very bright specimen in the shrub border.
L. amurense, the Amur Privet, is similar to California Privet, and very hardy.
All varieties of privet stand seaside planting well.

LILAC (Syringa)—H.S. Average loam or clay-loam with lots of humus, pH 6.5. Height up to 15 ft. White, cream, lilac, crimson or purple blooms in May-June. Named varieties best propagated from layers or by grafting on Common Lilac or Privet rootstock. Flower heads should be removed after blooming, and old or weak wood pruned out at that time.

S. persica, the Persian Lilac, is a shapely bush about 5 ft. high with lavender-pink trusses in May. A fine border shrub.

S. vulgaris, the Common Lilac, is a large shrub that grows to 15 ft. bearing large clusters of white or mauve fragrant flowers in May-June.

S. sinensis, the Rouen Lilac, is a cross between the two previously mentioned varieties, and grows around 8 ft. high, with lilac-blue single flowers in May.

The French Hybrids are varieties of the Common Lilac, and come with single or double flowers in April-May.

SINGLES	DOUBLES
Marie Legraye (White)	Mme. Lemoine (White)
Hugo Koster (Dark blue)	Michael Buchner (Lilac blue)
Souv. de L. Spath (Purple)	Chas. Joly (Dark reddish-purple)

The Preston Hybrids are a fine group of hardy lilacs resulting from crossing two Chinese kinds, *S. villosa* and *S. reflexa.* They bear large fragrant pyramidal spikes of flowers in June. Hiawatha (rose), Coral (pink), and Redwine (red), are good examples.

The Clark Hybrids are another fine group with very large trusses, and florets often exceeding an inch across. Clarke's Giant (blue), Esther Staley (pink), and Monique Lemoine (white), are three good varieties. Primrose is the only yellow lilac yet developed.

LILIUM (Lily)—H.B. Light loam, pH 5.5-6.5. Height varies from 1 ft. to 10 ft., according to variety, and bulbs vary in size from 1/2 in. diameter to the size of a large orange. May be propagated from seed, offsets (scales) or stems. See Part II (H)— Bulb Information chart. Excellent for cut flowers and border planting. Most varieties tolerate partial shade. There are so many hybrids now available, in a startling array of colors and flowers forms that it is not possible to list them here.

LILY OF THE VALLEY (*Convallaria majalis*)—H.P. Average moist soil, pH 6.0. White or pink-tinged bell-like flowers in April-May, about 8 in. high. Highly fragrant. Propagated from seed or root divisions. A useful ground cover in shade.

LILY OF THE VALLEY SHRUB (See Andromeda).

LINDEN (Tilia)—H.T. Loamy moist soil, pH 6.0-6.5. Height up to 100 ft. Propagated from seed or by graftage. Won't stand drought well.

T. cordata, the Little Leaf Linden, is an excellent pyramid shade tree, up to 50 ft. high with a 40 ft. spread, and fragrant yellowish flowers in June-July.

T. platyphyllos, the European Linden, is a tall large-leaved shade tree with fragrant flowers in June. Often used for avenue planting.

T. petiolaris, the Weeping White Linden, will reach 50 ft. but usually stays smaller, and has a very graceful habit with its very large green leaves on pendulous branches.

LIQUIDAMBAR STYRACIFLUA (Sweet Gum)—H.T. Moist, loamy soil, pH 6.0. Height up to 100 ft. but usually stays smaller. A shapely pyramidal tree with glossy green maple-like leaves that color beautifully in autumn. Propagated by seed or by graftage.

LIRIODENDRON TULIPIFERA (American Tulip Tree)—H.T. Will grow up to 100 ft., but usually stays much smaller. A shapely, quick-growing tree with fiddle-shaped leaves and greenish-yellow tulip-like flowers in June. Some varieties have variegated foliage, and one variety, *fastigatum,* has a compact columnar growth habit like the Lombardy Poplar. Propagated by seeds or graftage. A very beautiful tree for large gardens.

LOBELIA—H.A. Rich, well-drained soil, pH 6.0-6.5. Height 6 in. Seed sown in heat in February will bloom outdoors in July-Aug. A fine edging plant in white, light or dark blue, and crimson.

H.P.—The perennials prefer rich loam and will grow to 3 ft. They are erect stout-stemmed plants with reddish or green leaves and pink, blue or scarlet flowers. Ideally suited for cool Pacific northwest temperatures.

LOCUST, SUNBURST (See Gleditsia).

LOGANBERRY (See Blackberry)—A half hardy cane fruit that grows best in well-drained loam, pH 6.0. Propagated from tip layers. Cut out old fruiting canes after harvest. Don't tie up new cane growth until the following March. Fine fruit for pies, jam, canning or freezing.

LONICERA (See Honeysuckle).

LUPINUS (Lupine)—H.A. Fairly rich, loamy soil, pH 6.0. Height up to 4 ft., in blue, white, yellow, pink and purple. Seed sown outdoors in March will bloom in June-July. Sun or partial shade.
H.P.—The Russell strain of herbaceous lupines grows up to 4 ft. in a wide range of colors. Fine subject for the background of a perennial border. Prune back year-old shoots about half way in Feb.-March.

MAGNOLIA—H.T. Moist, rich, sandy loam, pH 5.5. Height 10 ft. to 50 ft., according to variety. Good lawn and border specimens. Propagated from seed, layering or grafting.
M. denudata, the Yulan Magnolia, grows to 30 ft. with pure white blooms, very early.
M. Soulangeana, the Saucer Magnolia, is the most commonly known in the Pacific northwest. Large saucer-like flowers, pinkish-purple outside, white inside, appear in May, before the foliage. Variety nigra has purple flowers. Height averages 20 ft.
M. stellata, the Star Magnolia, forms a shapely bush 10-15 ft., and produces abundant star-shaped, sweetly-scented white or pale pink flowers in April, before the leaves appear.
M. virginiana, the Sweet Bay Tree, is a tall glossy-leaved partly evergreen tree with creamy-white fragrant flowers in June.
M. grandiflora, the Southern Magnolia, is a 50 ft. evergreen with large leathery leaves and lemon-scented creamy-white large flowers in June. Not hardy in some Pacific coast areas.

MAIDENHAIR TREE (See Ginkgo).

MALUS (See Apple, Crabapple).

MAPLE (See Acer).

MARGUERITE (See Chrysanthemum).

MARIGOLD—H.H.A. Average soil, pH 6.0-6.5. Height varies from 6 in. to 36 in. Colors mostly yellow, red, orange, or variations. Seed sown in heat during March will bloom in June-July. Tall or dwarf African varieties have blooms resembling pompom chrysanthemums. The tall or dwarf French Marigold may be single or double small flowers in many color combinations. Fine edging and border plants.

MAY TREE (See Cratageus).

MECONOPSIS (Blue Poppy)—H.P. Rich, sandy soil, pH 6.0. Grows 3-5 ft. and blooms in midsummer. Likes shelter from strong wind and full sun. Propagated from seed sown in autumn.

MEXICAN ASTERS (See Cosmos).

MEXICAN ORANGE (See Choisya).

MIGNONETTE—H.A. Light loam, pH 6.5. Grows 12 in. high. If sown outdoors in March it will bloom in late June. Highly fragrant.

MOCK ORANGE (Philadelphus)—H.S. Average soil, pH 6.0-6.5. Height varies from 5 ft. to 10 ft. Single or double, white, scented flowers appear in May-June. Easily propagated from hardwood cuttings. Adaptable to sun or shade. Very useful for border planting. Many named hybrids have been developed from the variety P. coronarius.
P. hybrid Atlas is a large (3 in.) single white. Upright, 8 ft.
P. hybrid Belle Etoile is a single white with a maroon centre and a spicy scent. About 8 ft.
P. hybrid Manteau de Hermine is a 4 ft. dwarf with creamy-white very fragrant flowers.
P. hybrid Snowflake is a fragrant double white, to 5 ft.
P. hybrid Virginale is a semi-double fragrant white, to 10 ft.

137

MONKEY PUZZLE (See Araucaria).

MONKSHOOD (See Aconitum).

MONTBRETIA—H.B. Light, well-drained soil, pH 6.0. Yellow, red, or orange flowers on spikes up to 3 ft. high in June-July. Best propagated from offsets. Favor a sunny position.

MONTEREY CYPRESS (See *Cupressus*).

MORNING GLORY (See Convolvulus).

MOUNTAIN ASH (*Sorbus*)—H.T. Average well-drained soil, pH 6.0. Creamy-white flowers appear in flat clusters in May, followed by orange, red, yellow or pink berries. Height varies from 25-40 ft.

S. Aucuparia, the Rowan Tree, or European Mountain Ash, is best known and is widely planted as a boulevard or border tree. Berries are red or orange-red and are a favorite fruit of birds. Subvarieties have yellow berries, or white berries tipped red, and variations in habit and foliage.

S. americana, the American Mountain Ash, is a small tree up to 25 ft., with a stiff growth habit, large pinnate leaves and red berries.

S. aria majestica, the Whitebeam Tree, is somewhat taller than those previously mentioned, with a wide spread, and the foliage is not divided and is silvery underneath. Dense white flower heads appear in May, followed by large orange and red oval berries.

MOUNTAIN LAUREL (See Kalmia).

MUSCARI (See Grape Hyacinth).

MYOSOTIS (See Forget-Me-Not).

NARCISSI (See Daffodil).

NASTURTIUM—T.A. Average soil, pH 6.0. Height of bush variety varies from 1 ft. to 2 ft. and the climbing variety reaches 3 ft. Colors are yellow, red, and maroon, with variations, in single or double blooms. See sown outdoors in March will bloom in June-July. The Gleam Hybrids are very satisfactory.

NECTARINE—H.T. Medium, well-drained loam, pH 6.0-6.5. The tree is identical to the peach and the fruit is the same, without fuzz. Like peaches, bloom is subject to early frost in less sheltered areas. Propagated from grafting. Nectacrest, Gower, and Stanwick are a few good varieties.

NEMESIA—T.A. Average soil, with plenty of humus, pH 6.0. Four inches to 15 inches high. Many lovely colors. Seed sown in February indoors and set out in May will bloom June-July.

NEPETA (Catmint)—H.P. Light soil, pH 6.5. Height 12-18 in. Grey foliage, with graceful sprays of blue or lavender flowers in summer. Easily propagated from root divisions in April. A good rockery plant.

NICOTIANA (Flowering Tobacco Plant)—H.A. Average soil, pH 6.0. Height 2-3 ft. White, cream, pink, purple and crimson star-shaped flowers. Very fragrant.

NYMPHAEA (Water Lily)—Rich, loamy soil, pH 6.0, with water above. Plant rhizomes in wire basket in spring, and sink where wanted. There are many hardy hybrids in red, pink, yellow and apricot. They bloom in June-July. Best propagated by division of rhizomes in spring.

OAK (Quercus)—H.T. Loam or clay-loam, pH 5.5-6.5. Height averages 35-50 ft. There are many types, deciduous and evergreen, but few are suited for the average garden. Propagated from seed or graftage.

Q. borealis maxima rubra, the American Red Oak, is a rapid growing tall tree, up to 100 ft. with good leaf coloration.

Q. palustris, the Pin Oak, is a fine pyramid tree, around 50 ft. with slightly drooping branches, and brilliant fall leaf coloration. A fine shade tree.

Q. coccinea splendens, the Scarlet Oak, is a slow-growing tree, up to 50 ft., with the most brilliant leaf coloration of any type. It grows on drier soils than most. Good seaside tree.

Q. robur fastigiata, the Pyramidal English Oak, is a columnar tree, up to 40 or 50 ft. for use where space is at a premium. The subvariety *Concordia* has distinctly golden foliage.

Q. garryana, the Garry Oak, or Oregon Oak, is a native tree in a limited area of the Pacific northwest. It varies from 25 ft. to 75 ft. in height in a very irregular branching habit. Stands drought conditions and seaside planting.

OLEARIA (Daisy Shrub)—H.S. Sandy soil, pH 6.0. Height 4 ft. to 15 ft. Evergreen leaves with masses of white flowers in summer. Propagated from cuttings. Likes sun and is a good seaside shrub.

O. Haastii is a round 4 ft. shrub, with small, leathery green leaves, silvery under-neath, and clusters of small white flowers in July-Aug. May be used for a low hedge.

O. traversi is a fast growing, large-leaved evergreen up to 15 ft. A good windbreak.

OSMUNDA (See Fern).

PACHYSANDRA TERMINALIS (Japanese Spurge)—H.S. Moist, well-drained soil, pH 6.0. Small white flowers in July, with lustrous evergreen foliage. About 6 in. high. Does best in shade. Propagated from cuttings. A good ground cover.

PAEONIA (Peony)—H.P. Rich, well-drained soil, pH 6.0-6.5. Height 2-4 ft. Bloom in May-June. Many named varieties, single or double. Propagated from seed or root divisions, usually the latter. They thrive in sun or part shade and are one of the most popular of all border perennials.

MAY FLOWERING PEONIES
Alba Plena—Double pure white
Rosea Plena—Double pink
Rubra Plena—Double dark red.

JUNE FLOWERING PEONIES
Festiva Maxima—A fine early double white, flecked crimson.
Jules Elie—An early flowering double pink, fine for cutting.
Karl Rosenfield—A fine mid-season crimson.

JAPANESE PEONIES—May-June flowering
Hakodate—Pure white, pink stigma
Mr. G. F. Hemerik—Pink with large yellow centre
Mikado—Deep crimson.

PAEONIA SUFFRUTICOSA ARBOREA (Tree Peony)—H.S. Average well-drained loam, with plenty of humus. Height 3-5 ft. Single or double, large white, pink, red, yellow or purple blooms in May-June. Best propagated by root graftage.

PAMPAS GRASS (See Cortaderia).

PANSY—Hardy biennial. Average moist loam, pH 6.0. Height 6 in. Wide color range. Seed sown in July, transplanted in September will bloom the following April. Prefers shade. To extend bloom, keep removing dead flower heads. The Swiss Giants are one of many fine strains.

PAPAVER (Poppy)—H.A. Prefers sandy loam, pH 6.5. Height from 6 in. to 4 ft. Sow outdoors from March onwards, for midsummer bloom. Shirley Mixed are a good strain, 1½ ft.

H.P. The perennial Oriental Poppy (*Papaver orientale*) is a showy border plant that bears brilliant flowers in early summer. Doesn't like being disturbed after planting. May be grown easily from seed.

H.B. The Iceland Poppy (*Papaver nudicaule*), is a fine flower in a large rockery. White, orange and yellow blooms appear in May and June from seed sown the previous summer. (See *Meconopsis* for the Himalayan Blue Poppy).

PARTHENOCISSUS (Boston Ivy, Virginia Creeper)—H.C. Average well-drained soil, pH 6.0. Popular climbers for walls and trellises. Propagated from cuttings or layers. Foliage has brilliant fall coloration.

P. tricuspidata (Boston Ivy)—Clings to walls with sucker-like tendrils.

P. quinquefolia (Virginia Creeper)—More useful against the trunks of trees, or on trellises, as it doesn't cling.

PEA, SWEET—H.A. Rich, well-drained loam, pH 6.5-7.0. Height from 8 in. in the bush type to 10 ft. in climbing varieties. Seed should be inoculated with nitrogen before being planted. Sow outdoors in late February. The Spencer or Cuthbertson strains offer many choice color variations. Soil must be kept moist and fertile.

PEACH, FRUIT—H.H.T. Prefers light rich loam, pH 6.5-7.0. Must be pruned each year to keep open, and sprayed with a fungicide in December-January to prevent leaf curl. Propagated by budding on seedling peach rootstocks. Dwarf varieties are budded on Kroojen plum understocks. (See Part I (C) for varieties).

PEACH, FLOWERING (*Prunus persica*)—Light loam, pH 6.5-7.0. White, pink or red flowers in early spring on trees that grow up to 15 ft. Pink charming is a good deep pink, Iceberg a good white, and Cardinal is a double rose-crimson. Fine border trees in sheltered areas.

PEAR, FRUIT (Pyrus)—H.T. Will do well on moist clay-loam, pH 6.0. Needs constant pruning to keep height down. Standard varieties are budded on pear seedling stocks, dwarf varieties on quince stocks. (See Part I (C) for variety planting table).

PEARLBUSH (See Exochorda).

PELARGONIUM (See Geranium).

PENSTEMON—H.P. Light sandy loam, pH 6.5. Height 6 in. to 4 ft. A fairly wide range of colors in June-July. Propagated from seed, or fall cuttings. A useful plant for the perennial border in full sun. The Hartwegi Mixed strain grows about 3 ft. *P. Davidsonii*, a 6 in. red dwarf, is an excellent alpine.

PERIWINKLE (Vinca Minor or Myrtle)—H.P. Average soil, pH 6.0. Height 1-2 ft. Blue, purple and white flowers in midsummer. Foliage evergreen, dark and lustrous. Propagated from seed or cuttings. A good ground cover in sun or shade.

PERNETTYA MUCRONATA (Prickly Heath)—H.S. Moist, peaty loam, pH 5.0. Height 2 to 5 ft. Small, leathery evergreen leaves, with white flowers in May, followed by pink, white, red or purple berries in winter. A useful rockery or planter box subject. Propagated from layers or cuttings.
Bell's Seedling is a self-fertile variety with red berries.
Pink Bell is a self-fertile pink-berried variety.
Most other varieties require both male and female plants to set berries.

PETUNIA—A tender perennial treated as an annual. Light rich loam, pH 6.0-6.5. Height 1-2 ft. Seed sown in heat during February will bloom in June-July. Many fine colors have been developed through hybridization, both in single and double blooms, plain or ruffled. The new F1 Hybrids are exceptionally showy and the Fringed California Giants produce magnificent double blooms. There is no better annual for mass plantings in borders in full sun.

PHILADELPHUS (See Mock Orange).

PHLOX DRUMMONDI—H.A. Average moist soil, pH 6.0-6.5. Height 6 in. to 18 in. Seed sown outdoors in April will bloom in July. Wide color range. Likes sun.

PHLOX PANICULATA—H.P. Average soil, pH 6.0-6.5. Height 2-3 ft. Many Named varieties in a wide selection of color combinations. Blooms in June-July. Propagated from summer cuttings or root divisions. A fine border perennial, best planted in groups.
Spitfire—Salmon red, doesn't fade.
Sweetheart—Rose pink, white eye.
Blue Moon—Lilac blue.
Snowdrift—White.

PHLOX SUBULATA (Creeping Phlox)—H.P. Average soil, pH 6.5. Height 4-6 in. Blooms in April-May. Propagated from summer cuttings or root divisions. A good rockery plant, often used as a groundcover, especially in partial shade.
G. F. Wilson—Lavender blue.
Vivid—Deep rose.
Longiflora—Lilac pink.

PICEA (Spruce)—H.T. Moist, light loam, pH 5.0-6.0. Height from 6 ft. to 100 ft. or more. Propagated from seed, cuttings or graftage. Many choice ornamental varieties.

SOME HOME GARDEN VARIETIES:

P. Engelmanni (Engelman's Spruce)—A symmetrical, bluish-green conifer that grows up to 100 ft.

P. pungens glauca (Colorado Blue Spruce)—A shapely tree with bluish foliage, slow growing to 70 ft. A good hedge tree.

P. pungens glauca Kosteriana (Koster's Blue Spruce)—The well known grafted blue spruce. Slow growing to 60 ft. Beautiful soft blue color. A fine specimen for the larger garden.

P. excelsa conica (*Norway Spruce*)—A dense, light green, conical shaped tree, with long pendulous cones. Average height on the Pacific coast is around 30 ft. A fine tree for a shelter belt or high hedge.

P. excelsa ohlendorffi is a compact, dwarf form of Norway Spruce that makes a 4 ft. dense green mound.

P. excelsa nidiformis (Nest Spruce)—A dense green dwarf, resembling a large pin cushion.

P. glauca albertiana conica (Alberta Spruce)—A compact, conical dwarf, to 8 ft. Slow growing. A good foundation plant or rockery subject.

PIERIS (Andromeda)—H.S. Moist, peaty loam, pH 5.0-5.5. A rounded evergreen bush, 3-6 ft. with small oval leaves and drooping clusters of white, lily-of-the-valley type flowers in early spring.

P. Japonica is widely grown along the Pacific coast. It prefers afternoon shade. The subvariety, *variegata*, has smaller leaves, margined with white. Propagated from cuttings taken in late summer.

PINKS (See Dianthus).

PINE (Pinus)—H.T. Light sandy soil, pH 5.5-6.0. Height from 3 ft. to 100 ft. Propagated from seed or by grafting. Many ornamental forms. Stands drought well. A good seaside subject.

SOME HOME GARDEN VARIETIES:

Pinus strobus (White Pine)—A fine blue-green conifer, up to 70 ft. A rapid grower and an excellent windbreak. Subject to rust in some areas. Many ornamental variations such as *P. parviflora* (Japanese White Pine), and *P. Cembra,* (The Swiss Stone Pine).

P. nigra Austriaca (Austrian Pine)—A symmetrical, pyramidal tree, up to 70 ft. Stiff green, large-needled foliage. Stands limed soils and seaside planting.

P. sylvestris (Scotch Pine)—Similar in color and habit to the White Pine. Yellowish bark. Suitable for dry, poor soils. The dwarf form, *nana,* is an excellent rockery subject.

P. mugho mughus (Swiss Mountain Pine)—A useful semi-dwarf, 10 ft., for specimen planting in large rockeries. Stands dry conditions. Variety *pumilio* is slower growing, with smaller needles, up to 4 ft. An excellent foundation plant.

PLUM, FRUIT—H.T. Well-drained loam or clay-loam, pH 6.0-6.5. Most fruiting plums reach a height of 20 ft. unless budded on dwarf understock like yellow Kroojen plum, or the Sand Cherry, *prunus Besseyi.* Many European varieties, like the Italian Prune, Green Gage and Yellow Egg, are self-fertile, and a few Japanese varieties like Beauty, Climax and Santa Rosa, are partially self-fertile, but Japanese-American hybrids are all self-sterile and require pollenizers. (See Part I (C) for variety table).

PLUM, FLOWERING (Prunus)—H.T. Average well-drained soil, pH 6.0-6.5. Height of ornamental plums varies, but seldom exceeds 20 ft. Propagated from grafting or budding. Excellent lawn or boulevard tree.

P. cerasifera pissardi nigra is a purple-leaved plum with single pale pink flowers in March-April.

P. cerasifera Blireana has bronze-purple leaves and large, double rose-pink flowers in March-April. One of the showiest and most popular flowering trees for boulevard or specimen planting.

POLYGONUM (See Fleece Vine).

POPLAR (See Cottonwood).

POPPY (See Papaver).

PORTUGAL LAUREL (See Laurel).

PORTULACA—H.H.A. Average soil, pH 6.0. Seed sown in heat during February will bloom in June-July. Height around 6 in. Mixed colors in long double flowers. A sun lover.

POTENTILLA (See Cinquefoil).

PRIMULA (Primrose)—H.P. Average well-drained soil, pH 6.0, with plenty of humus. Height from 4 in. to 15 in. A wide range of colors in many choice hybrid strains. Propagated from seed or root divisions. Good in sun or shade. Fine border plants or rockery specimens. Bloom from Feb.-April.
P. vulgaris, the English Primrose, bears flowers singly on stems arising from the base of the plant. Colors are mostly yellow, blue and violet. The bunch-flowered Primrose, or Polyanthus, *P. polyantha,* is a cross between the English Primrose, the Cowslip and the Oxlip, which has resulted in many fine strains with large blooms and a wider color range.
P. denticulata, from the Himalayas, forms clumps of large leaves and flower stems a foot high bearing clusters of rose, white, crimson, or lavender blooms.
P. Auricula, the Alpine Primula, has broad leaves and strong stems that bear heads of perfumed flowers in purples, browns and yellows.
P. japonica, the bog Primula, has great clumps of leaves with 18 in. stems carrying tiers of showy blooms in pink, crimson, and white. Likes moisture and partial shade.

PRIVET (See Ligustrum).

PRUNUS (See Plum, Cherry, Almond).

PYRACANTHA (See Firethorn).

PSEUDOTSUGA (See Douglas Fir).

PYRETHRUM (Painted Daisy)—H.P. Average well-drained soil, pH 6.0. Height varies from 1-2 ft. Blooms from April-June in white, red and yellow, single or double flowers. Propagated from seed or root divisions.

PYRUS (See Pear).

QUERCUS (See Oak).

QUINCE, FRUIT (*Cydonia oblonga*)—H.T. Loam or clay-loam, pH 6.0. Height rarely exceeds 15 ft. Propagated by budding on Quince seedlings or Angers Quince rootstock. Fruit valued for making jams and jellies. The Orange Quince is a good variety. It is self-fertile.

QUINCE, FLOWERING (See Chaenomeles).

RANUNCULUS (See Buttercup).

RASPBERRY—H.S. Rich, well-drained loam, pH 6.0. Raspberries are easily increased by means of suckers. Cut out old canes after fruiting. When planting new canes, cut back to 8 in. Shorten new cane growth to 5 ft. in spring. (See Part I (C) for varieties).

RED CURRANT (See Currant).

RED HOT POKER (See Kniphofia).

RETINOSPORA (See Chamaecyparis).

RHODODENDRON—H.S. Moist, but well-drained peaty loam, pH 5.0-5.5. Height varies from a few inches in dwarf species to 15 or 20 ft. in Ponticum and other species. Hybridization has been extensive and there are hundreds of named varieties in white, yellow, pink, red, blue and purple, blooming from January through April, May and June. Propagated from seed, layers, cuttings or graftage. There are so many species and hybrids that we cannot begin to list them here.
A SELECTION OF HARDY HYBRIDS:
Mrs. A. T. de la Mare—Pure white, fragrant, midseason.
Unique—Pale yellow waxy flowers, midseason.
Queen Mary—Deep pink, early.
Souv. de Dr. S. Endtz—Deep pink, midseason.

Pink Pearl—Shell pink, midseason.
Louis Pasteur—Light red, light pink centre, late.
Fabia—Orange-salmon, midseason.
Unknown Warrior—Light red, early.
Jean Marie Montague—Deep scarlet, early.
Madame de Bruin—Midseason, bright red.
Brittania—Bright scarlet, midseason.
Blue Peter—Lavender-blue, purple blotch, midseason.
Purple Splendor—Rich dark purple, late.

SOME GOOD DWARF HYBRIDS:
Blue Diamond—Medium blue, compact, very dwarf.
Oudyk's Favorite—Deep, purplish-blue, 10 in. high, compact.
Humming Bird—Large rosy-red bells, 15 in. high.
Yellow Hammer—Yellow, small tubular flowers, 18 in. high.

SOME GOOD DWARF SPECIES:
Impeditum—dwarf to one foot, purplish-blue, compact.
Praecox—lilac-pink, very early and free flowering, to 3 ft.
Williamsianum—shell-pink bells, heart-shaped foliage, to 3 ft.

RHUS (Sumac)—H.T. Light, rich soil, pH 6.0. Average height on Pacific coast is 10-15 ft. Propagated from seed, cuttings or layers. The large pinnate leaves are very decorative, and color beautifully in the fall.
R. Typhina (Staghorn Sumac)—A shrubby tree with leaves up to 2 ft. in length. Brilliant red fall coloring.
R. Typhina laciniata—The same habit as the Staghorn Sumac, but the leaves are finely serrated. Both have red plume-like flowers.

RHUS COTINUS (Smoke Tree)—Hardy shrub or small tree, sometimes placed under the separate genus, *cotinus*. Prefers well-drained soil, on the sandy side, pH 6.0. Propagated from seeds, root cuttings or layers. Masses of plumed, silky flower stalks (smoke), appear in June. The variety *cotinus coggygria rubrifolius* has purplish flower panicles and outstanding red foliage coloration in the fall.

RIBES (See Currant, Alpine).

ROCK CRESS (See Arabis).

ROCK ROSE (See Cistus).

ROCK SPRAY (See Cotoneaster).

ROSA (Rose)—H.S. Well-drained clay-loam, with lots of humus, pH 5.5-6.0. Roses vary in height from 8 in. miniatures to 5 ft. grandifloras. Roses may be propagated easily from cuttings but are usually budded on hardy rootstocks in June-July. There are scores of species and hundreds of named varieties, in a color range that covers everything but dark blue. (See Part I (F) for groupings and variety selections).

ROSMARINUS (Rosemary)—H. S. Light average well-drained soil, pH 6.5. Evergreen, fragrant leaves, and blue and white flowers in early summer. Propagated from seed, layers or cuttings, usually the latter.
R. officinalis is a dense branching shrub, up to 6 ft. with lavender blooms in May.
R. officinalis humilis is a spreading form of the other, and there is a variety, *albiflorus,* with white flowers.

ROSE OF SHARON (See Hibiscus).

RUSSIAN OLIVE (See Eleagnus).

SALIX (Willow)—H.T. Moist loam, pH 6.0. Height up to 60 ft. Easily propagated from hardwood cuttings. Needs space, and most varieties are too large for the smaller garden. Does well in damp places.
S. alba vitellina pendula (Golden Weeping Willow)—The most popular garden variety, with yellow bark and drooping branches. It reaches thirty feet, or more.
S. pentandra (Laurel Willow)—A 60 ft. tree with lustrous green laurel-like foliage.

S. Matsudana tortuosa (Permanent Wave Tree)—A curious ornamental tree, up to 30 ft. high, with contorted branches and twigs.

There are a number of attractive dwarf Willows suitable for the rock garden. E.g. *S. herbacea* and *S. Bockii*.

SALPIGLOSSIS—T.A. Sandy loam, pH 6.0-6.5. Height 18 in. to 3 ft. Colorful trumpet-shaped flowers, July to September from sowings in heat during February-March. Likes sun. Good for mass border plantings.

SALVIA (*S. Splendens*)—H.H.A. Rich friable loam, pH 6.0-6.5. Height 10 in. to 2 ft. Seed sown in heat Feb.-March will bloom July-Sept. A very showy bright red border plant.

SALVIA (*S. azurea grandiflora*)—H.P. A beautiful perennial plant, up to 4 ft. high, with long spikes of blue flowers in September. Likes well-drained loamy soil and full sun.

SAXIFRAGA (Saxifrage)—H.P. Well-drained sandy loam, pH 6.0-6.5. Height from a few inches to 2 ft. Colors in white, pink, yellow and scarlet. Blooms from January to July, according to variety. Propagated from seed or root divisions. Doesn't like to be disturbed. Particularly valuable for the rock garden. The Kabschia hybrids include many choice subjects, with cushions of blue-grey leaves and white, pink or yellow blooms.

SCABIOSA (Pincushion Flower)—H.A. Average soil, pH 6.0, with good drainage. Height of the annual is about 3 ft. Seed sown in March outdoors will flower in midsummer. The blue, rose, purple, yellow or white flowers are excellent for cutting.

H.P. The perennial, in white, blue or violet, is also a good plant for cut bloom. Propagated from seed or root divisions.

SCHIZANTHUS (Butterfly Flower)—H.H.A. Average soil, pH 6.0. Height 1½-2 ft. The small flowers, like butterflies, appear in many colors in June-July, if sown in heat during February. Sow outdoors in April for late bloom.

SCILLA (Squill)—H.B. Average well-drained soil, pH 6.0. Height 4 in. - 12 in. White, rose, red or blue flowers in early spring. Propagated from offsets.

SEDUM (Stonecrop)—H.P. Average to poor light soil, pH 6.0-6.5. Height from 2 in. to 2 ft. Propagated from seed, cuttings or root divisions. Suitable for rock walls, flagstone crevices, border edging or rockery pockets. Flowers are mostly white, yellow and pink.

S. spathulifolium is a native of the Pacific northwest. It forms cushions of grey-green leaves which send up heads of golden flowers on 4-6 in. stems in May-June.

S. Sieboldi is one of several distinctive Japanese varieties with rosy-purple flowers in August-September.

SERVICE BERRY (See Amelanchier).

SKIMMIA JAPONICA—H.S. Fairly heavy moist soil, pH 5.5. Height 3-4 ft. Large, aromatic leathery leaves, white flowers in April, followed by scarlet berries. A good evergreen for shade. Propagated from seed or cuttings. Male and female flowers produced on different plants.

SMOKE TREE (See *Rhus Cotinus*).

SNAPDRAGON (See Antirrhinum).

SNOWBALL (See Viburnum).

SNOWDROP (See Galanthus).

SOLIDAGO (See Goldenrod).

SORBUS (See Mountain Ash).

SPANISH BROOM (See Broom).

SPEEDWELL (See Veronica).

SPINDLE TREE (See Euonymus).

SPIRAEA—H.S. Average moist soil, pH 6.0. Height 1 ft. to 8 ft. White, pink, or red blooms, April to June, according to variety. Propagated from cuttings or root divisions. Prefers sun.

S. Thunbergi—A 4-5 ft. shrub with wiry branchlets, small leaves and white star-like flowers in March-April.

S. Vanhouttei—A 6 ft. shrub with arching branches and clusters of white double flowers in April-May.

S. prunifolia flore pleno (Bridal Wreath)—A 6 ft. graceful shrub with narrow leaves and small double white flowers. Foliage colors beautifully in the fall.

S. Bumalda Anthony Waterer is a 4 ft. shrub with flat-topped heads of deep pink flowers in July-August.

S. bullata Newmanni is a 12 in. dwarf, with pink flowers in July, an excellent rock garden subject.

SPRUCE (See Picea).

SPURGE (See Pachysandra).

SQUILLS (See Scilla).

STOCKS—H.A. Light, friable loam, pH 6.0-6.5. Height 1 ft. to 3 ft. Colors in white, pink, yellow, red, and lavender. Seed sown in heat during February will bloom outdoors in June. Very fragrant.

H.B. Brompton Stocks, a biennial, should be sown in August to flower the following spring. All stocks like full sun.

STRAWBERRY—H.P. Light, well-drained loam with plenty of humus, pH 5.5-6.0. Both June-bearing and everbearing varieties need good air drainage and an ample supply of moisture. Best planted in early spring from runners (layers) either left in the ground over winter, or stored in cold storage. Three years is the life of bearing plants in average soil. (See Part I (C) for varieties and planting table).

SUMAC (See Rhus).

SUNFLOWER (See Helianthus).

SUN ROSE (See Helianthemum).

SWEET CHESNUT (See Castanea).

SWEET PEAS (See Pea).

SWEET WILLIAM (*Dianthus barbatus*)—H.B. Average soil, pH 6.0. Sow outdoors in June-July to flower the following summer. Height 6 in. - 18 in. Wide range of colors. Alpine and dwarf varieties are suitable for borders or rockeries. May be propagated from layers or root divisions as well as seed.

SWEET GUM (See Liquidambar).

SYRINGA (See Lilac).

TAMARIX (Tamarisk)—H.S. Light, sandy soil, pH 6.0. Height 8-10 ft. Asparagus-like foliage, with plumes of pink or crimson flowers in midsummer. Propagated from cuttings. A good seaside plant.

T. tetranda—May flowering with pink bloom.

T. odessana Pink Cascade—Fall flowering, with pink bloom.

T. pentandra rubra—Summer flowering with red bloom.

Prune all varieties hard back in spring to maintain form and promote new flowering wood.

TAXUS (Yew)—H.T. Good moist loam, pH 6.0-7.0. Many varieties, upright or spreading, green or golden. Propagated from seed or cuttings. An evergreen extensively used for foundation planting and general landscaping. Thrives in sun or quite dense shade.

SOME HOME GARDEN VARIETIES:

T. baccata (English Yew)—Dark green foliage, loose upright habit to 25 ft. Used extensively for hedging.

T. baccata repandens—Same deep color as above, with prostrate habit and arching branches. A good foundation plant.

T. baccata stricta (fastigiata)—The Irish Yew is a very erect column of green, up to 15 ft. There is a golden form, *aurea,* with the same habit. Both have attractive red berries.

T. cuspidata nana—The dwarf Japanese Yew. Dense, bushy form suitable for low hedges or foundation planting.

T. media Hicksi—An English-Japanese hybrid. Upright form, 6-10 ft. A useful landscaping variety.

THUYA (See arborvitae).

THYMUS (Thyme)—H.S. Average light soil, pH 6.0. Height 2 in. to 18 in. Purple or white fragrant flowers in June-July. Propagated from seed or root divisions. A good rockery plant or groundcover, as well as an herb used for flavoring.

T. Serpyllum or Creeping Thyme, has tiny dark green leaves and heather-purple flowers in June.

T. lanuginosus or Silver-Grey Thyme, is an excellent carpeter for an alpine lawn or ground cover.

T. nitidus is a twiggy shrub about 18 in., with small grey-green leaves and lilac-colored flowers in June-July.

TILIA (See Linden).

TOBACCO PLANT (See Nicotiana).

TORCH LILY (See Kniphofia).

TROLLIUS (See Globeflower).

TSUGA (See Hemlock).

TULIPA (Tulip)—H.B. Average light loam, pH 6.0. Height from 6 in. to 2 ft., according to variety. Propagated from seed or offsets, usually the latter. Many colors and types, blooming April and May. (See Part II (B) for varieties and planting table).

TULIP TREE (See Liriodendron).

ULMUS (See Elm).

VACCINIUM (See blueberry).

VERBENA (*V. hortensis*)—H.A. Good rich loam, pH 6.0-6.5. Seed sown in heat in February will bloom outdoors June-July. Colors in white, rose, scarlet, lilac and purple. Fragrant.

(*V. canadensis*)—H.H.P. Sometimes called the Clump Verbena. It grows 18 in. high, with pink, crimson and white flowers. Propagated by root division.

VERONICA (Speedwell)—H.P. Average soil, pH 6.0. Height 4 in. to 24 in. White, pink or blue flowers, April to July. Propagated from seed, cuttings or layers. A fine rockery or edging subject.

V. latifolia (V. prostrata)—A prostrate evergreen with 4 in. spikes of bright blue in midsummer.

V. spicata 'Minuet'—Grey-green foliage, 12 in. pink spikes, July-August.

NOTE: Most of the New Zealand plants commonly called Veronicas come under the genus *Hebe,* but we will list some of them here:

H. buxifolia—Pale green small leaves, white flowers. A neat shrub, 2-4 ft.

H. cupressiodes—A round bush, 2-4 ft. resembling a dwarf Cypress. A useful border or planter box subject.

H. Hectori—Called Whipcord Veronica on account of its foliage, which is golden-green. Grows 2 ft. high, with white flowers.

VIBURNUM—H.S. Average soil. Deciduous varieties favor acidity around pH 6.5, while some of the evergreens prefer some peat and more acidity. Height ranges from 4 ft. to 10 ft. White or rose pink flowers, often fragrant, from January-June, according to variety. Propagated best from cuttings or layers.

Some home garden varieties:

V. Opulis sterile (Snowball Tree)—A 10 ft. shrub with large round white flowers in June, and fine fall leaf coloration.

V. Tomentosum sterile (Japanese Snowball)—A 10 ft. shrub with flat clusters of white flowers in May-June. Red berries turn black in winter.

V. fragrans—A 10 ft. deciduous shrub with fragrant white or pink flowers January-March.

V. Carlcephalum—A Carlesii hybrid, 4-8 ft. with heart-shaped, grey-green leaves and huge clusters of white flowers in April-May. Very fragrant.

V. Burkwoodii—Another Carlesii hybrid, 6 ft., with glossy dark evergreen leaves, pinkish fragrant flowers in June.

V. Tinus (Lauristinus)—A well-known evergreen up to 12 ft. with reddish buds in late summer that open white during winter and early spring. Suitable for hedging.

V. Davidii—A dwarf evergreen, 2-3 ft., with long leathery leaves, white flowers in late spring, followed by blue berries. A good rockery plant, preferring some shade.

VINCA (See Periwinkle).

VIOLA (Violet—See Pansy)—H.P. Average soil, pH 6.0. Height from 3 in. - 18 in. White, blue, yellow, rose, apricot and crimson flowers. Seeds sown in January in heat, transplanted in May, will bloom the first year. Propagated from root divisions also. Fine border or edging plants. Besides the bedding violas there are numerous varieties of alpine violas and violets suitable for rockeries and green covers.

The Sweet Violet, *V. odorata,* likes partial shade and cool moist soil, and blooms from early spring into summer.

VIRGINIA CREEPER (See Parthenocissus).

VISCARIA—H.A. Average soil, pH 6.0. Height 9 in. - 12 in. Red, pale blue or dark blue flowers. Sow seed in heat during February to bloom outdoors June-July.

VITIS (See Grape).

WALLFLOWER (See Cheiranthus).

WALNUT (See Juglans).

WATER LILY (See Nymphaea).

WEIGELA—H.S. Average well-drained soil, pH 6.0. Height 4-6 ft. Propagated from cuttings or root divisions. White, pink, or red trumpet-shaped blooms in May-June. Prefer sun. Prune out old shoots after flowering. Some of the best hybrids are Abel Carriere, rose-pink, Bristol Ruby, deep pink, Eva Rathke, crimson, Candida, white, and Rosea Nana Variegata, pink with gold and green foliage.

WILLOW (See Salix).

WINTER JASMINE (See Jasmine).

WISTERIA SINENSIS (Chinese Wisteria)—H.S. Average well-drained soil, pH 6.0-6.5. A twining climber with racemes of mauve, pea-like flowers in May-June. A rampant grower, it needs an arbor or trellis for support. May be trained as a weeping tree. Propagated by root grafting or layering.

WITCH HAZEL (See Hamamelis).

YEW (See Taxus).

YUCCA—H.P. Rich, light soil, pH 6.5. Creamy-yellow flowers on a long 3-4 ft. stem, in midsummer. Propagated from cuttings or offsets. Stands heat well.

Y. filamentosa (Adam's Needle)—A low-growing kind suitable for rock gardens or borders. Leaves are 2½ ft. long, up to 2 in. wide, with grayish, thread-like filaments attached. Large cream-white flowers grow on stems 4 to 5 ft. high.

ZINNIA—T.A. Deep rich loam, pH 6.5. Height 1 ft. to 3 ft. in brilliant mixed colors. There are large blooms like dahlias, or small pom pom flowers like chrysanthemums. Seed sown in heat in March, planted out in May, will bloom July-August. Likes full sun.

General Index